THE REGIONAL DIMENSION IN EUROPEAN PUBLIC POLICY

The Regional Dimension in European Public Policy

Convergence or Divergence?

Reiner Martin

First published in Great Britain 1999 by
MACMILLAN PRESS LTD
Houndmills, Basingstoke, Hampshire RG21 6XS and London
Companies and representatives throughout the world

A catalogue record for this book is available from the British Library.

ISBN 0–333–74671–6

First published in the United States of America 1999 by
ST. MARTIN'S PRESS, INC.,
Scholarly and Reference Division,
175 Fifth Avenue, New York, N.Y. 10010

ISBN 0–312–21702–1

Library of Congress Cataloging-in-Publication Data
Martin, Reiner, 1966–
The regional dimension in European public policy : convergence or divergence? / Reiner Martin.
p. cm.
Includes bibliographical references and index.
ISBN 0–312–21702–1 (cloth)
1. Regional planning—European Union countries. 2. European Union countries—Economic conditions—Regional disparities. 3. European Union countries—Economic policy. I. Title.
HT395.E8M375 1999
338.94—dc21 98–50835
CIP

---

10 9 8 7 6 5 4 3 2 1
08 07 06 05 04 03 02 01 00 99

Printed and bound in Great Britain by
Antony Rowe Ltd, Chippenham, Wiltshire

To my family

Contents

List of Tables

List of Figures

List of Boxes

Acknowledgements

I would like to thank Thomas Straubhaar, my PhD supervisor, for continuous encouragement, support and constructive criticism through all stages of this work.

Students and staff at the Europa-Kolleg Hamburg, especially Reinhard Felke, Philip Nölling, Kolya Rudzio, Mathias Schulze Steinen and Marc Suhrke, provided intellectual support and created a most enjoyable social environment.

My thanks go also to Peter Fischer for excellent co-operation and to Christof Schoser for numerous detailed and useful comments on all parts of this work.

A Junior Research Fellowship at the Centre for European Policy Studies in Brussels proved to be most beneficial in many respects. In particular, I would like to thank Daniel Gros for extremely valuable comments and intellectual stimulation and Anne Harrington for correcting an earlier draft of this work.

The staff of the European Policies Research Centre, notably Douglas Yuill, who acted as second examiner for my PhD, and Fiona Wishlade proved that peripheral location, research excellence and high quality of life go easily together.

Andries Brandsma of the European Commission's DG II helped to make a Commission stage a very productive working period, and Elisabeth Helander of DG XVI commented extensively on various parts of this work.

Financial support for this work was provided by the Deutsche Forschungsgemeinschaft through the 'Graduiertenkolleg Integrationsforschung' at the Europa-Kolleg Hamburg.

Finally, I would like to thank all those friends and family, who for a long time accepted a far smaller share of my time and attention than they deserved. Their collective moral support was crucial for the successful completion of this work.

List of Abbreviations

CAP	Common Agricultural Policy
CEC	Commission of the European Communities
CEEC	Central and East European Country
CF	Cohesion Fund
CI	Community Initiative
CRS	Constant returns to scale
CSF	Community Support Framework
CTP	Common Transport Policy
DG	Directorate-General
DOM	Départements d'outre Mer (French overseas departments)
DRS	Decreasing returns to scale
EAGGF	European Agricultural Guarantee and Guidance Fund
EC	European Community
ECU	European Currency Unit
ECSC	European Coal and Steel Community
EEC	European Economic Community
EIB	European Investment Bank
EIF	European Investment Fund
EMU	Economic and Monetary Union
ERDF	European Regional Development Fund
ESF	European Social Fund
EU	European Union
FDI	Foreign direct investments
FIFG	Financial Instrument for Fisheries Guidance
FP	Framework Programme
FPE	Factor price equalisation
FRG	Federal Republic of Germany
GDP	Gross Domestic Product
GNP	Gross National Product
HOS	Heckscher–Ohlin–Samuelson
IMP	Integrated Mediterranean Programme

IRS	Increasing returns to scale
ISPA	Instrument for Structural Policies pre-Accession
JRC	Joint Research Centre
MNC	Multinational corporation
NTB	Non-tariff barrier to trade
NUTS	Nomenclature des Unités Territorales Statistiques
OCA	Optimum currency area
OECD	Organisation for Economic Co-operation and Development
OJ	Official Journal (of the European Communities)
OLS	Ordinary least squares
OP	Operational Programme
PPS	Purchasing Power Standards
R&D	Research and Development
SEA	Single European Act
SEM	Single European Market
SF	Structural Funds
SME	Small and medium sized enterprises
SPD	Single Programming Document
TETN	Trans-European-Transport Network
TEU	Treaty on European Union
UK	United Kingdom of Great Britain and Northern Ireland
US	United States of America

1 Introduction

The political and economic integration of Europe, a process that started nearly 40 years ago, has become one of the most important determinants of the political and economic situation in Europe. Whereas only six countries, France, Germany, Italy and the Benelux states, signed the founding documents in the 1950s, the European Union (EU)[1] now encompasses 15 member states. A single European market (SEM) came into existence in 1992, the 1997 Treaty of Amsterdam streamlined some of the decision-making procedures and brought progress towards a Common Foreign and Security Policy, and European economic and monetary union (EMU) started at the beginning of 1999. The large number of countries from Central and Eastern Europe, as well as the Mediterranean, that have applied for membership shows that the Union still exerts considerable attraction for third countries. Further deepening and widening is therefore the most likely future for the EU.

There is widespread agreement that the integration of Europe led to substantial economic and political benefits for the Union as a whole. It is less clear, however, whether the integration process has had positive effects on all parts of the Union. Especially with regard to the cohesion countries, whose level of economic and social development is significantly below that of the EU average, it is sometimes argued that the negative integration effects have outweighed the benefits.

The uncertainty surrounding the spatial effects of integration is of much more than academic interest. It is the basis for a long-standing political debate between rich and poor member states of the EU about transfers from the former to the latter. This debate led to the development of EU regional policy which, from modest beginnings in 1975, has developed into the second most important policy area of the Union, at least in terms of its share of the budget.

The present study investigates two closely related sets of questions. Chapters 3 and 4 provide theoretical and empirical analyses of the question whether an automatic ('natural') reduction of EU spatial socio-economic disparities can be expected in the foreseeable future. It turns out that this reduction is unlikely to occur. In the absence of fast, 'natural' convergence, however, the EU has a legal obligation to employ public policies in order to reduce socio-economic disparities within the Union. This is established in Chapter 5, which provides an overview of EU regional policy.

Chapter 6, 7 and 8 are devoted to the question of whether European regional policy is sufficiently co-ordinated with other European and national policies that have an impact on the regional distribution of economic activity. There are similarities between this study and the European Commission's First Cohesion Report (Commission of the European Communities (CEC), 1996a), but there are also important differences. Whereas the Cohesion Report tries to provide an encompassing survey of relevant EU and national policies, the present study is restricted to three policy areas which are of particular interest for regional economic developments in Europe, namely R&D, transport infrastructure and productive investment support. For these three areas an in-depth analysis of the co-ordination with EU regional policy is provided.

It should be kept in mind that the present study does not intend to develop an alternative grand scheme for regional policy or to show that it would be economically more meaningful to do away with it altogether. While the latter solution has to be taken seriously from the point of view of aggregate economic welfare, politically it is unthinkable for the foreseeable future. Alternative redistribution schemes are easy to find, in theory as well as in practice, but a drastic change in the current system of EU regional policy is unlikely to occur. For the time being, it seems much more useful to accept the main features of EU regional policy and to identify ways to improve the current system.

Chapter 2 provides some background information for the main parts of the book. First, the development of the EU is summarised with special reference to the growing heterogeneity of the Union due to the various enlargements. Second, the European regional nomenclature system used for all empirical investigations in the book is introduced. Finally, the extent of regional income and labour market disparities in the EU is illustrated.

Drawing on economic theory, the third chapter analyses whether economic integration between locations is more likely to contribute to an equalisation or a divergence of economic conditions in these areas, focusing mainly on per capita income. Increasing equalisation is predicted by the neoclassical school of economic thinking (convergence theory), whereas the second line of argumentation is associated with the divergence school -- a less coherent theory focusing on economic phenomena such as economies of scale, external effects and transport costs.

On theoretical grounds, the dispute between convergence and divergence theory remains undecided, which leads to the empirical investigation of income convergence or divergence in European regions during the 1980s and early 1990s. In a first step (Chapter 4.1), important aspects of the macroeconomic development of the four EU cohesion countries (Greece, Spain, Ireland and Portugal) are presented. In a second step (Chapter 4.2), the growth performance of EU regions is examined with special reference to the impact of human capital and infrastructure on regional growth. This analysis provides useful information as to which regional policy instruments are likely to speed up the intra-European convergence process. Chapter 4 lends some empirical support to the convergence school, although it shows that a fast, automatic catch-up process of lagging European regions is unlikely and that regional policy instruments can have a positive impact on regional convergence.

Chapter 5 starts off by looking at the EU's legal obligations to work towards a reduction of regional socio-economic disparities. These obligations are contained in the European treaties, which implies that regional policy will remain indispensable for the foreseeable future. Chapter 5 looks also at possible economic rationales for regional policy and asks why regional policy should be pursued at the European rather than the member state level. The second section of this chapter provides a critical review of European regional policy, its origins, its present operation and the plans recently announced by the Commission for the post-1999 period.

Chapter 6 looks at European and national support for productive investments. The comparison of national and European support payments contained in this chapter illustrates the insufficient co-ordination between national and EU investment support policies and casts doubts on the relation between EU regional policy and EU state aids policy.

Chapter 7 is devoted to a particular aspect of human capital, namely R&D. Following the approach adopted in Chapter 6, the spatial distribution of national and EU expenditures across European regions is analysed. As far as European R&D support is concerned, two separate policy areas are investigated. First, expenditures within the framework of regional policy; and second, the regional distribution of EU-supported R&D projects. This allows an empirical investigation of the widespread assumption that European support for research and development contributes to regional divergence.

The distribution of infrastructure endowments and transport infrastructure investments across European regions is investigated in Chapter 8. Following a review of the relevant theoretical literature, differences in regional infrastructure endowments across the EU are presented. This is followed by an analysis of the national and regional distribution of member states' transport infrastructure expenditures. In the last section of Chapter 8, the spatial impact of the three pillars of European transport policy are presented: (1), the liberalisation of transport services, (2), infrastructure investments as part of the Structural Funds, and (3), the 'Trans-European Transport Networks' (TETNs).

Although it has to be emphasised that good co-ordination between EU regional policy and other policies that have an impact on the spatial distribution of economic activity is not sufficient to guarantee that European regional policy is effective and efficient, co-ordination is certainly a necessary condition for efficacy as well as efficiency. The difference between these two concepts is quite important. Efficacy means that regional policy succeeds in achieving its main objective, namely a reduction of the regional socio-economic disparities in the EU. In contrast to that, efficiency implies that this objective is achieved with minimum costs, which is a much more ambitious aim than efficacy. As the analysis will show, some aspects of EU regional policy are at present clearly inefficient due to a lack of policy co-ordination. In some cohesion countries insufficient co-ordination even poses a threat to the efficacy of regional policy.

Part I

Regional Convergence or Divergence in the European Union?

2 European Economic Integration and the Growth of Regional Heterogeneity

The first section of this chapter sketches briefly the historical development of European integration with particular reference to the emergence of spatial economic imbalances within the EU; Section 2.2 outlines the regional organisation of the Union; and Section 2.3 illustrates regional income and labour market disparities during the 1980s and early 1990s. This is important in order to understand why regional policy has become such a leading EU policy area.

2.1 A SHORT HISTORY OF EUROPEAN ECONOMIC INTEGRATION

During the first phase of the EU, regional policy was not an important policy issue because, in terms of their spatial income distribution, the founding members of the EU (France, Italy, Germany, Belgium, the Netherlands and Luxembourg) were a fairly homogeneous group. The only area with major regional problems was southern Italy, the so-called Mezzogiorno. This problem was mainly, although not very successfully, addressed by Italian regional policy. The European Social Fund (ESF), a relatively small financial instrument of the EU aimed at labour market problems, also focused its activities on the Italian South. Until the 1970s, the labour market problems of the Mezzogiorno had also been eased by large-scale migration from this region to northern Italy as well as to other EU member states, especially Germany.[1]

The regional problem was intensified by the first enlargement in 1973, when Denmark, the Republic of Ireland and the United Kingdom (UK) joined the Union. Whereas Denmark did not differ much from the original member states in terms of its per capita income and regional balance, some of the UK regions, especially the

North of England and Northern Ireland, were experiencing major unemployment problems with a low per capita income compared to the rest of the EU. Taken as a whole, however, the income level of the UK at the time of accession was comparable to that of EU6. It was only the third new entrant, the Republic of Ireland, that was significantly poorer than the original member states. Its per capita income in 1973 was just about half of the EU6 average. Things were made worse by the fact that the first oil crisis and the international stagflation that followed it clouded growth prospects throughout the Union. The economic problems within the EU led to a proliferation of internal non-tariff barriers to trade (NTBs), restricting the free flow of goods. Migration also lost some of its safety-valve function because the potential receiving countries reduced recruitment of foreign labour. Henceforth, in 1975, shortly after the first enlargement, the European Regional Development Fund (ERDF) was founded. For more than a decade, however, the scale of its operations remained very modest.[2]

Spatial disparities became a much more important issue following the 'southern' enlargement. Greece joined the EU in 1981, followed by Spain and Portugal in 1986. The accession of these countries added a new dimension to European regional issues. Although the richest parts of the new members were better off than the Republic of Ireland, they were still poor compared to the Union average.[3] Moreover, the sheer size of the new poor member states, around 60 million inhabitants compared to around 260 million in the pre-1981 member states, dwarfed the pre-1981 situation.

The two last geographical accessions also contributed to the regional problems of the EU, although to a smaller extent than the southern enlargement. The incorporation of the former German Democratic Republic into the Federal Republic of Germany added an area inhabited by 17 million people whose average income in 1990 was only 35 per cent of the Union average. Due to massive intra-German transfers, and – to a lesser extent – due to EU support, this discrepancy has since been significantly reduced, but significant unemployment and structural adjustment problems remain.

The 1995 northern enlargement, which brought Finland, Sweden and Austria into the EU, was much less problematic. Expressed in purchasing power standards (PPS) Finland's 1993 per capita income was 89 per cent of the Union average, Sweden's 98 per cent and Austria's per capita income exceeded the EU average by 12 per cent. On the basis of 1993 data, only two regions in the new member states would have qualified as 'lagging' regions although, mainly due to political reasons, large parts of the new member states have become eligible for European regional support. This point will be taken up again in Chapter 5.

Over the years, the enlarged number of member states has transformed the Union into an increasingly heterogeneous group of countries with persistent spatial economic imbalances. This long-run process is the basic rationale for the development of EU regional policy, discussed in more detail in Chapter 5. Before turning to regional socio-economic disparities in more detail, the following section will define what constitutes a region in the context of the EU.

2.2 THE REGIONAL ORGANISATION OF THE EUROPEAN UNION

In principle, the term 'region' can define any geographic entity, irrespective of whether this entity corresponds with national or sub-national boundaries or a group of countries. For regional policy purposes, however, regions refer to national or sub-national administrative areas.

Due to the growing importance of regional policy, the EU has increased its efforts to improve the structure, availability and comparability of regional statistical material. EUROSTAT, the Statistical Office of the European Commission, has defined various levels of regional disaggregation which are applicable in all EU member states. The 'nomenclature des unités territoriales statistiques' (NUTS) used to have four levels (NUTS 0 to III), with NUTS 0 being the member states. In order to make it more suitable for the analysis of small areas, two additional levels (NUTS IV and V) have recently been added (Decand, 1996). For the purposes of the analysis below, however, these new levels are not relevant.

Most analyses of regional disparities are based on the NUTS II level of regional disaggregation. There are 206 regions at this level, including Denmark, Ireland and Luxembourg. These member states have not designated NUTS II regions, which means that statistical analyses usually have to be made at the national level. In the UK, most data are available only at the NUTS I level.

NUTS II regions differ significantly in terms of size and population. Excluding the UK NUTS II regions, the average population is 1.9 million but the standard deviation (1.7 million) is very high.

Table 2.1 Correspondence between EU Regions and National Administrative Divisions

	NUTS I	NUTS II	NUTS III
Belgium	régions	provinces	arrondissements
Denmark	./.	./.	Amter
Germany	Länder	Regierungsbezirke	Kreise
Greece	NUTS II groupings	development regions	nomoi
Spain	NUTS II groupings	comunidades autonomas	provincias
France	ZEAT + DOM	régions + DOM	départements + DOM
Ireland	./.	./.	planning regions
Italy	NUTS II groupings	regioni	provincie
Luxembourg	./.	./.	./.
Netherlands	landsdelen	provincies	COROP-Regio's
Austria	Gruppen von Bundesländern	Bundesländer	Gruppen von Politischen Bezirken
Portugal	NUTS II groupings	Comissôes de coordenaoçâô regional + Regiôes autónomas	groupings of concelhos
Finland	Manner-Suomi/a Ahvenanma	Suuralueet	Maakunat
Sweden	./.	Riksområden	Län
United Kingdom	standard regions	NUTS III groupings	counties, local authority regions

Source: EUROSTAT (1997a).

The smallest NUTS II region are the Åland Islands with 25,000 inhabitants whereas the largest NUTS II region, Île de France, has nearly 11 million inhabitants. For analytical reasons, a higher level of disaggregation than NUTS II would be desirable, but data availability below the NUTS II level remains very restricted (di Palma and Maziotta, 1998).

Despite the undeniable progress that has been made, the availability of regional data still leaves much to be desired, especially when it comes to regionalised national expenditure data. Moreover, most of the available material covers only the period after 1980. This limits the possibility of analysing regional long-run developments.

2.3 REGIONAL ECONOMIC DISPARITIES WITHIN THE EU

2.3.1 Regional Income Disparities

Per capita income levels are the most commonly used indicator for differences in economic development. On a national as well as a regional level, such income disparities are very considerable within the EU. Figure 2.1 shows the 1988 and 1996 per capita income of the EU member states relative to the EU15 average (100). In order to account for differences in relative purchasing power, income is measured in PPS.

The figure indicates a narrowing of income disparities at the national level. The performance of Ireland in particular is remarkable. In PPS terms the country is now above the EU average per capita income. Portugal, Spain and Greece also made some progress, whereas some of the northern member states – Sweden, Finland and, following reunification, Germany – experienced a relative decline in per capita income. Luxembourg managed to increase its lead vis-à-vis the Union average, but given its size (0.4 million inhabitants) it clearly represents a special case.

Income disparities are considerably wider at the NUTS II level of regions. The ratio between Luxembourg, the richest member state, and Greece, the poorest member state, was only 2.6 to 1 in 1996. The ratio

Figure 2.1 Relative per capita Income in EU Member States, 1988 and 1996

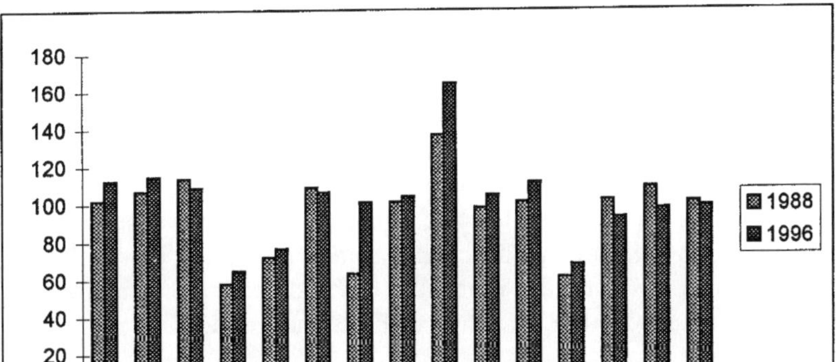

*PPS; EU average = 100
Source: CEC (1997a).

Figure 2.2 Relative per capita Income in EU NUTS II Regions, 1994*

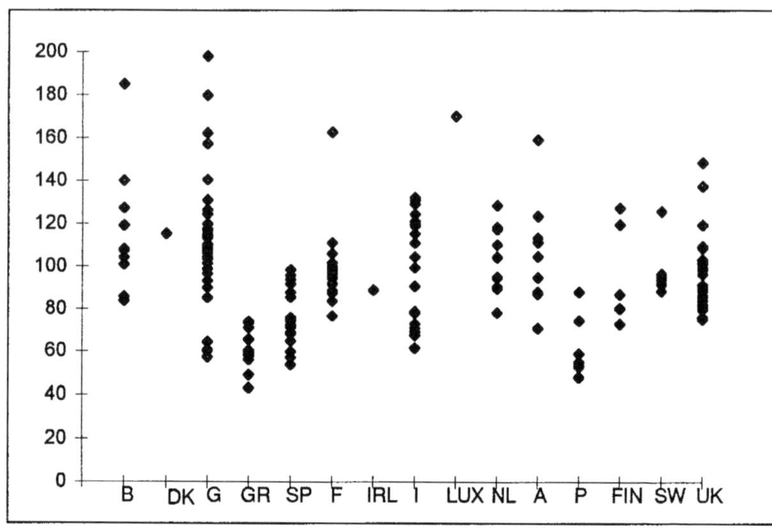

*PPS; EU average = 100
Source: EUROSTAT (1997b).

between Hamburg, the richest NUTS II region, and its poorest counterpart, Ipeiros (Greece), however, was more than 4.5 to 1 in 1994. Figure 2.2 provides an overview of 1994 PPS per capita in NUTS II regions.

A closer look at Figure 2.2 reveals various recurrent features. First is the leading position of national political and economic centres like Brussels, Île de France/Paris, Vienna and Stockholm. Another interesting aspect is the large intra-national income variation in some of the big member states. Italy, with its notorious North–South divide, features very prominently, but the most striking case is post-reunification Germany with the new *Länder* being well below the EU average. Income levels in France, the UK and Spain are comparatively homogeneous, with the exception of Paris and London.

Box 2.1 Indicators of Regional Income

Gross domestic product (GDP) is the most widely used indicator for regional income. It measures the value of goods and services produced in a particular region. However, not all people benefiting from this income reside within the region. In Hamburg, for example, many commuters live outside its boundaries which statistically increases the city's per capita GDP. Similar effects occur in areas where multinational companies (MNCs) are an important element of the economy. Irish gross national product (GNP), for example, is estimated to be around 10–12 per cent *less* than its GDP (Barry and Bradley, 1997). Although GNP would thus be a more accurate regional income indicator than GDP, it is not available at regional level in the EU and therefore cannot be used for regional policy purposes.

GDP values are frequently expressed in Purchasing Power Standards (PPS) rather than currency terms. In principle this is a meaningful procedure in order to account for differences in the costs of living, but it has also its weaknesses. PPS 'exchange rates' exist only on a national basis, although intra-national differences in the costs of living can be considerable. In Germany, for example, a recent investigation into the costs of living in 50 cities has identified differences of up to 12 per cent (Ströhl, 1994). Since these differences are highly correlated with intra-German differences in per capita income, the 'real' PPS values are not as different as the EUROSTAT-figures suggest.

It should also be borne in mind that GDP values do not include financial transfers within the member states, although it is estimated that regional disparities in disposable income are 20–40 per cent lower than disparities in GDP once the redistributive effect of national policies is taken into account (CEC, 1996a). However, since the main aim of EU regional policy is not redistribution but improvements in regional competitiveness, it can be argued that GDP is a more meaningful indicator for the purposes of regional policy than disposable income.[4]

Unlike income disparities on the national level, regional disparities tended to widen slightly during the last decade. The standard deviation of income disparities at NUTS II level has increased from 26.8 in 1983 to 27.2 in 1993. The same is true for intra-national regional income disparities with the exception of the Netherlands, Finland and the UK (CEC, 1996a). While the reasons for the weakening of internal cohesion are clearly not uniform, it is argued that the impact of allocative member states policies like R&D strongly favour their core regions.[5] Moreover, national regional policy has been significantly reduced in some countries (Yuill et al., 1995). This point will be further analysed in Chapter 6.

2.3.2 Regional Labour Market Disparities

Unemployment is another important indicator for the assessment of regional socio-economic disparities. Figure 2.3 shows relative national unemployment rates for the EU member states in 1987 and 1996.

The most striking developments have taken place in Ireland, which managed to reduce its relative (as well as its absolute) level of unemployment significantly, and in Finland, where relative and absolute unemployment has dramatically increased. The relative performance of the Netherlands and the UK is also positive although to a lesser extent than that of Ireland. It has to be kept in mind, however, that the average absolute level of unemployment in the EU has increased. The 1987 average EU15 unemployment rate was 9.8, the average value in 1996 10.9. The relative position of the poor EU member states is quite mixed. Whereas unemployment appears to be less of a problem for Portugal and Greece, the unemployment rate for Spain is extremely high and shows little tendency to fall.

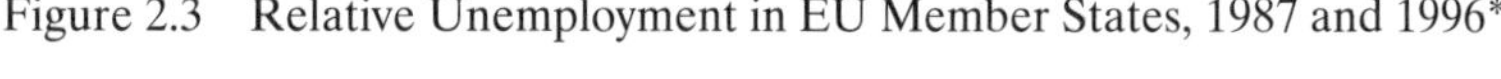

Figure 2.3 Relative Unemployment in EU Member States, 1987 and 1996*

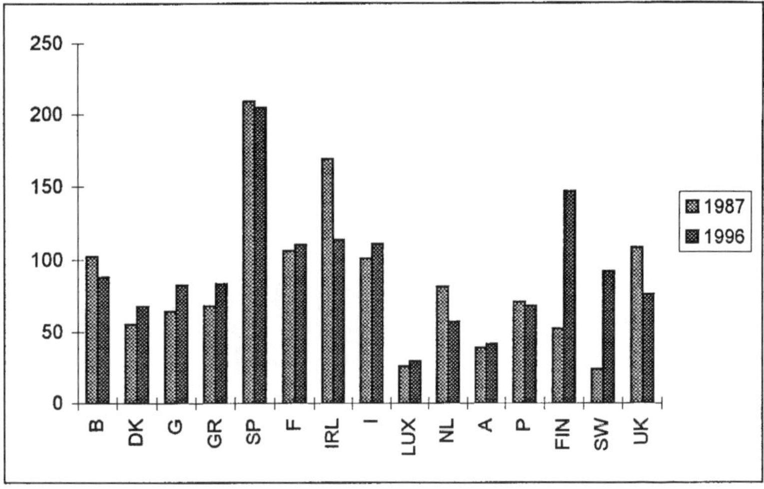

* EU Average = 100
Source: (CEC 1997a).

Figure 2.4 Relative Unemployment in EU NUTS II Regions, 1995*

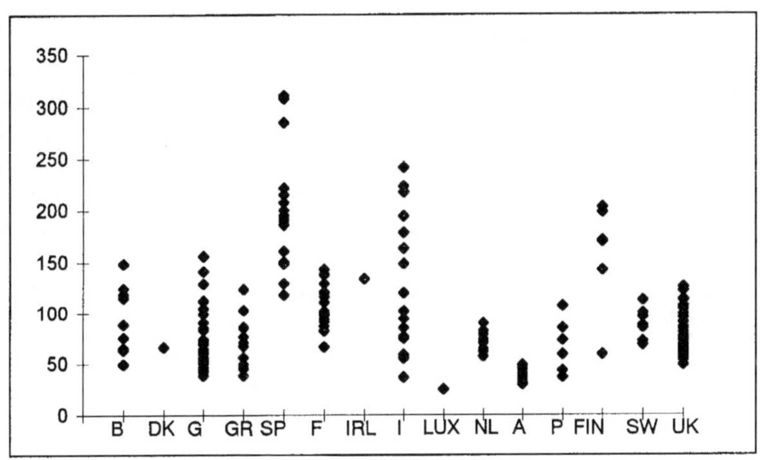

*EU Average = 100
Source: EUROSTAT (1997b).

As for per capita income, unemployment differences are also more pronounced at the NUTS II level of regions than at member state level.

In 1995 Luxembourg had the lowest unemployment rate (2.7 per cent), whereas the Spanish region of Andalucia was the worst affected region with an unemployment rate of no less than 33.3 per cent in 1995. Intra-national differences are particularly significant in Spain, Italy and Sweden, whereas unemployment rate differences in other countries, for example France and the UK, are surprisingly low. However, regional unemployment disparities also tended to widen over time with the standard deviation of all NUTS II regions increasing from 4.2 in 1983 to 5.6 in 1995.

2.3.3 Links between Regional Income, Employment and Productivity

Inter-regional differences in per capita income can be disaggregated into differences in productivity and differences in the activity rate of the regional population. For the purposes of the following analysis, productivity is defined as GDP per person employed whereas the activity rate is the ratio between the number of employees in a particular region and its total population. All values are relative to the

EU15 average (EU = 100) and GDP values are expressed in PPS. The analysis is conducted at the NUTS II level except for the UK where NUTS I regions had to be used. The total number of regions is 176. All data refer to the year 1993.

Figure 2.5 and Figure 2.6 both indicate a clear, positive link between per capita income on the one hand, and the activity rate as well as productivity on the other hand. The scatterplots suggest an even stronger correlation between regional productivity and per capita income than between income and the activity rate. This is confirmed by econometric analysis.

In a first step, productivity (PROD) and the activity rate (ACTIV) are used as separate variables in order to explain relative regional income. The regression results show that productivity differences explain about 60 per cent of the total variation in per capita income whereas differences in the activity rate explain about 40 per cent. In separate regressions for the 49 Objective 1 regions, in other words those regions with a relative per capita income of less than 75 per cent of the EU average, productivity differences also explain about 60 per cent of the variation. The activity rate ceases to be statistically significant, a result that is mainly determined by the high relative activity rates in Portuguese regions.

In a second step, relative per capita income is simultaneously regressed on productivity and the activity rate. The regressions also

Figure 2.5 Relative per capita Income in NUTS II Regions and Relative Activity Rate in 1993 (logged)*

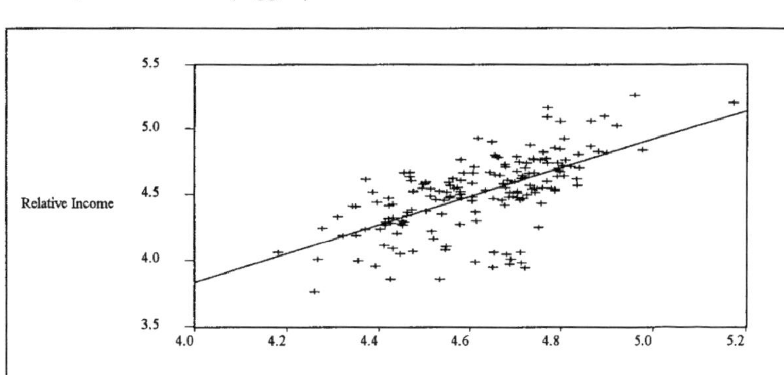

*Relative income in PPS

Source: EUROSTAT (1997b); own calculations.

Figure 2.6 Relative per capita Income in NUTS II Regions and Relative Productivity in 1993 (logged)*

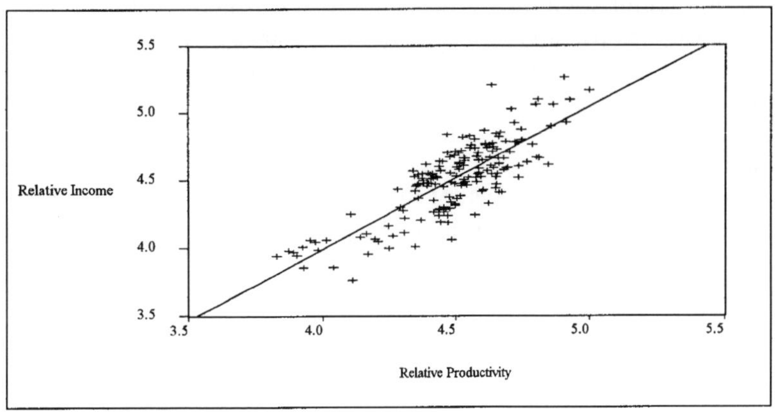

*Relative income in PPS
Source: EUROSTAT (1997b) and own calculations.

include country dummies in order to account for country-specific differences. The *t*-statistics for the different variables are given in brackets.

All Regions

$$\text{INCOME} = \underset{(-33.88)}{-107.91} + \underset{(63.70)}{0.98}\ \text{ACTIV} + \underset{(84.82)}{1.09}\ \text{PROD} \qquad (2.1)$$

$R^2 = 0.99$; DW = 1.4; SE Reg. = 9.52; n = 176

Objective 1 Regions

$$\text{INCOME} = \underset{(-14.73)}{-62.14} + \underset{(23.99)}{0.71}\ \text{ACTIV} + \underset{(35.88)}{0.88}\ \text{PROD} \qquad (2.2)$$

$R^2 = 0.99$; DW = 1.7; SE = 1.4; n = 49

The results indicate that increases in regional productivity as well as increases in the activity rate lead to a roughly proportionate increase in regional per capita income. Comparing the two variables, however, the results show that an increase in productivity results in a slightly larger increase in income than an increase in the activity rate. This result holds for the full sample of regions as well as for the Objective 1 regions. For the latter, the income effect of changes in regional productivity and the regional activity rate are slightly below the comparable values for the full sample.

Most country dummies turn out to be insignificant. Only the dummies for Luxembourg and, more surprisingly, Greece are weakly significant in Regression 2.1. The coefficients indicate that per capita income in these countries is about 7 percentage points above what one would expect on the basis of their relative productivity and the participation of the population in the economy. A possible explanation for Luxembourg is the importance of financial inflows. The result for Greece is more likely to be caused by the poor quality of the available statistical information.

All in all regionalised income and unemployment data demonstrate clearly the existence of significant socio-economic disparities within the EU. These disparities exceed comparable values for other large economic areas like the United States significantly and they are at the heart of EU regional policy.[6] However, it is not clear whether the regional disparities within the EU are likely to be permanent or whether they can be expected to disappear in the foreseeable future. This question is addressed in the next two chapters.

3 Economic Theory and the Convergence versus Divergence Debate

Economists have been unable to agree whether regions within an economically integrated area will tend to converge to a common level of per capita income. This chapter thus provides an overview of the convergence and divergence approaches of economic theory. Convergence theory, based on neoclassical economic reasoning, predicts that factor incomes in all parts of an integration area will eventually converge provided that sufficiently strong adjustment mechanisms within the integration area exist. Divergence theory, however, predicts an increasingly uneven spatial distribution of economic activity due to economic phenomena such as increasing returns to scale, positive agglomeration externalities and transport costs.

3.1 CONVERGENCE THEORY

3.1.1 The Neoclassical Approach to Growth and Convergence

In order to be able to deduct universally applicable results, neoclassical economic theory is based on a set of rigid assumptions, the most important of which are given below:

1. production technologies are identical and exogenously given across countries;
2. returns to scale are constant; and
3. production factors are (imperfect) substitutes.

The usual starting point for a review of modern economic growth theory is the Solow model (Solow, 1957). His analysis is based on the following production function:

$$Y = eT^{*} F(K,L) \qquad (3.1)$$

Y equals total output, produced with a given quantity of the production factors labour (L) and capital (K); eT is the total factor productivity variable, representing the technology used in the economy. Neoclassical theories assume that technology spreads rapidly and can therefore be regarded as identical in all countries or regions (Assumption 1). Changes in the technology variable are exogenously determined. Assuming that the functional form of Equation 3.1 is Cobb–Douglas, the equation reads as follows:

$$Y = eT * K(t)^{a} L(t)^{1-a} \tag{3.2}$$

The specification that a + (1 – a) = 1 satisfies Assumption 2 above. Constant returns to scale (CRS) means that a doubling of both production factors together exactly doubles the output produced. Individually, however, the production factors yield decreasing returns to scale ($a < 1$; $(1 - a) < 1$). In other words, the more one increases the input of only one factor, the lower is the marginal return from this increase.

These assumptions in the Solow model lead to the conclusion that there is an optimal ratio between capital and labour, denoted k*. Once k* is reached, per capita growth is only possible due to technological progress, assumed to be exogenous to the economy (Assumption 1). The identity of k and k*, however, is assumed to be the exception rather than the rule. Whenever locations are imperfectly integrated, spatial differences in relative factor endowments are likely to exist which in turn explains spatial disparities in wages, interest rates and prices. If, for example, an economy uses a production technology which requires relatively more capital than the country has at its disposal, production cannot be efficient because labour has to act as an imperfect substitute for capital (Assumption 3).

If k is smaller than k*, individuals can optimise k by increasing their savings rate and using these savings for investments. If k is larger than k*, people can reduce savings and investments. The relative scarcity or abundance of capital and the capital remuneration based on relative scarcity are a strong incentive to save or dissave until k equals the technologically determined optimal level k*. However, changes in the savings rate or the growth rate of the workforce take time. Alternative and faster adjustment mechanisms are factor movements or, since goods and services can be regarded as transformed factors of production, goods movements between different countries or regions. According to neoclassical theory it is, therefore, an important task of the state to make sure that these adjustment mechanisms are not obstructed, for example due to trade and migration restrictions.

Provided sufficient adjustment mechanisms exist, neoclassical growth theory predicts an inter-regional and international convergence of factor incomes. This prediction, however, is based on a rather mechanistic analysis of the model. Only on the basis of the assumptions that technology is identical in all locations, that differences in the economic structure do not matter and that sufficient mobility of goods and/or factors of production exists, will absolute convergence take place. These assumptions are clearly not very realistic. If the persistence of technological differences is acknowledged, or if the adjustment mechanisms remain insufficient, conditional as opposed to absolute convergence will occur, which is a more likely prediction.

Besides safeguarding the abovementioned adjustment mechanisms, the role of governments in neoclassical growth theory is very limited. Some authors relax the assumption that technology is identical in all locations. They argue that the diffusion of technology is time-consuming and costly and should be eased by governmental action. It is also argued that a sufficient degree of education of the workforce is necessary in order to use the available technology as efficiently as possible. Mankiw, Romer and Weil (1992), for example, extend the classic Solow growth model by including human capital as an additional factor of production. While they demonstrate theoretically and empirically the importance of human capital for growth, they leave the assumption of exogenous technological progress untouched. Possibly the most important task of the state, however, is the creation of a 'market-friendly' economic environment.

> ... the appropriate role of government is to ensure adequate investments in people, provide a competitive climate for private enterprise, keep the economy open to international trade, and maintain a stable macroeconomy. Beyond these roles, the report agrees, governments are likely to do more harm than good. (World Bank, 1991)

As argued above, the existence of sufficient adjustment mechanisms is of crucial importance for the inter-locational convergence of factor prices. In the following we shall analyse how international economic integration affects these adjustment mechanisms.

3.1.2 Adjustment Mechanisms and the Theory of Factor Price Equalisation

3.1.2.1 Goods Movements

Imagine a model world with two locations, two goods and two production factors (capital and labour). Location 1 (the core) is relatively well endowed with capital ($k_t > k^*$) and location 2 (the periphery) is relatively well endowed with labour ($k_t < k^*$). If the core specialises in the good that is most efficiently produced by making relatively intensive use of capital whereas the periphery produces the labour-intensive good, the two locations can trade their products until the product mix best suits their local demands.

Reasoning along these lines is the basis for the Heckscher–Ohlin–Samuelsen (HOS) model of international trade. Locations specialise in the production and export of the good in which they have a comparative advantage. This in turn is the good which requires relatively intensive use of the location's relatively abundant factor of production (HOS theorem).

The Factor–Price–Equalisation (FPE) theorem predicts that in a free trade situation the remuneration for the factors of production is the same in both locations. At first sight this makes intuitive sense, since the degree of relative scarcity or abundance of factors is equalised due to trade. A brief look at the distribution of factor incomes across Europe, however, shows that factor incomes still differ significantly across countries and regions (Langhammer, 1987; EUROSTAT, 1994).

To some extent this problem is not only caused by the abovementioned restrictive assumptions but also by some assumptions that are specific to HOS trade theory.

1. All goods are tradable.
2. Production factors are fully mobile between different economic sectors and within countries or regions.[1]
3. Production factors are fully immobile between countries or regions.

Assumption 1 denies the existence of natural or artificial barriers to trade and is not normally satisfied. Although institutional arrangements like a common market lead to the abolition of artificial trade barriers like tariffs, quotas or technical regulations, natural barriers to trade like transport costs remain in place.

Another reason why full FPE is unlikely to come about is Assumption 2. Most factors of production, labour in particular but also parts of the capital stock, are neither fully mobile within locations nor between economic sectors. It is sometimes argued that in the long run capital and labour can change from one sector to the other. This is not entirely true. Substantial parts of the labour force will not be able to move from, say, agriculture to software development. Furthermore, natural resources and land are fully immobile factors of production which also influences the returns to capital and labour.

3.1.2.2 Factor Mobility

In the section above, it was argued that trade in goods and services amounts to an exchange of factors of production in processed form. This implies that factor movements can substitute goods movements whenever trade is impossible or too expensive due to high transport and transaction costs. Within the framework of neoclassical theory, it is easy to demonstrate that international factor movements also lead to a convergence of factor prices.

Migration Imagine again two different economic areas, the core (C) and the periphery (P). Due to exogenous reasons both locations are unable to produce at the utility-maximising capital intensity k^*. Initially, P is relatively labour-abundant ($k_1^P < k^*$), and C is relatively capital-abundant ($k_1^C > k^*$). Due to the relative scarcity of labour in C, the initial equilibrium wage in C (w_1^C) is higher than the equilibrium wage in P (w_1^P).[2]

Neglecting more sophisticated micro-foundation of migration decisions,[3] it can be assumed that people move to where wages are higher, provided that migration is costless. Moreover, it has to be assumed that neither capital movements nor trade between the two locations are possible. Provided that labour is perfectly mobile and the labour markets in C and P fully integrated, immigration from P to C increases relative labour supply in C. The wage level in C decreases to the new equilibrium wage (w_2^*), which is identical in P and C. Labour in P benefits from a relative income redistribution away from the owners of capital and towards workers because emigration makes labour scarcer in relation to the (fixed) stock of capital. The total compensation for the production factor labour increases. In C, however, immigration makes labour relatively more abundant and induces a reduction in labour compensations relative to the returns on capital.

These are the short-run direct labour market effects of migration on the total labour force. In practice, however, it is important to analyse the labour market effects of migration on the situation of the native population in C. If it is assumed that immigrant and native workers can substitute each other perfectly, total employment in C will increase, but employment of natives will initially fall due to migration (quantity effect of migration). From the above introduction into the basic framework of neoclassical production and growth theory, however, it can be deducted that the improved production input factor intensities k_2^P and k_2^c are closer or equal to k*. This allows a more efficient production and therefore an increase in output in P and C. This allocational effect of migration will increase the wage level in both, P and C from w_2^* to w_3^*. Employment in P and C will also increase and offset the short-term negative employment effects in C.

Admittedly, this is a very positive assessment. The effect of immigration on the wages and employment of natives always depends on the relative importance of the quantity and allocation effects. While differences in the magnitude of these effects have repercussions on the political acceptability of migration, they do not change the conclusion that, according to neoclassical theory, international labour mobility is a strong force of macroeconomic convergence.

There is some empirical evidence for the equalising effects of migration on factor returns. Boyer et al. (1993) argue that the massive emigration from Ireland prior to the First World War contributed significantly to the convergence of real wages between Ireland, the UK and the US. The convergence power of free labour movement is also emphasised in Williamson and Taylor (1994). Like Boyer et al. they investigate international migration prior to the First World War, a period when international migration was relatively strong. At present, however, international mobility within and between industrialised countries is very limited. Within the EU each year only about 0.5 per cent of the population move from one country to another. For most individuals, the substantial costs of migration seem to outweigh its potential benefits. Migration is not only a suitable mechanism to equalise long-run international income differences but it can also balance out the effects of nation and region-specific macroeconomic shocks. This point is taken up in the section on monetary adjustment mechanisms.

Capital Mobility As far as capital movements are concerned, the equalising mechanism is very similar to that for migration. Again, the two locations core (C) and periphery (P) are unable to produce at the utility-maximising capital intensity k*. At the beginning P is relatively labour-abundant ($k_1^p < k^*$), and C is relatively capital-abundant ($k_1^c > k^*$). Due to the relative scarcity of labour in this location, the initial equilibrium interest rate in C (i_1^c) is lower than the equilibrium interest rate (i_1^p) in P.

This time it is assumed that capital is perfectly mobile whereas labour is perfectly immobile. Trade remains non-existent. Capital will now be transferred to P where interest rates decrease until the new equilibrium interest rate i_2^* equalises capital returns in P and C. Capital owners in C benefit from a relative income redistribution away from labour because capital has become relatively less abundant, capital owners in P face an initially reduced interest rate.

Beyond these short-run effects, the neoclassical framework foresees that the new, optimal production input factor intensity k^* allows a more efficient production and improved output in P and C which raises the (identical) capital return level in P and C.

Empirically one has to distinguish between financial and physical capital mobility. Financial capital mobility is often two-way, say from Germany to Luxembourg, and vice versa. There are various motives for this form of capital mobility, for example the distribution of risks or the intermediation services provided by international financial centres such as London and Frankfurt. These flows increase the efficiency of capital markets, but are unlikely to foster the equalisation of factor endowments and returns between different locations.

Physical capital mobility, however, can contribute to such an equalisation. An important form of this kind of capital mobility are Foreign Direct Investments (FDIs). Economic integration theory predicts an increase of such flows due to institutional integration and the corresponding reduction of barriers for physical capital. Empirical evidence on intra-EU FDI flows show indeed a clear upward trend in capital mobility between different parts of the European Union with economically lagging member states being net recipients. We will come back to this point in Chapter 4.1.

3.1.2.3 Monetary Adjustment Mechanisms

Exchange rate changes do not directly alter production factor ratios but they influence trade and capital flows, which in turn can work towards an equalisation of production factor ratios and factor incomes. Generally speaking, however, monetary adjustment mechanisms are mainly important to balance asymmetric economic shocks and are therefore important for the debate on the economic effects of EMU.

The starting point for most approaches to define optimum currency areas (OCA) is to investigate whether the demand shocks affecting the different parts of a common currency area are predominantly symmetric or asymmetric. If, for example, the periphery P is affected by a negative demand shock whereas demand in the core C remains stable, P can depreciate its currency which increases its exports and offsets the negative demand shock. The more asymmetric the shocks in different areas are, the more useful it is to maintain exchange rate flexibility between the different areas as a (short-term) adjustment tool. The three classic approaches to OCA theory are briefly summarised below. For more detailed surveys, see for example Gros and Thygesen (1992) and Traud (1996).

- Mundell (1961) argues that a high level of factor mobility within a currency area can make good for the loss of the exchange rate mechanism. As shown above, migration and capital mobility can be a source of long-run convergence, but the same mechanism can also be used for short-term shocks.
- For McKinnon (1963), the decisive feature of countries forming a currency union should be their openness. He argues that countries with a high foreign trade share are more likely to offset asymmetric domestic demand shocks by means of increased exports. Moreover, McKinnon argues that the effectiveness of exchange rate changes as an instrument of economic policy diminishes for very open economies. Higher prices for imports, expressed in local currency after a depreciation, quickly offset the positive effects that depreciation may have on exports.
- According to Kenen (1969), countries with a diversified economic production structure are better prepared for monetary integration than countries which rely on just a few products because they will not be as severely affected by asymmetric shocks.

According to these criteria, monetary union will be most beneficial for highly open, diversified economies with a high degree of intra- and international factor mobility.[4]

Since the EU embarked on its way to EMU, a substantial number of empirical studies investigating whether the EU is an OCA or not have been published. Bayoumi and Eichengreen (1992) find that only a core of EU countries are exposed to shocks, which in terms of symmetry are comparable to the US. They argue accordingly that the EU as a whole 'may find it more difficult to operate a monetary union than the US' (Bayoumi and Eichengreen, 1992: 36). Caporale (1993) also finds evidence for considerable asymmetries, but not for a clear core–periphery pattern among EU member states. De Grauwe and Vanhaverbeke (1993) look at adjustment mechanisms for European regions and find that at present real exchange rate variability between countries is quite significant, whereas labour mobility is more important between regions of the same country.

All in all, there is a substantial amount of disagreement about whether the whole or parts of the EU are an OCA. As far as lagging regions are concerned, one has to distinguish between those areas that are part of a rich member state, and member states such as Greece which in their entirety are lagging. Only the latter can make direct use of the monetary adjustment mechanism and may thus find EMU more problematic than the present exchange rate regime. For the former, an independent exchange rate policy was never feasible.

Table 3.1 summarises this overview of various channels of adjustment. As long as international factor mobility is given, neoclassical theory predicts that FPE will come about eventually.

Although one might think that trade and factor mobility between different locations of an integrated area like the EU should be sufficient to induce FPE, this is not necessarily the case. As argued above, factor mobility within Europe is still quite low. Even a perfect functioning of the adjustment mechanisms described above, however, would not necessarily guarantee the convergence of factor incomes in all parts of the EU. After all, it has to be kept in mind that the prediction of FPE is still based on the neoclassical set of assumptions which disregards important economic phenomena such as increasing returns to scale or external effects.

Table 3.1 Factor Mobility and Factor Price Equalisation

		Barriers to Trade	
		YES	NO
International Factor Mobility	YES	Full FPE	Full FPE
	NO	No FPE	Convergence stops short of full FPE due to non-tradables.

3.2 DIVERGENCE THEORY

New approaches to economic theory relax the rigid assumptions of neoclassical economics. In the following section, some of the concepts used to explain a divergent economic development between different locations are reviewed. On the basis of these concepts, those forms of governmental intervention that might be invoked to alter the spatial distribution of economic activity are analysed.

3.2.1 Technological Differences between Locations

A first strand of divergence theory is based on the argument that technological progress does not spread evenly across all economic locations. This is a significant change compared to the original neoclassical assumption that production technologies are identical and exogenously given across countries. Put in formal terms, this yields the following equation:

$$Y = eT * K(t)^{\alpha} L(t)^{1-\alpha} \quad \text{with} \quad eT_c > eT_p \qquad (3.3)$$

The total factor productivity variable for the core C (eT_c) is higher than the corresponding variable for the periphery P (eT_p). It does not matter why the production conditions in the core are more favourable. It suffices to assume that factor productivity in C is absolutely superior to factor productivity in P. This implies that any given combination of input factors will produce a higher output in the core than in the periphery. Correspondingly, there is more output with which to compensate input factors. Labour and capital will be better paid in C than in P.[5] Given this situation, the question arises, what happens if labour and capital are mobile? As long as factor proportions do not become too unfavourable in C, and as long as the technology remains superior in the core, it will be beneficial for production factors to emigrate to the core.

Whereas in Section 3.1 factor mobility equalised factor returns and was a source of convergence, it now becomes a source of divergence. In the long run, assuming that capital and labour are fully mobile, the periphery faces a total outflow of production factors unless immobile, location-specific factors are taken into account. Since this radical solution is not realistic, it is appropriate to introduce immobile, location specific factors. This alters Equation 3.3 to:

$$Y = eT * K(t)^{\alpha} L(t)^{\beta} A^{\gamma} \quad \text{with} \quad eT_c > eT_p \qquad (3.4)$$

where A^{γ} represents location specific, immobile input factors. Given the above assumption that technology is superior in the core, C can still produce more output to compensate its factors of production. Given similar initial factor proportions in both locations, mobile factors of production like capital are better off if they move from P to C. Factor mobility will therefore make capital in C scarcer and the return on investment in this region has to increase. This, however, will decrease wages and the compensation of location-specific factors, which in turn increases migration incentives for the remaining mobile factors.

Due to the existence of immobile, location-specific factors and due to the assumption of constant returns to scale, development in this economy is still stable. Once the mobile factors capital and (mobile) labour have become sufficiently scarce, wages and capital returns will equalise across both locations. The return for immobile factors in the core, however, will be higher than the return for immobile factors in the periphery. Moreover, P will have lost a large share of its original endowments with capital and (mobile) labour.

Not only factor movements but also trade between locations can be a source of divergence if we allow for technological differences. In the preceding section, it was argued that factor movements can substitute for goods movements in order to achieve FPE. This, however, holds only as long as we do not allow for differences in the production techniques of different locations. Among the first to explore these arguments was Markusen (1983).

Imagine again region C and P producing two different goods with two factors of production. There is not only inter-regional trade but also inter-regional factor mobility. C has a technological advantage over P in the production of a specific good. Due to this technological advantage and despite the absence of a factor endowment difference, C will export this good to P and the rate of return for the factor used relatively intensively in the production of this good will be higher in C than in P. This incentive causes factors used relatively intensively in the production process of the traded good to move from P to C, which in turn creates a previously absent difference of factor endowments which further amplifies the trade flow. The shift of factors from P to C and the country's specialisation will not stop until either C is completely specialised in the production of its export good or P has been emptied of this factor. If technological differences exist, trade and factor movements are therefore no longer substitutes but complements. Factor movements become a prerequisite for increases in trade.

Although this is a highly oversimplified model it has real life relevance to it. Imagine, for example, capital being removed from peripheral parts of an integration area in order to be invested in more central locations where industries have acquired superior production skills. Immobile factors are left behind and the ratio between mobile and immobile factors in the periphery becomes more and more unfavourable. This means that prices for immobile factors in the periphery – mainly wages – will be significantly lower than in the core.

The policy implications of this reasoning for regions that are technologically disadvantaged are obvious. It is important to close technological gaps as soon as possible in order to prevent disruptive outflows of mobile factors of production like capital and highly qualified labour. This argument has become one of the core rationales for regional policy measures designed to improve the endogenous technological potential of disadvantaged regions and to disseminate knowledge more quickly, for example by means of technology transfer centres.

3.2.2 Increasing Returns to Scale and External Effects

In the previous section the impact of technological differences on aggregate output and productivity was investigated. In this section the neoclassical assumption of constant returns to scale is being dropped. This changes the aggregate effects of integration as well as the spatial distribution of economic activity significantly.

From a theoretical point of view output can be produced at constant returns to scale (CRS), decreasing returns to scale (DRS) or increasing returns to scale (IRS). As far as IRS are concerned, three different forms can be distinguished, namely firm-specific IRS, industry-specific IRS and location-specific IRS.

3.2.2.1 Firm-Specific Increasing Returns to Scale

Firm-specific IRS are the most intuitive form of returns to scale. Setting up and operating a car plant, for example, requires large fixed costs. The production of 100,000 cars in this plant is therefore cheaper per unit than the production of just 1,000 because fixed costs can be divided. This is only possible, however, if the market is big enough. For a small location, trade is therefore a prerequisite for firm-specific IRS and the exploitation of previously unexploited IRS was an important motive for, as well as an effect of, European economic integration (Owen, 1983; CEC, 1988).

The final location of the production plants inside an integration area depends mainly on the plant's pre-integration size, which in turn determines the average production costs (Grubel and Lloyd, 1975). Since the average plant size in lagging European economies tends to be smaller than in the core countries, this finding is uncomfortable from a cohesion point of view. However, there are also limiting factors to the beneficial effects of firm-specific IRS. Production sites can become too big, which increases co-ordination costs and leads to a loss of flexibility. The turning point beyond which such negative scale effects dominate depends strongly on industry-specific factors, such as the fixed costs required to establish a production site.

3.2.2.2 External Effects

The second and third category of IRS, industry- and location-specific IRS, are closely related to external effects. These forms of IRS are less intuitive than firm-specific IRS. Here the argument goes that firms benefit from other firms' positive external effects (spillovers), either in the same industry or the same location. Location-specific IRS are therefore very similar to positive agglomeration effects as pioneered by Marschall (1890). Examples for such external effects are:

- technological developments which are beneficial for all firms in the industry;
- the forward and backward linkages that exist within an area of intense economic activity; and
- a well-trained and diversified labour force within an agglomeration.

On the other hand, agglomerations can also have negative external effects like the congestion of urban areas, overused transport facilities and a rise in factor prices.

A production function with location-specific IRS can look as follows:

$$Y = eT * K^{\alpha} L^{\beta} A^{\gamma} \quad \text{where } \alpha + \beta + \gamma > 1 \tag{3.5}$$

Besides labour (L) and capital (K) the production function now includes location-specific, immobile factors (A). T refers to the production technology used in the economy and e is an efficiency parameter. Given an optimal factor distribution, one finds now that the larger the total amount of inputs, the higher their productivity. What does that imply for the convergence or divergence effect of factor movements?

One can imagine two regions, core (C) and periphery (P), which are identical in everything but their size. Due to this difference, the marginal return and compensation of input factors in the bigger region C is higher than in P. If capital and labour can move from the periphery to the core, the size of C and hence its productivity advantage will increase even further, along with the wage and interest rate gap between P and C. This process stops when the scarcity of location specific factors A and corresponding redistribution effects eventually decrease periphery–core differences in mobile factors' return to such an extent that this difference is no longer a sufficient incentive for mobile factors to move to C.[6]

The predictions of this model are quite similar to the situation where we assumed technological differences between core and periphery. In this previous situation an initial technological advantage decided which region benefited from goods and factor movements. In the present model, based on IRS, the determining factor is the size of a location. Labour (or capital) will start to move to the larger region, which in turn strengthens the position of this location whereas the initially smaller region loses competitiveness.

How realistic is the idea of divergence based on differences in the size of locations? Whereas the example of a firm dividing fixed costs by a larger number of goods produced is convincing, the idea that German labour and capital have become more efficient simply due to German reunification makes less intuitive sense. Nevertheless, there is some empirical support for the existence of industry- and location-specific external effects.

Caballero and Lyons found fairly robust evidence in favour of external IRS at the national level in the US and a couple of European countries (Caballero and Lyons, 1990a). They estimated also international, intra-industry external IRS in Europe (Caballero and Lyons, 1990b). The results of these estimations, however, were not statistically significant.

Which policy recommendations can be derived from the existence of external effects? Generally speaking positive external or agglomeration effects lead to a situation where social factor returns outweigh private returns. The opposite applies for negative external effects. In both cases public interventions are required in order to maximise collective welfare (Balassa, 1961). If positive effects dominate, public intervention in order to counteract these effects is likely to reduce aggregate welfare. From the point of view of regional equality, however, things look different. External effects are likely to increase the differences between core and periphery. Public policies designed in order to reduce spatial imbalances should therefore try to make good for the relative disadvantages that lagging regions face due to positive external effects in the core. This problematic balance is addressed in more detail in Chapter 5.

The next section looks at a special but very important form of external effect by assuming that the amount of accumulated capital or human capital in a location has a beneficial effect on the technology used in the production process. This leads us back to section 3.2.1, where we looked at the convergence or divergence effects of technological differences. This time, however, these differences are endogenous rather than exogenous to the location.

3.2.3 New Growth Theory and Endogenous Technological Progress

The term new growth theory refers to a group of approaches that try to endogenise technology, previously assumed to be exogenously determined. A rather simple version of new growth theory argues that returns to capital do not have to be diminishing. This is a significant change compared to the neoclassical approach outlined above. Romer (1986) for example defines the following aggregate production function:

$$Y = AK^{\alpha + \gamma}L^{1 - \alpha} \tag{3.6}$$

Private returns to capital are represented by α, returns to labour by $1 - \alpha$. Due to positive externalities, there are not only private but also social returns to capital, denoted by γ. Provided that $\alpha + \gamma = 1$, capital has constant returns to scale and growth is no longer dependent on exogenous technological progress.

According to this reasoning the stock of capital and, according to some models, the stock of human capital in an economy becomes a crucial factor for the growth performance. This also alters the likely impact of economic integration on growth. Neoclassical analyses of integration effects, like CEC (1988), argued that the main consequence of the shift from a customs union to a common market is a one-off adjustment of the participating economies to a resource allocation that is closer to the optimal production factor ratio required by the prevailing production technology. Besides these allocational gains firm-specific scale effects of the kind outlined above can be realised. After these adjustments have taken place, however, there is no lasting change of the pre-integration growth path. This point of view was questioned by new growth theorists. They argued, that integration leads to an increase of the available capital stock, increased social returns to capital and hence to a permanent increase in the growth rate. Applying the arguments of new growth theory Baldwin (1989) projected that the Single European Market (SEM) project could lead to welfare gains of up to 13–40 per cent of pre-SEM GDP.

Growth models based on production functions like Equation 3.6 suffer from a substantial analytical problem. In order to yield realistic results, the combined private and social returns to capital must be exactly 1. If $\alpha + \gamma < 1$, the model collapses back to neoclassical theory; if it is more than 1, growth will steadily accelerate, which is not realistic (Solow, 1994).

The second approach of new growth theory is based on the assumption that technological progress depends crucially on human capital. This leads to the following aggregate production function proposed by Lucas (1988).

$$Y = eT(HC)\, K^{\alpha} L^{\beta} HC^{\gamma} \tag{3.7}$$

Output depends on the input of capital (K), labour (L), human capital (HC) and on efficiency (e), namely the degree to which the input factor mix is suitable for the level of technology (T) with which the economy operates. T depends in turn on the stock of human capital. If this model is correct, markets fail because they do not compensate people or firms who invest in skills for the collective external effect of human capital on technology. This is so important in this model because differences in the accumulation of human capital can explain persistent differences in the growth paths of locations.

It is not difficult to find some empirical support for the economic importance of human capital. Countries that invested heavily in human capital enjoyed on average higher growth rates than countries with a poor educational record (Sala-i-Martin, 1994). Despite this evidence, one has to be cautious when advocating governmental action. First, most innovations in an economy are stochastic and beyond the reach of planning or control. Second, governmental R&D support for private research is often likely to be just another form of subsidy which harms the overall efficiency of the economy rather than doing much good.

What are the implications of new growth theory for the convergence versus divergence debate? Provided that positive external effects of human capital and capital on factor productivity exist, agglomerations are likely to develop wherever regions have an initial advantage (Grossman and Helpman, 1994). This, however, means that regional growth paths can permanently diverge depending on whether a region was lucky enough to have a headstart in the race for human capital or production clusters. Only these regions will be able to develop a dynamic comparative advantage in high-tech, high value-added goods. Other economies will get stuck in a poverty trap, as described by Rebelo (1991).

Since total factor productivity and hence the remuneration of production factors in lagging regions remain below the remuneration in the technologically advanced agglomerations, outmigration of physical and human capital keeps their per capita capital stock always below a level where endogenous growth and hence a catch-up process could be sparked. The effect that the Lucas model attributes to brain drain, for example, differs fundamentally from the neoclassical approach of Mankiw, Romer and Weil (1992). For the latter, human capital is just an input factor like any other and the brain drain enforces convergence through the balancing of unequal distributions of human capital. In the Lucas model, the country that is most developed attracts human capital with higher returns, and the immigration of highly skilled specialists assures a further upswing of growth and development. Henceforth brain drain unambiguously lowers the growth rate of the emigration country.[7]

Although simple and uniform policy recommendations cannot be given, there is some evidence in favour of a threshold level of development, below which economic integration can have detrimental effects on the long-run growth prospects of locations.[8] Historical experiences, such as the ill-fated development process in the Mezzogiorno (Faini, 1983; Faini, Galli and Gianninni 1992), demonstrate that the integration of insufficiently competitive regions with more advanced economies, in the case of the Mezzogiorno unification with northern Italy, may have negative effects on the future prospects of the initially backwards areas. As far as possible regional policy interventions are concerned, new growth theory points also towards the importance of technology transfer facilities and investments in better education.

3.2.4 Location Theory

Location theory has long been neglected by mainstream economics. During the last few years, however, there has been a renewed interest in locational questions, pioneered by scholars like Krugman (1991 and 1992) and Giersch (1990). The focus of location theory is on the impact of transport costs. In light of the effects of economic integration on different locations it is important to differentiate transport and transaction costs. Transaction costs can be substantially reduced due to integration. Transport costs can also be reduced, for example by improvements in transport infrastructure, but they will not cease to exist, even within a highly integrated economic area.

Classic location theorists of the 1920s and 1930s stressed that the importance of transport costs differs substantially from one economic sector to the other. Predöhl (1925) looked at the ideal distance between the points of production and consumption of individual goods. At these points of substitution, the benefits to be obtained from lower labour and capital costs in the production location (due to IRS) are balanced out by the additional transport costs incurred. Christaller (1933) developed a hierarchy of central and peripheral places, which is also based on transport cost considerations. Different goods require different market sizes, which leads to the development of central places, offering all goods produced, as well as the development of increasingly peripheral places, offering a declining range of goods.[9]

Empirical investigations of the relative importance of different factors for locational decisions are frequently based on business surveys (CEC, 1990 and 1993a). Table 3.2 summarises some results of a large survey, asking firms which factors they perceived as critical or important for their locational decision (CEC, 1993a).

It turns out that most decisions are based on a complex interplay of numerous factors, some of which are important for the choice of the country within which a firm wants to locate; others are more important for the selection of the region within the country.

There are some obvious shortcomings to this investigation. Only those companies which have actually decided to relocate or to expand in a different location have been asked, which introduces a certain bias into the study. Nevertheless, some interesting features emerge from the analysis. The factor quoted most frequently – proximity to markets – cannot be influenced by public policies. Nearly all the other determinants, however, for example the availability, quality and costs of the workforce, the endowment with infrastructure and financial assistance, can be influenced by public policies, although most of them not in the short run. This in turn opens up the debate on locational competition and attempts by the state to influence the spatial pattern of economic activity.

Table 3.2 Most Important Location Factors for Manufacturing Plants

	Country		Region	
	Critical (%)	Important (%)	Critical (%)	Important (%)
Business factors				
Proximity to markets	34	51	19	31
Availability of raw materials	9	23	12	17
National and local characteristics				
Financial assistance or promotion	9	20	14	22
Official language and language skills	15	14	2	0
Corporate taxation	6	15	3	0
Labour factors				
General availability and quality of labour	8	24	12	31
Availability of skilled labour	9	19	11	22
Cost factors				
Costs of land and premises	5	17	11	18
Costs of labour	11	22	9	17
Infrastructure				
Quality of road/rail services	23	20	15	32
Proximity to major airports	9	14	6	31
Quality of life/personal factors				
Cultural factors	5	17	0	23
Schools and educational facilities	1	9	2	11

Source: CEC (1993a: Table 8.3); some figures are averages of two related indicators in the original table.

3.2.5 Locational Competition and Governmental Intervention

Giersch (1989) defines 'locational competition' as the competition among immobile factors of production for mobile factors, mainly

Table 3.3 Typology of Governmental Interventions to Improve Competitiveness

	Pro-Market	Contra-Market
Cost-neutral	De-regulations	Measures to Reduce Trade and Factor Mobility
Costly	Infrastructure Human Capital Formation	State Aids

capital. 'Competitiveness' can therefore be defined as the ability of countries or regions to attract respectively, to keep mobile factors of production in order to activate the immobile factors of production. What can countries or regions do in order to influence their relative competitiveness? Possible interventions can be classified along two major differentiations: (1), according to the relationship between the intervention and the market forces; and (2) according to the financial implications of the activities.

Contra-market measures that try to reduce trade and factor mobility, for example capital restrictions and tariff barriers, are second-best options and are likely to lead to substantial welfare losses. As argued above, however, it may be useful for locations at an early stage of economic development not to integrate too early into a larger economic area.

Most economists argue in favour of pro-market interventions with deregulation being the most preferable kind of intervention (Giersch, 1989; Sinn, 1989; and Lammers, 1992). Deregulation works in tandem with the market and is cost-neutral. It is easy to imagine examples of overregulation which can have detrimental economic effects. The introduction of European statutory minimum wages that are out of line with regional productivity levels, for example, would drive industries in lagging regions out of the market. Nevertheless, the discussion above has shown that overregulation cannot be made solely responsible for regional differences in economic performance and income levels. The options for other cost-free pro-market measures are limited. Governments can try to improve the general 'business climate' in their location. This is a laudable aim, but the regional 'business climate' is difficult to influence and depends to some extent on long-standing traditions and centuries-old historical processes (North, 1994; Leonardi, 1995).

What are the costly pro-market interventions that public authorities can pursue in order to improve the competitiveness of their location? First of all, they can try to improve the physical infrastructure. Second, they can try to enhance the quality of the regional workforce and the regions' overall human capital endowment. The rationales for these measures have been implicitly provided above. Improvements in physical infrastructure lower transport and transaction costs. Such a reduction can be a distinct advantage for enterprises, especially in peripheral locations. Investments in human capital do not only benefit the location in the short run but might also lead to positive external effects, which in turn might have a beneficial effect on the endogenous growth performance of the supported regions. The economic effects of these types of interventions will be further discussed in Chapters 7 and 8.

The most important costly contra-market intervention are state aids.[10] Whereas the above forms of support try to improve the underlying factors of regional competitiveness, state aids target the enterprises directly. They try to compensate for disadvantages which firms incur if they decide to move to or remain in a less-favoured region.

Although state aids lead to significant distortions of the market mechanism (Soltwedel et al., 1988; Seidenfuß, 1989) they remain the primary regional policy instrument in most EU member states (Bachtler, 1995). This is mainly due to the fact, that state aids can achieve short-run effects, e.g. the relocation of companies. Changing the underlying determinants of regional competitiveness, however, takes a long time.

3.3 CONCLUSIONS: THE AMBIGUITY OF THEORETICAL PREDICTIONS

The economic theories reviewed above leave one with predictions that are sometimes diametrically opposed. According to the neoclassical school of economic thinking, economic integration is not only likely to increase the aggregate welfare of the participating locations, it will also lead to an equalisation of factor returns within the integration area provided that sufficiently strong adjustment mechanisms, namely goods or factor movements between the integrated locations, exist.

The different approaches of divergence theory lead to radically different conclusions. It is still predicted that the integration process will lead to aggregate welfare gains. Within the integration area, however, technological differences, external effects and transport costs will lead to the development of a heterogeneous economic landscape made up of agglomerations as well as lagging areas with a low level of economic activity. Wages and returns to capital in the different regions will vary significantly, which results in substantial out-migration of mobile factors from some regions.

Supporters of divergence theory, as well as those convergence theorists that relax the assumption of identical technologies across all locations, provide rationales for governmental efforts in education and, despite reservations in view of the danger of rent-seeking, R&D. Divergence theory also stresses the importance of transport costs for economic activity. The overlap between geographical peripherality and below-average income within the EU supports that point of view and points towards the importance of investments in transport infrastructure.

4 Regional Convergence within the EU: an Empirical Analysis

The present chapter provides an empirical analysis of income convergence in the European cohesion countries. It is mainly based on the neoclassical convergence approach (Barro and Sala-i-Martin, 1991). The basic caveat of this approach is the assumption that growth will be faster in regions that are further away from their steady-state level of income. Given the assumption that this level of income should be identical in all parts of the EU, poorer regions should thus have higher growth rates than the richer areas of the Union (natural income convergence). This chapter goes beyond previous empirical assessments of convergence theory by testing the importance of regional policy variables such as human capital and infrastructure for regional income convergence across all 12 pre-1995 EU member states. Since investments in human capital and infrastructure are two of the cornerstones of EU regional policy, the present analysis amounts to an implicit qualitative evaluation of the convergence effects of European regional policy.

Section 4.1 looks at differences in the national economic performance of the four cohesion countries, Spain, Portugal, Ireland and Greece (EU4). Section 4.2, the principal section of this chapter, uses an extended convergence approach to analyse regional convergence in the EU. The concluding section summarises the findings.

4.1 NATIONAL ECONOMIC PERFORMANCE IN THE COHESION COUNTRIES

There are various ways to define and measure income convergence and, during the last few years, numerous theoretical and empirical studies on this issue have been published. A simple indicator for convergence within the EU is to look at whether the relative per capita income level in cohesion countries has approached the EU average. Figure 4.1 shows the development of this indicator for Portugal, Spain,

Figure 4.1 Relative Income in EU Cohesion Countries, 1960–97*

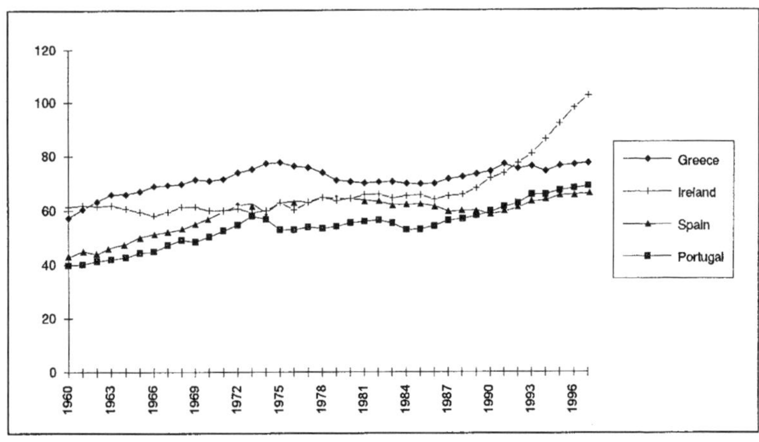

*Purchasing power standards. EU15 = 100
Source: CEC (1997a).

Greece and Ireland over the 1960–96 period. Income is expressed in purchasing power standards (PPS) relative to the EU15 average.

Since 1960 all cohesion countries have managed to narrow the gap to the EU15 average significantly, but there are considerable differences between these four member states. Greece, Spain and Portugal have narrowed the gap by 23.6 per cent, 20.3 per cent and 29.1 per cent respectively. Ireland, the success story among the cohesion countries, increased its relative income by no less than 41.3 per cent and is now above the EU15 average.

The catch-up process varied significantly over time. Table 4.1 provides average annual catch-up figures for the periods 1960–85 and

Table 4.1 Average Annual Catch-up in the Cohesion Countries, 1960–97

	Greece	Spain	Ireland	Portugal
1960–85	0.8	0.5	0.1	0.6
1986–97	0.4	0.7	3.5	1.3

Source: CEC (1997a); own calculations.

1986–97 respectively. From 1986 onwards all four cohesion countries were EU member states, which increases the comparability of their performance.

On average Greece was the fastest growing country of the EU periphery during the 1960–85 period. In fact, most of Greece's catch-up took place during the 1960–73 period when the average annual value was around 1.5 per cent. During the 1986–97 period, however, Greece was the worst-performing country, whereas Portugal and especially Ireland reduced their income gap very rapidly. These differences are largely attributable to differences in the cohesion countries economic policy.

It is beyond the scope of this chapter to survey the cohesion countries' macroeconomic policy in detail, but there is clearly a close link between macroeconomic performance and income convergence.[1] In the following we will use gross fixed capital formation and labour costs in order to demonstrate the differences in cohesion countries' macroeconomic policies.

Gross fixed capital formation is of crucial importance for the prospects of lagging economies like Portugal, Greece, Spain and Ireland to increase their relative competitiveness (Levine and Renelt, 1992: 943). Provided one follows neoclassical economic theory in assuming that the capital/labour ratio in lagging economies is below corresponding levels in more advanced countries, investment ratios in lagging European economies should be above the average level of EU15 in order to equalise this ratio and bring about a convergence of factor incomes.

Figure 4.2 shows that the Greek investment performance worsened considerably from the mid-1970s onwards. During the 1956–73 period the average investment rate was 22 per cent. During the 1975–92 period, however, it dropped to 18 per cent. Alogoskoufis (1995) argues that from the mid-1970s misguided economic policies destroyed 'the reputation of the government as co-operating in a high-investment, high-growth equilibrium' (Alogoskoufis, 1995: 170) which led to the abovementioned decline in the investment rate. On top of that, public investment declined simultaneously in quantity and quality during the 1980s.

The investment performance of Portugal and – since the mid-1980s – Spain, was more positive than that of Greece. Investment conditions in both countries were improved by successful adjustments of the public sector as well as by policies designed in order to render the labour markets more flexible (Larre and Torres, 1991).

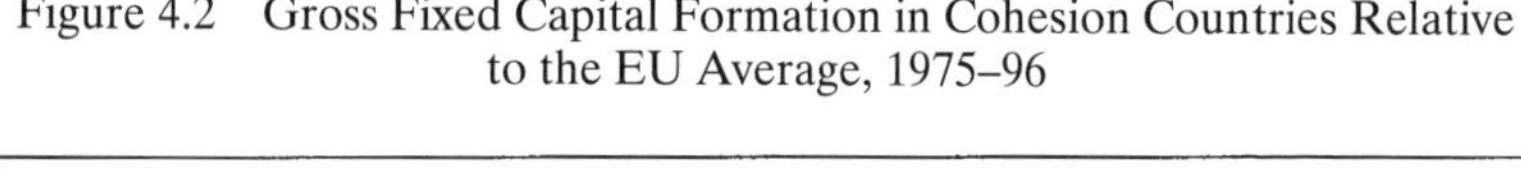

Figure 4.2 Gross Fixed Capital Formation in Cohesion Countries Relative to the EU Average, 1975–96

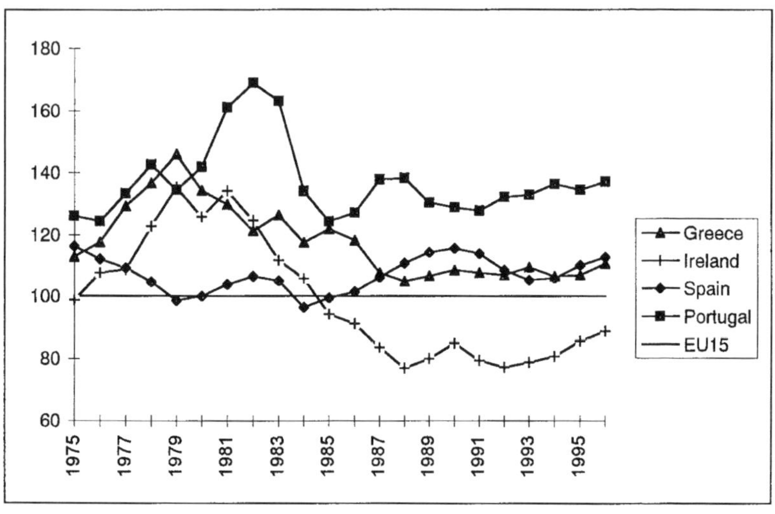

Source: CEC (1997a); own calculations.

Looking at relative labour costs, the differences within the European periphery are also striking.

Portugal clearly uses low relative labour costs in order to improve its competitiveness within the EU. The picture is less clear for Spain and Ireland. Until the mid-1980s their relative real unit labour costs were mostly above the Union average. By now, however, they are very close to or even below the EU15 mark. The value for Greece has been below the EU15 average until the early 1980s but above the average for most of the 1980s and early 1990s. Once again misguided economic policies, this time with regard to the labour market, are the main reason for this development (Katseli, 1990). Over a long period wage increases in Greece exceeded productivity growth, thereby weakening the competitiveness of the Greek economy.

Given the definition of 'competitiveness' provided in Chapter 3, the amount of inward FDI a country receives is a good indicator of its competitiveness.

Table 4.2 shows striking differences between the four countries. On a per capita basis, Ireland received more than 13 times more FDI than Greece and between three and four times the amount of Spain and

Figure 4.3 Real Unit Labour Costs in Cohesion Countries Relative to the EU Average, 1975–96

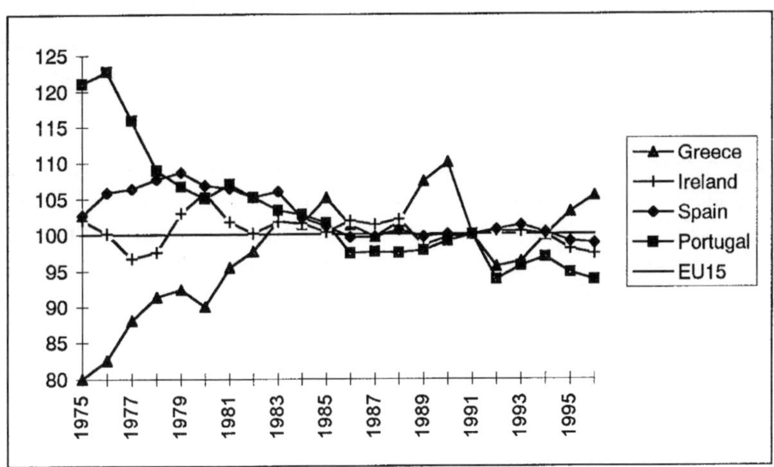

Source: CEC (1997a); own calculations.

Table 4.2 Net FDI Flows into the Cohesion Countries, 1986–91

	Greece	Spain	Ireland	Portugal
Million ECU	1670	29012	7669	6028
ECU per capita	160	740	2190	610

Source: CEC (1994a: Table 9).

Portugal. According to Barry and Bradley (1997), the favourable supply-side conditions in Ireland, a highly educated and trained labour force, improvements of the physical infrastructure and a stable macroeconomic environment are the keys to its success in attracting FDI, which in turn played a crucial role in the transformation of the Irish economy.[2] The importance of FDI for the modernisation of the Spanish and Portuguese economy is also considerable and both countries are actively and successfully pursuing policies to attract inward investments (OECD, 1994a). The lack of inward FDI in Greece reflects the abovementioned shortcomings of macroeconomic policy, the insufficient quality of the workforce and the poor level of infrastructure. The relative position of the different cohesion countries with regard to education and infrastructure will be discussed below.

Summing up this short glance at macroeconomic indicators for EU4, it emerges that their economic development over the last 20 years has been very heterogeneous. Ireland comes closest to the ideal of a dynamic, catching-up economy, although it should be kept in mind that this is essentially a phenomenon of the 1990s. Until the 1980s, Irish economic history was clearly not a success story (O Grada and O'Rourke, 1996). After a prolonged period of governmental intervention and unsustainable public debt levels the economic damage was only repaired during the macroeconomic adjustment period of the 1980s when Irish economic policy was characterised by tough fiscal policy and participation in the European Monetary System from 1978 onwards. This led to a significant reduction of the Irish inflation rate and the budget deficits and created a stable, growth-promoting macroeconomic environment.

The Greek macroeconomic indicators make the poor performance of this country with regard to per capita income easier to understand. In recent years some progress towards a more growth conducive macroeconomic environment has been made. Inflation and interest rates were significantly reduced but labour market flexibility remains limited (CEC, 1996a) and the country is only at the beginning of a fiscal consolidation process (OECD, 1996b).

Macroeconomic developments in Portugal and Spain are located somewhere between these two extremes, although structural reforms in both countries are by now far advanced, especially in Portugal (CEC 1996a).

4.2 DETERMINANTS OF REGIONAL CONVERGENCE

4.2.1 Convergence as a Spontaneous Process?

An intuitive indicator for regional convergence in the EU is to see whether per capita income in regions that were lagging behind at the beginning of an observation period had come closer to the EU average. Table 4.3 groups those NUTS II regions that had Objective 1 status during the 1989–93 period into four categories:

1. Regions that caught up during the 1980–7 as well as during the 1988–94 period.

Table 4.3 Changes in Relative Income of Objective 1 Regions during the 1980–94 Period

Group	Region	Country	Income Change 1980–94	Relative p.c. Income 1994
(I)	Anatoliki Makedonia	GR	9.7	58.7
Catch-up 1980–7	Ionia Nisia	GR	11.4	60.4
and 1987–94	Voreio Aigaio	GR	6.5	49.2
	Notio Aigaio	GR	19.8	73.9
	Kriti	GR	18.5	70.9
	Extremadura	SP	9.0	54.0
	Comunidad Valenciana	SP	2.9	74.1
	Canarias	SP	17.5	75.9
	Ceuta y Melilla	SP	18.6	68.8
	Ireland	IRL	28.8	89.1
	Campania	I	1.1	69.1
	Abruzzi	I	3.9	90.8
	Molise	I	1.1	78.1
	Calabria	I	2.4	61.6
	Sicilia	I	2.2	70.9
	Sardegna	I	5.5	78.9
	Lisboa e Vale do Tejo	P	8.8	88.0
(II)	Dytiki Makedonia	GR	2.7	56.2
Catch-up 1980–7	Ipeiros	GR	–1.8	43.1
only	Murcia	SP	3.5	68.1
(III)	Kentriki Makedonia	GR	3.7	65.6
Catch-up 1987–94	Thessalia	GR	3.0	60.4
only	Peloponnisos	GR	–3.8	57.9
	Attiki	GR	2.6	73.2
	Galicia	SP	–0.8	59.8
	Asturias	SP	–4.4	72.3
	Cantabria	SP	–3.2	75.2
	Castilla y León	SP	1.4	71.3
	Andalucia	SP	0.9	57.2
	Basilicata	I	–3.7	67.5
	Norte	P	8.5	59.0
	Centro	P	8.1	55.1
	Alentejo	P	1.4	53.8
	Algarve	P	19.5	74.4
	Northern Ireland	UK	0.2	80.3
(IV)	Sterea Ellada	GR	–20.5	65.5
No Catch-up	Corse	F	–30.1	76.6
	Puglia	I	–2.8	72.8

Source: EUROSTAT (1997b); own calculations.

2. Regions that caught up during the 1980–7 period but fell back during the 1987–94 period.
3. Regions where the change was the other way around.
4. Regions that fell back during both periods.

The picture is dominated by two groups of regions: those that converged constantly towards the EU average and those that caught up during the second period only. Just three regions lost ground during both periods and three others converged towards the average during 1980–7, but faced a reversal of this trend during 1987–94. A closer look at the table reveals further details:

- Regional convergence is closely related to national economic well-being. Whereas all Portuguese regions except Lisbon caught up during the second period only, most Italian regions have consistently caught up although at a much slower pace. The performance of the Greek regions is more varied, but also more disappointing. It is mainly the island regions that have caught up during both periods, presumably due to the growth-inducing effects of tourism. Many of the mainland areas, however, despite improving their performance during the second seven-year period, have made little progress or even lost ground vis-à-vis the EU average.
- On the whole the performance is extremely mixed. Whereas seven regions show double-digit catch-up figures, a large number of Objective 1 regions remained more or less static during the 14-year period under review.

Another simple convergence approach is to look at the development of per capita income dispersion within a sample of locations. Barro and Sala-i-Martin (1991 and 1995) call this σ-convergence. This indicator of convergence can be easily influenced by short-term asymmetric economic shocks, thereby clouding whether convergence or divergence takes place in the long run. Looking at the development of σ-convergence within the EU during the 1980s, Neven and Gouyette (1994: 9) found that the standard deviation of per capita income is consistently much lower for a group of northern EU regions than for regions located in the South. Moreover, the standard deviation for the complete sample is slowly falling since 1984, which suggests a reduction in inter-regional income differences.

Beyond these approaches there are three convergence hypotheses on which most of the theoretical and empirical debates have focused.[3]

The first two are normally referred to as β-convergence hypotheses, arguing that growth will be faster in regions that are further away from their steady-state level of income.

1. Absolute convergence hypothesis. Per capita income levels of countries converge to one another in the long-run independently of their initial conditions.
2. Conditional convergence hypothesis. Per capita income levels of countries that are identical in their structural characteristics (for example, preferences, technologies, rates of population growth, government policies, etc.) converge to one another in the long run independently of their initial conditions.
3. Club convergence hypothesis. Per capita income levels of countries that are identical in their structural characteristics converge to one another in the long run provided that their initial conditions are similar as well.

The following analysis will focus on the first two hypotheses, called by Sala-i-Martin the 'classical approach because ... it is the basis of reference and target of criticism of all other methodologies and it has survived the challenges of more modern and "surrealist" movements' (Sala-i-Martin, 1996: 1019–20).

The standard econometric specification for the test of the absolute convergence hypothesis mentioned above is an equation of the form:

$$\Pi \ Y_{i,t} = \alpha - \beta \ Y_{i,0} + u_t \tag{4.1}$$

where $\Pi \ Y_{i,t}$ refers to the average per capita growth rate of region i during period t, $Y_{i,0}$ is the region's income level at the beginning of the observation period, u_t is the error term. Testing for the conditional rather than absolute convergence hypothesis Equation 4.1 is modified to:

$$\Pi \ Y_{i,t} = \alpha - \beta \ Y_{i,0} + \Phi \ X_i + u_t \tag{4.2}$$

where $\Phi \ X_i$ is a vector including potential determinants of steady-state income, assumed to be different between locations. In one of the first empirical studies on regional convergence, Barro and Sala-i-Martin (1991) used regional dummies for groups of US states and sectoral variables in order to capture the impact of differences in locations' industrial structure. For the EU, the equivalent to regional dummies are country dummies for the member states.

A significant number of empirical studies look at convergence or divergence of income levels within a sample of locations. Most of them use national rather than regional data and find that the presence or absence of convergence depends strongly on the sample of countries selected. Grossman and Helpman (1994) argue that 'countries appear not to be converging to a common level of per capita income as they must be in the neoclassical model' (Grossman and Helpman, 1994: 27). According to Barro and Sala-i-Martin (1995: 7), however, conditional 'convergence does appear if we limit attention to more homogeneous groups of economies, such as the states in the US, regions of several European countries, and prefectures in Japan'. Within the OECD, convergence has also been identified. Levine and Renelt (1992) summarise a vast amount of literature on cross-country growth regressions and find robust evidence for the conditional convergence hypothesis for the 1960–89 period, but not for the 1974–89 period. They also find that very few economic indicators used in these studies are robustly correlated with growth. Among the few exceptions are investment as a share of GDP and an indicator for human capital.

A number of studies look specifically at β-convergence among EU regions, for example Blanchard and Katz (1992), Neven and Gouyette (1994), Thomas (1997) and Armstrong (1995a and 1995b). Although their methodology is similar, there are small differences in the sample of regions as well as the observation period. While these differences cause some variation in the size and significance of the β-coefficient, most empirical investigations find evidence in favour of convergence among European regions. During the 1980s, however, the convergence process has slowed down.[4]

The Barro and Sala-i-Martin-type of convergence regressions have been criticised by supporters of the club convergence hypothesis for largely neglecting the dynamics of changing regional (or national) income distributions (see, for example, Quah, 1993 and 1996). It is argued that the spatial distribution of income shows a tendency towards 'twin peaks', 'a two-camp world, divided between haves and have-nots, where escaping from the poverty trap is a low-probability proposition, either over short- or long-runs' (Quah, 1993: 433).

Looking at empirical evidence for the EU (Quah, 1997), the most important feature of income development across NUTS II regions is persistence. Inequality increases at the NUTS III level of regions, but mainly because rich regions in the cohesion countries become richer rather than poor regions become poorer. Portugal, Spain and Greece do not show an emerging polarisation of rich and poor regions, a tendency that is discernible in Italy, but increases only slowly. All in all, the club convergence evidence is certainly weaker for the EU than for more heterogeneous groups of countries. Despite the well-founded criticism of the club convergence school against the more conventional 'conditional convergence hypothesis', it is thus defensible to use the Barro and Sala-i-Martin approach in the analysis below.

The estimations below cover the period 1980–94. Longer time-series cannot be constructed for the Objective 1 regions. Nevertheless, the period 1980–94 is long enough to ensure that the results are not excessively influenced by short-term changes in the economic situation. Three different groups of regions are investigated: (1) the complete sample of 145 NUTS II regions; (2) the 39 Objective 1 regions; and (3) the 106 non-Objective 1 regions.

Figures 4.4–4.6 depict graphically the link between relative regional per capita income in 1980, expressed in PPS (logged) and the average annual regional growth rate during the 1980–94 period (logged).

The scatterplots show a negative link between the starting level of relative regional income in 1980 and the regional growth performance during the 1980–94 period. In other words, regions that were relatively poor in 1980 tended to grow faster. This finding supports the convergence hypothesis.

Figure 4.4 Income and Growth in NUTS II Regions, 1980–94

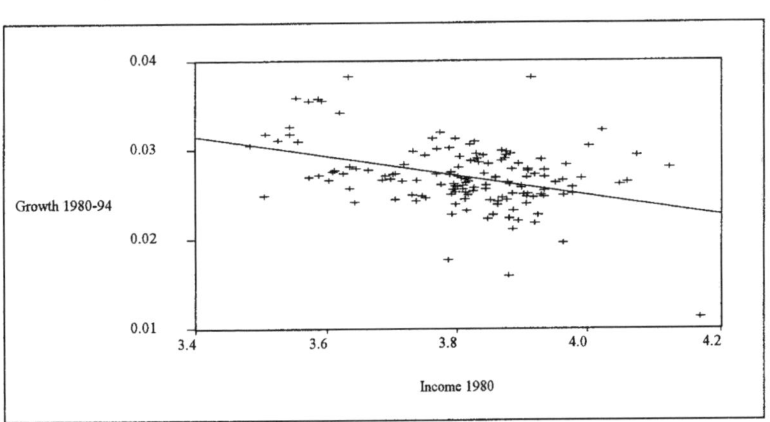

Source: EUROSTAT (1997b); own calculations.

Figure 4.5 Income and Growth in Objective 1 NUTS II Regions, 1980–94

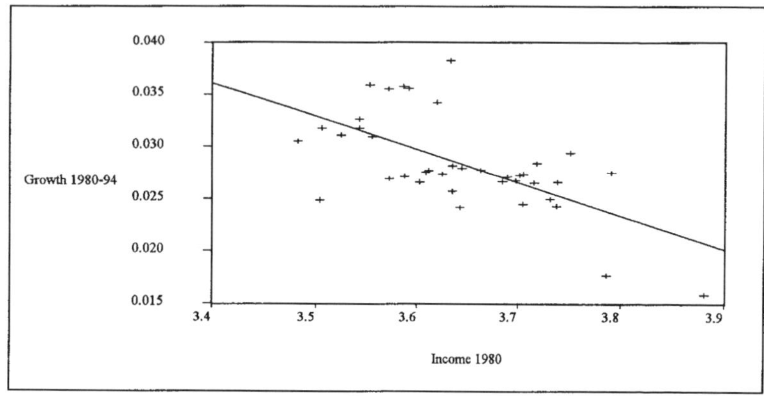

Source: EUROSTAT (1997b); own calculations.

Figure 4.6 Income and Growth in Non-Objective 1 NUTS II Regions, 1980–94

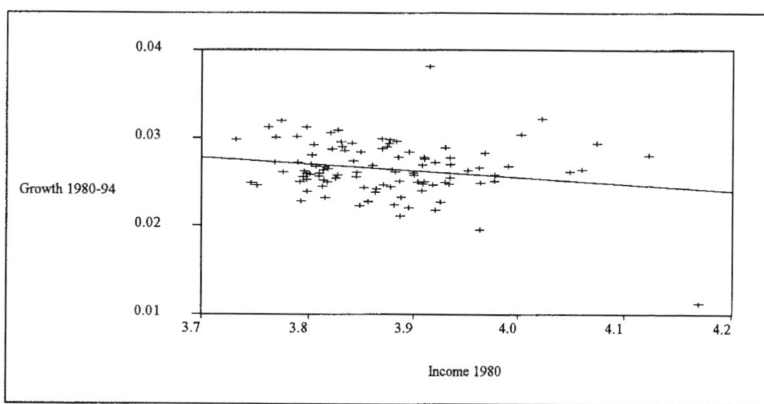

Source: EUROSTAT (1997b); own calculations.

The Objective 1 regions fall into two clusters. A group of 12 fast-growing regions with average annual logged growth rates above 0.03 (around 2 per cent) and one where average annual growth was below that level. While the convergence hypothesis holds for the Objective 1 sample as a whole, initial income is no longer a significant explanatory variable within these sub-samples. It should be kept in mind, though, that a division of the Objective 1 group into fast- and slow-growing lagging regions yields very small sub-samples and this limits the explanatory value of regression analysis. The elimination of the high-income outliers Corsica and Sterea Ellada does not significantly alter the regression result for the full Objective 1 sample.

For non-Objective 1 regions, the picture is less heterogeneous than for the lagging regions, although there are two outliers: Luxembourg was by far the fastest-growing region during the 1980–94 period, whereas Groningen was the richest region in 1980 but had a very low rate of growth.[5] The omission of these regions does not significantly alter the regression result.

Table 4.4 summarises the results of a number of convergence regressions for the three different groups of regions (all NUTS II regions, Objective 1 regions and non-Objective 1 regions), different time periods and different equation specifications. The first figure in each box is the β coefficient of the initial income variable in the equation, the figure in brackets is the *t*-statistics for the β coefficient and the last figure is the R^2 value of the equation. The unconditioned regressions are based on Equation 4.1 above. The equations reported in the second row were conditioned by country dummies for the EU member states and those in the third and forth rows include country dummies as well as variables indicating the relative importance of agriculture and services in the regional economies.

The regressions reported in Table 4.4 provide evidence for conditional as well as unconditional convergence for all three groups of regions. This result, as well as the magnitude of the β coefficients are in line with the results of the abovementioned studies on EU regional convergence. There are, however, important differences between the results for the three investigation periods, the groups of regions and the specifications.

Looking at all regions and the unconditioned model (no dummies to capture country-specific effects), the impact of initial income on growth was clearly stronger during the 1987–94 period than during the 1980–7 period. This is even more noticeable for the Objective 1 regions. For the richer regions of the EU, however, the opposite effect can be observed. A relatively lower regional income had a significantly positive effect on growth during the first period but not during the second, which suggests that growth within the contrast group of regions was more homogeneous during that time. The main findings of this first set of equations – strong impact of initial income on growth

Table 4.4 Empirical Tests of Convergence Hypotheses for European NUTS II Regions, 1980–94

		All Regions (n = 145)			Objective 1 Regions (n = 39)			Contrast Regions (n = 106)		
		1980–94	1980–87	1987–94	1980–94	1980–87	1987–94	1980–94	1980–87	1987–94
Income only	β	0.011	0.008	0.016	0.032	*0.025*	0.052	0.008	0.013	*0.001*
	t	(5.21)	(2.52)	(4.87)	(4.87)	*(1.91)*	(4.72)	(2.09)	(2.76)	*(0.16)*
	R^2	0.159	0.042	0.142	0.391	*0.090*	0.376	0.040	0.068	*0.000*
Income + Dummies (CDs)	β	0.012	0.015	0.012	0.028	*0.029*	0.044	0.013	0.016	*0.007*
	t	(4.44)	(3.08)	(3.21)	(3.56)	*(1.68)*	(3.65)	(3.85)	(3.22)	*(1.80)*
	R^2	0.476	0.219	0.583	0.574	*0.305*	0.627	0.477	0.249	*0.598*
Income + CDs + Agriculture	β	0.017	0.027	0.011	0.034	0.043	0.049	0.016	0.026	*0.001*
	t	(4.97)	(4.62)	(2.22)	(4.35)	(2.69)	(3.40)	(3.63)	(3.95)	*(0.27)*
	R^2	0.496	0.283	0.583	0.638	0.453	0.632	0.483	0.286	*0.610*
Income + CDs + Services	β	0.010	0.012	0.012	0.021	*0.021*	0.043	0.012	0.015	0.009
	t	(4.02)	(2.58)	(3.39)	(3.21)	*(1.25)*	(4.00)	(4.31)	(3.42)	(2.46)
	R^2	0.618	0.306	0.644	0.731	*0.363*	0.708	0.645	0.439	0.655

Note: Figures in italics are β coefficients that are not significant at the 5 per cent level.
Source: Own calculations.

for the group as a whole, strong impact on growth in Objective 1 regions during the second seven-year period, and vice versa for the non-Objective 1 regions – are confirmed when country dummies are included in the regressions. Only two of the dummy variables, namely those for Ireland and Luxembourg, are consistently (positively) significant. The coefficients of the dummies for these two countries approach the magnitude of the initial income variable. In the case of Ireland, for example, this means that the magnitude of country-specific factors fostering growth is comparable to natural convergence, the 'catch-up bonus' for all lagging EU regions during the 1980–94 period.

The inclusion of a variable for the relative importance of the agricultural sector increases the coefficients of the income variable significantly. For the Objective 1 regions it also has a strong impact on the income variable's statistical significance. For the full sample and the lagging regions the agriculture variable itself is significant during the 1980–94 and the 1980–7 periods, but its coefficient is much smaller than that of the initial income variable. The intuition behind this result is that structural backwardness is a significantly negative factor in periods of sluggish growth whereas it becomes less of an obstacle during periods of faster economic expansion. As above, the country dummies for Ireland and Luxembourg remain statistically significant and their coefficients remain essentially unchanged.

The inclusion of a service sector variable has an effect on the non-lagging regions that is similar to that of the agriculture dummy for the lagging regions. For the 1987–94 period, initial income becomes a statistically significant determinant of growth for the contrast regions if differences in the relative size of the service sectors are taken into account. The coefficient of the service sector variable is larger than that of the income variable. For the Objective 1 regions the service sector variable is also significant but its coefficient is smaller than that of the income variable. The dummies for Portugal and Ireland retain their statistical significance. For the contrast regions, finally, the service variable is very strongly significant and its coefficient is about twice that of the income variable and that of Luxembourg, the only significant country dummy.[6]

Box 4.1 The Structure of Regional Economies

Within the EU, there are significant differences in the regional employment structure. These differences can be interpreted as indicators for more encompassing differences in regional economic development and competitiveness. As far as the cohesion countries are concerned, Greece has by far the highest relative levels of agricultural employment (385 per cent of the EU average in 1995). The importance of agricultural employment in Spain, Ireland and Portugal is roughly comparable (175, 226 and 217 per cent of the EU average respectively) and closer to the European average. With regard to service sector employment, the four countries are all below the EU average but the difference is much less striking. Relative employment shares are between 87 (Greece) and 94 per cent (Spain) of the Union average.

The link between agriculture and growth is ambivalent. On the one hand, an above-average share of agriculture can be problematic for the regional growth potential because prospects for growth in agricultural demand are limited and positive external effects for the regional economy are likely to be small. On the other hand, a high share of employment in the primary sector can point towards a large growth potential as a large number of employees can move to higher value-added activities.

Figure 4.7 Relative Income Growth in NUTS II Regions, 1980–94, and Relative Agricultural Employment, 1980 (logged)

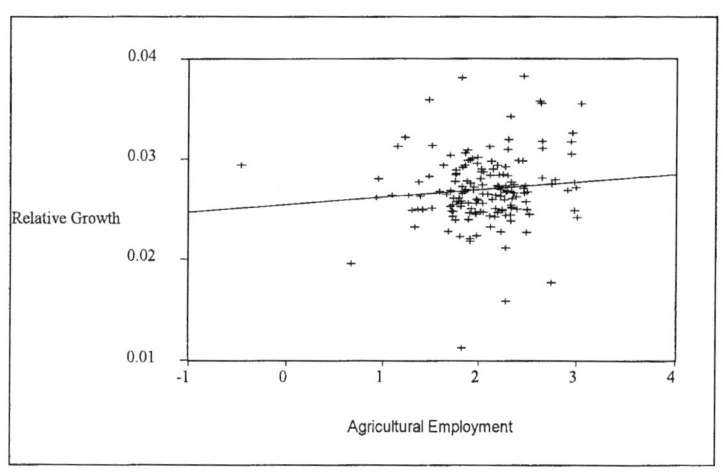

Source: EUROSTAT (1997b); own calculations.

Figure 4.8 Relative Income Growth in NUTS II Regions, 1980–94, and Relative Service Sector Employment, 1980 (logged)

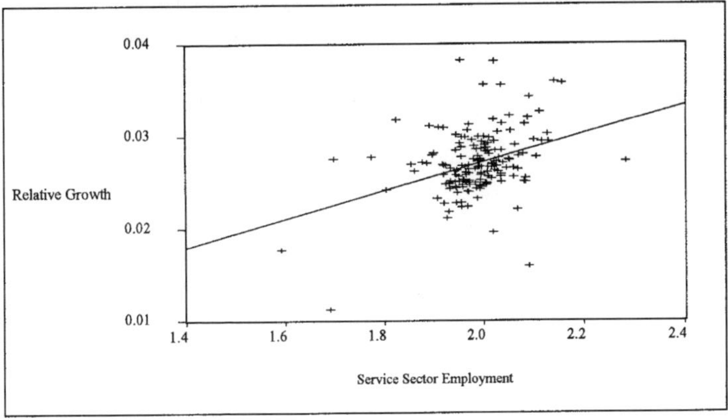

Source: EUROSTAT (1997b); own calculations.

Figure 4.7 shows a weakly significant positive correlation between growth during the 1980–94 period and agricultural employment at the beginning of this period. This indicates that the growth-inducing effects of agriculture are slightly stronger than the growth-reducing effects mentioned above. For the Objective 1 regions, however, this effect cannot be observed.

Unlike agriculture, a high relative share of services in regional employment can be interpreted as an indicator for a more advanced, diversified and dynamic regional economy. One would therefore expect a positive link between services and growth which is confirmed by Figure 4.8.

The correlation between service sector employment in 1980 and growth during the 1980–94 period is slightly weaker for the lagging regions, but remains statistically significant. In order to understand the lesser importance of the service sector for lagging regions, it has to be kept in mind that the service sector is very heterogeneous as far as the required qualifications and the wage level are concerned. Especially in lagging regions, a large portion of service sector jobs are in comparatively low-skill, low value-added activities such as retail and tourism, which lowers the growth potential of the service sector.

These results, together with previous research, point towards some degree of absolute as well as relative convergence among EU regions but the convergence process depends largely on the general macroeconomic climate. Lagging regions tend to grow faster during periods of high aggregate growth. In periods of sluggish overall economic performance, however, their structural backwardness, proxied by the agricultural variable, hampers their growth performance.

The convergence process is also very slow. The 2 per cent per annum convergence rate ($\beta = 0.02$) found by Barro and Sala-i-Martin and confirmed here means that 35 years are required to close one-half of the initial income gap. Such a long adjustment period, however, creates political pressures in favour of policies designed to speed up the convergence process. In other words, the absence of fast significant automatic reductions of the socio-economic disparities outlined in Chapter 2 provides a political case for regional policy efforts to work towards such a reduction of disparities (Begg, Gudgin and Morris, 1995).

4.2.2 The Impact of Regional Policy Variables on Growth

In this section, we analyse whether the regional policy variables 'human capital' and 'infrastructure' had a noticeable impact on the growth performance of EU regions during the 1980–94 period. Although the impact of human capital and infrastructure is a question of utmost importance in the context of regional policy, it has not yet been given much attention in the empirical regional convergence literature, mainly due to the fact that any empirical analysis of this question is plagued by serious data problems. The explanatory variables used in the present analysis, for example, are either purely cross-sectional, which means that they refer to one particular year only (infrastructure, educational attainment) or they cover only a short period of time (R&D). The main advantage of the data used in this section, however, is that they are available for all pre-1995 EU member states including the cohesion countries, which is of course of particular interest in the context of regional policy.[7]

4.2.2.1 Human Capital Endowments

In this section, two indicators for regional human capital endowments are used, namely the educational attainment of the workforce and activities in the field of research and development (R&D). A well-qualified workforce is generally assumed to be a major asset for any location and likely to be beneficial for regional growth prospects. This point of view is supported by the results of business surveys outlined in Chapter 3 (CEC, 1990 and 1993a), as well as by empirical research on growth and convergence at the national level (Levine and Renelt, 1992).

Although the importance of education is undisputed, regionalised data that allow comparisons of the educational attainment of the workforce across several countries are not easily obtainable. EUROSTAT has only recently started to publish figures of this kind, differentiating between low, medium and high levels of qualification. The earliest available data at NUTS II level refer to the year 1993. While earlier data would of course be preferable, educational attainment levels are unlikely to change significantly in the short run. The available data provide therefore a reasonable approximation of the situation at the beginning of the 1980s.

Another indicator for the human capital endowment of regions is the number of R&D personnel operating in the region. From a theoretical point of view, one would also expect a high relative intensity of R&D operations to have positive effects on regional growth, especially in light of the arguments of new growth theory presented in Chapter 3. Once again, comparable regionalised data on R&D personnel have only recently been published by EUROSTAT. For most member states the available data cover the years 1988–93, which allows the construction of a six-year average figure. For the present analysis public sector R&D has been singled out in order to identify the effect of public R&D efforts.

Table 4.5 provides an overview of relative regional education levels and public R&D personnel. Education 1 (Educ.1) refers to the relative share of the workforce with a low level of education, Education 2 (Educ. 2) refers to an intermediate, and Education 3 (Educ. 3) to a high level of education. Where applicable, separate figures for Objective 1 regions are provided.

Differences between the member states and between the Objective 1 and non-Objective 1 regions are very significant. In all cohesion countries and regions, the share of workers with a low level of education is far above the EU average. The opposite applies to the share of workers with intermediate and high levels of education. Only Ireland's share of workers with a high level of educational attainment approaches the EU average. The same applies to R&D activities.

Table 4.6 summarises the results of regional convergence regressions that include the abovementioned human capital indicators as

Table 4.5 Educational Attainment of the Workforce and Public R&D Personnel in EU Regions, 1993*

	Education 1		Education 2		Education 3		Public R&D Personnel	
	All	Obj. 1	All	Obj. 1	All	Obj.1	All	Obj.1
Belgium	112	./.	77	./.	120	./.	287	./.
Denmark	39	./.	151	./.	125	./.	341	./.
Germany	46	./.	151	./.	110	./.	453	./.
Greece	141	141	72	72	70	70	29	29
Spain	178	187	31	28	75	64	94	39
France	100	154	105	62	90	65	409	16
Ireland	132	132	69	69	95	95	103	103
Italy	157	161	72	67	38	36	199	67
Lux.	141	./.	54	./.	105	./.	n.a.	./.
NL	54	./.	144	./.	110	./.	291	./.
Portugal	193	193	26	26	55	55	33	33
UK	122	127	74	79	105	85	678	134

* Figures are relative to the EU average (100).
Sources: Education: EUROSTAT (1997b and unpublished data for Italy); R&D: EUROSTAT (1995); own calculations.

well as country dummies in order to capture member state-specific effects. Each box in the table refers to one equation but only the coefficients and *t*-statistics for the initial income lag and the regional policy variable (education or R&D) are given. Figures in brackets are *t*-statistics. Income is relative regional per capita income in 1980, RP-Variable refers to the regional policy variable. Figures in italics indicate variables below the 5 per cent significance level. The standard error of all reported regressions is around 0.002.

The results are in line with the theoretical predictions outlined above and in Chapter 3. It was argued that a well-qualified workforce and a high degree of R&D activities have a positive impact on the location's growth performance whereas a poor educational record of the workforce is likely to depress prospects for growth.

The coefficients and *t*-statistics for the income variable remain essentially unchanged. As far as the human capital variables are concerned, there are strong differences between the results for the full sample and the lagging regions on the one hand, and the contrast group on the other hand.

Table 4.6 Human Capital and Regional Convergence in Europe, 1980–94

	All Regions (n = 145)			Objective 1 Regions (n = 39)			Non-Objective 1 Regions (n = 106)		
	Inc.	RP-Variable	R^2	Inc.	RP-Variable	R^2	Inc.	RP-Variable	R^2
Educ. 1	–0.016	–0.133	0.511	–0.034	–0.030	0.631	–0.016	–0.009	0.503
	(–5.4)	(–3.3)		(–4.3)	(–2.1)		(–4.5)	(–2.3)	
Educ. 2	–0.015	0.015	0.536	–0.041	0.022	0.719	–0.013	*0.009*	0.492
	(–5.7)	(4.28)		(–5.6)	(3.93)		(–3.9)	*(1.69)*	
Educ. 3	–0.015	*0.005*	0.485	–0.031	*0.008*	0.597	–0.015	*0.004*	0.487
	(–4.8)	*(1.92)*		(–3.8)	*(1.29)*		(–4.1)	*(1.39)*	
R&D*	0.010	0.002	0.540	0.025	*0.002*	0.622	*0.005*	0.002	0.493
	(3.29)	(3.77)		(3.38)	*(1.90)*		*(1.21)*	(3.01)	

* For the R&D variable the full sample comprises 108 regions and the non-Objective 1 sample 69 regions because R&D data for Belgium and the Netherlands are only available on a national level and for Germany only on NUTS I level. Data for Luxembourg is not available.
Source: Own calculations.

A high share of workers with a low level of education has a significantly negative impact on growth in all three samples. The coefficient for this variable is particularly large if all regions are investigated. A high share of workers with secondary education has a strong positive impact on growth, especially in the full sample and for the lagging regions, and a large share of workers with tertiary education has a positive but only weakly significant impact.

The explanatory value of the education variables is particularly weak for the non-Objective 1 regions, mainly because the variations in the level of educational attainment between these regions appear limited. It is likely that a more detailed differentiation system would identify more significant differences between the non-Objective 1 regions but on an EU-wide basis such a system is not available, at least not on a regional level.

Whereas growth in lagging regions seems to benefit most from a relatively well-qualified workforce, the results for the contrast group indicate that in non-Objective 1 regions, the relative level of R&D activities has the strongest impact on growth.[8]

After all, variations in R&D activity within the contrast group are much stronger than variations in the educational endowment of the workforce. The coefficient of the R&D variable, however, is comparatively small, about the size of the standard error of the regression.[9]

4.2.2.2 Infrastructure Endowments

The impact of infrastructure on growth has also been studied quite extensively and was usually assessed as positive. Most research looks at the US where the federal system allows the construction of sufficiently large infrastructure expenditure data sets to use time-series or panel data estimation techniques. For the EU, the availability of regional infrastructure expenditure data is much poorer and even the availability of regional infrastructure indicators is limited. The present study uses primarily indicators compiled by Dieter Biehl (CEC, 1986), which take not only the quantity but also the quality of the infrastructure into account. For the present analysis, an updated version of the Biehl study (Biehl et al., 1991), has been used in order to construct a physical infrastructure indicator, encompassing the categories transport, telecommunications and energy supply. Since the data refer to the year 1981, the indicator is well suited for an analysis of regional growth during the 1980–94 period.

Table 4.7 shows that the physical infrastructure endowment in lagging countries and regions is clearly below the EU average, especially in Greece and Portugal.

Table 4.7 Physical Infrastructure Endowments of EU NUTS II Regions Relative to the EU Average, 1981*

	All Regions	Objective 1
Belgium	228.5	./.
Denmark	150.4	./.
Germany	177.2	./.
Greece	68.9	68.9
Spain	96.9	72.4
France	149.8	n.a.
Ireland	77.5	77.5
Italy	84.7	69.6
Luxembourg	264.9	./.
Netherlands	187.7	./.
Portugal	41.5	41.5
UK	116.0	84.6

* Figures are relative to the EU average (100)
n.a. = Not available.
Source: Biehl et al. (1991); own calculations.

Table 4.8 is very similar to Table 4.6. The estimated equations are conditioned by country dummies. Only the coefficients for the initial income level and the infrastructure indicator are reported, together with the *t*-statistics and the R^2 value. Figures in brackets are *t*-statistics, Inc. is the relative income in 1980, Inf. refers to the infrastructure variable. The standard errors of the regressions are close to 0.002.

Table 4.8 Infrastructure and Regional Convergence in Europe, 1980–94*

All Regions (n = 142)*			Objective 1 Regions (n = 37)			Non-Objective 1 Regions (n = 105)		
Inc.	Inf.	R^2	Inc.	Inf.	R^2	Inc.	Inf.	R^2
–0.015	0.005	0.467	–0.025	0.006	0.530	–0.015	0.003	0.431
(–4.89)	(3.30)		(–3.46)	(2.10)		(–3.71)	(2.02)	

* The indicator used in this analysis is not available for Corsica. Ceuta y Melilla and Berlin which reduces the total number of regions to 142.
Source: Own calculations.

The econometric results summarised in Table 4.8 suggest that a relatively good infrastructure endowment contributes significantly to regional growth. Initial income – the 'catch-up variable' – remains strongly significant with coefficients and *t*-statistics for the complete sample and the contrast group being in line with the original regressions reported in Table 4.4 above.

As in the section on human capital, the coefficients suggest that the impact of the initial income level exceeds that of the regional policy variable significantly. However, the positive coefficient of the infrastructure variable for the complete sample (the Objective 1 sample) is 2.5 (3) times that of the standard error of the regression. For the contrast group of regions, the impact of infrastructure on growth is the least significant. As for the educational attainment above, the variations of this comparatively crude indicator among non-Objective 1 regions are relatively small.

4.2.3 The Impact of Regional Policy Variables: a Multivariate Approach

In this last part of the empirical analysis, the different regional policy variables introduced above are used simultaneously in a multivariate approach to regional growth and convergence. Relative regional income in 1980 still provides the 'base' variable, on top of which additional variables are used in order to explain regional growth. Whereas the equations described above looked only at the impact of one regional policy variable at a time, the multivariate approach used here allows a comparative assessment of the importance of the different elements of regional policy. As above, the equations reported in Table 4.9 are conditioned by country dummies in order to capture country-specific effects. The three education variables are obviously highly correlated and therefore not used simultaneously. Figures in italics are not significant at the 5 per cent level. Figures in brackets are *t*-statistics. R&D data are only available for 108 regions, of which Berlin had to be excluded because the infrastructure variable is not available. This reduces the number of regions for a multivariate analysis to 107. Given the changed sample, the results reported below are not directly comparable with the univariate regressions reported in the tables above.

The results differ strongly between the three samples. For the full sample, R&D and physical infrastructure are positive and significant, although the coefficients of these indicators are just slightly above or equal to the standard error of the regression. The educational attain-

Table 4.9 A Multivariate Approach to Regional Convergence in Europe, 1980–94

	All Regions			Obj. 1 Regions			Non Obj. 1 Regions		
Income	–0.014	–0.015	–0.013	–0.028	–0.038	–0.024	*–0.005*	*–0.002*	*–0.003*
	(–4.23)	(–4.67)	(–3.80)	(–3.44)	(–4.42)	(–3.13)	*(–1.04)*	*(–0.56)*	*(–0.63)*
Educ. 1	*–0.006*			*–0.015*			*–0.008*		
	(–0.97)			*(–0.94)*			*(–1.30)*		
Educ. 2		*0.008*			0.018			*0.009*	
		(1.98)			(2.42)			*(1.48)*	
Educ. 3			*0.000*			*0.000*			*0.002*
			(0.103)			*(0.01)*			*(0.52)*
R&D	0.002	0.002	0.002	*0.002*	*0.001*	*0.002*	0.002	0.002	0.002
	(2.75)	(2.94)	(3.25)	*(1.07)*	*(0.47)*	*(1.63)*	(2.63)	(3.09)	(3.38)
Infra.	0.003	0.003	0.003	0.006	*0.004*	0.005	*0.001*	*0.001*	*0.001*
	(2.54)	(2.68)	(2.46)	(2.16)	*(1.81)*	(2.09)	*(0.36)*	*(0.46)*	*(0.33)*
R^2	0.601	0.613	0.597	0.595	0.562	0.582	0.610	0.614	0.601
S.E.R.	0.002	0.002	0.002	0.003	0.003	0.003	0.001	0.001	0.001
n	107	107	107	39	39	39	68	68	68

Note: Figures in italics are β coefficients that are not significant at the 5 per cent level.
Source: Own calculations.

ment level indicators have the expected sign but are all below the 5 per cent level of statistical significance – in the case of the relative share of secondary education, however, just narrowly. The initial income lag appears to be the strongest growth-inducing factor – not only in terms of significance but also in terms of the coefficient. The dummy for Ireland remains positive and significant; Luxembourg had to be excluded from these equations because R&D data for this country are not available.

For the Objective 1 regions, relative income in 1980, infrastructure and the relative share of workers with secondary education are statistically significant. The relative share of R&D personnel docs not appear to be a factor that contributes significantly to growth although this result should be interpreted with great caution. In most lagging regions, very little R&D activity takes place, which limits the explanatory power of the R&D variable for Objective 1 regions. After all, regressions of this kind cannot predict the effect of a variable that was essentially absent in many of the observations.

In contrast to the lagging regions, R&D is highly significant in the non-Objective 1 regions. In fact, it is the dominant explanatory variable for this third group of regions. Infrastructure and the education variables lose their significance completely and the impact of initial income is strongly reduced. These results make intuitive sense because the catch-up potential within the third sample is by definition reduced and, as argued above, the educational endowment differences between these regions are less pronounced than within the other samples.

Summing up, two stylised facts emerge:

1. In the regressions for all regions and Objective 1 regions, the initial income level is significant and has the largest coefficient of all the explanatory variables. This points clearly towards some 'natural' income convergence among European regions.
2. The sign of the coefficients for the human capital and infrastructure variables always corresponds with the theoretical predictions and points towards a positive impact of education, R&D and infrastructure on regional growth.

The second result suggests that improvements of the infrastructure and human capital endowment of regions are likely to foster growth. However, there are strong differences in the usefulness of these instruments for different types of regions.

4.3 CONCLUSIONS: CAN REGIONAL POLICY FOSTER CONVERGENCE?

In this chapter the problem of regional convergence and divergence was approached from a national as well as a regional perspective. The analysis of national determinants of economic competitiveness has shown that there are clear differences between the EU cohesion countries. Whereas the macroeconomic performance of Ireland is good, at least from the late 1980s onwards, the performance of Spain and Portugal is mixed, and that of Greece disappointing. The differences in national economic performance are also reflected in the convergence or divergence performance of Objective 1 regions during the 1980–94 period.

What are regional factors that determine growth? Can it be argued that human capital and infrastructure foster regional growth and are therefore effective instruments of regional policy?

- The analysis shows that a relatively good endowment with human capital and infrastructure is most likely to have a positive influence on regional economic development. This is not only in line with theoretical predictions and a similar recent study on regional growth in Spain (de la Fuente and Vives, 1995) but also with the results of various business surveys investigating the determinants of location decisions within the EU.
- The econometric analysis suggests, however, that the influence of the regional policy variables is smaller than that of the initial income gap. For the Objective 1 regions it is mainly a relatively good endowment with a well-educated workforce and a sufficient infrastructure that are important for the growth performance. For non-Objective 1 regions, however, differences with regard to these more basic location requirements become less important. For the better-off regions of the EU it is mainly differences in the R&D efforts that have a significant impact on growth.

The results of this chapter certainly suggest that macro-policies are of considerable importance for national economic success and the growth performance of regions located within these countries. The Greek example of a high-inflation, low-growth economy during the 1980s demonstrates that regional policy, even if one assumes that the right instruments are chosen and that the policy is well implemented, can not compensate for the absence of a stable, growth-promoting macroeconomic environment. Ireland, in contrast, has managed to create such an environment, at least from the late 1980s onwards. While it seems that regional policy can contribute to regional convergence, it can only do so if the macroeconomic framework in the supported areas is conducive for growth.

Summing up the course of the argument so far, Chapter 2 has established that there are significant socio-economic disparities between the regions of the European Union which do not seem to change rapidly. The theoretical survey in Chapter 3 did not provide clear guidance as to whether these disparities are likely to increase or decrease in the future. The last chapter of the first part approached the problem of convergence and divergence from an empirical point of view. It established that country-specific economic developments in the four EU cohesion countries vary significantly which has a strong impact on regional growth. Beyond the member state level, however, there are region-specific aspects of growth. Relatively poor regions tend to grow faster than relatively rich ones, but regional growth can also be influenced by regional policy instruments, namely the promotion of human capital and infrastructure.

In the second part of the book the regional distribution of public support across the EU will be investigated empirically, using state aids, R&D expenditures and transport infrastructure investments as case studies. This in itself does not allow a quantitative analysis of regional growth prospects, However, it is possible to analyse which parts of the EU are the major beneficiaries of European and national public assistance. Provided it turns out that all or some of the lagging regions are the main recipients, these regions have a good chance to catch up. In case rich European regions are the main beneficiaries of public support, however, the prospects for the lagging regions to close the socio-economic gap between 'rich' and 'poor' in the EU are worsened by public policies.

Part II

European Regional Policy and the Problem of Policy Co-ordination

The preceding chapters showed that even if regional per capita income levels in the EU will converge automatically, the convergence process will take a couple of decades. Henceforth, one has to ask whether there are economic or legal rationales for public policies designed to promote regional income convergence? This issue is addressed in the first section of Chapter 5. The second section of Chapter 5 presents the historic development of European regional policy and a critical account of its present structure and operations.

The other three chapters of Part II are devoted to the issue of co-ordination between European regional policy and other national and European policies that influence the regional distribution of economic activity within the EU. Each chapter provides a case-study concerning one of the three main pillars of EU regional policy. Chapter 6 looks at EU support for productive investments and national regional incentive schemes. Chapter 7 investigates national and European R&D policy. Chapter 8, finally, focuses on transport infrastructure. The period covered by the analysis is the first regional policy programming period, 1989–93. The new member-states Austria, Finland and Sweden which joined the EU in 1995 are therefore not included.

5 The Regional Policy of the European Union

5.1 RATIONALES FOR EUROPEAN REGIONAL POLICY

5.1.1 Why Regional Policy in the First Place?

When it comes to rationales for regional policy, the literature usually provides a blend of social, political and economic arguments (Armstrong and Taylor, 1993). Among the most frequently stated aims and rationales are:

1. Flattening 'unjust' spatial income distributions (equity or fairness argument).
2. Easing adjustment problems for economies undergoing major transformations or economic shocks.
3. Welfare increases due to the activation of previously unused factors of production.
4. Optimising the spatial allocation of production (for example, by internalising external agglomeration effects).

A clear separation of the different aims and rationales is often impossible. Literature on the growth effects of income distributions, for example, links equity and efficiency arguments by saying that there is a negative link between economic growth and inequality (Alesina and Rodrik, 1994; Galor and Zeira, 1993). The results of these studies, however, support inter-personal rather than inter-regional distribution policy.[1] Rationale (2) is also essentially a socio-political argument. In the context of the EU, however, adjustment problems can become an obstacle for integration. Imagine a member state that is likely to experience a major rise in unemployment due to deeper integration because large parts of its industry are not competitive without protection. This member state is unlikely to support deepened integration although it might not only be beneficial for the economic area as a whole but, in the long run, for the member state itself. In light of this danger, it becomes economically meaningful to compensate the country for its adjustment problems.

The last two points are direct economic arguments for regional policy. Argument (3) concerns the employment of unused resources. In areas where economic activity is insufficient, some factors of production, notably labour, are likely to remain unemployed or underemployed. Regional policy, so the argument goes, can reintegrate these factors of production into the economic process, thereby increasing aggregate welfare. In principle, this argument can be used as an economic justification for state intervention. However, it requires that:

1. the surplus factors of production are too immobile to move to other parts of the integration area; and that
2. the costs to activate them are lower than the welfare gains obtainable from their activation.

Condition (1) is by and large fulfilled in the EU. Despite the four freedoms, labour mobility in particular is very low. It should not be forgotten, however, that factor mobility, especially labour mobility, is frequently regarded as politically undesirable. Given the lack of political efforts to increase the spatial mobility of labour, however, factor immobility is to some extent politically determined rather than an unavoidable fact.[2]

Condition (2), the costs of activation have to be lower than the welfare gains to be obtained, is more difficult to tackle and requires the introduction of agglomeration externalities (Rationale 4). In the absence of external effects and on the basis of the assumption of rational behaviour, the market outcome must be the optimal spatial allocation of resources. In the presence of externalities, however, private welfare optimising behaviour is no longer equal to social welfare optimisation. A private decision to locate a company in an agglomeration, for example, can lead to negative side-effects, such as an increase in traffic congestion. The investor does not have to pay other economic subject's costs due to the increase in congestion that his decision has caused. These costs are external to him. Most authors are very careful in assessing the welfare implications of regional market failures. 'It is not immediately clear, whether they provide a case for regional policy. For example, if there are positive benefits from firms' agglomeration, this should not be discouraged, but it is easy to imagine situations where there is a case for policy' (CEPR, 1993: 151).

Generally speaking, the welfare costs of regional policy interventions have to be weighed against the welfare gains. Most interventions cause direct costs, opportunity costs and efficiency costs. An attempt to improve the productivity of a lagging region by means of infrastructure investments, for example, is costly (direct costs). The money is no longer available for similar action in core regions (opportunity costs) and price signals in the economy are being distorted (efficiency costs).

In order to identify the preferable instrument, two general rules should be taken into account.

- Measures that are trying to increase the underlying competitiveness of regions, for example, investments in human capital and infrastructure, are normally preferable to measures such as regional incentives that are directed at the firm level because the former lead to fewer distortions of the market mechanism (Soltwedel et al., 1988; and Seidenfuss, 1989).
- Regional policy should aim at increasing the endogenous potential of lagging regions rather than diverting existing activities from one location to another (Temple, 1994).

All in all, it has to be emphasised that the chances of regional policy to increase aggregate welfare by activating idle resources are very limited. Lammers (1992) argues that the marginal utility of factors of production in peripheral areas is almost by definition insufficient to generate a positive net welfare effect.

As far as allocative distortions due to external effects are concerned (fourth rationale), regional policy is normally a second-best solution. It is preferable to internalise external effects such as environmental pollution and traffic congestion, for example by road use charges for private transport.

Summing up, it is very difficult to find clear economic rationales in favour of regional policy. Equity arguments for regional policy are certainly more powerful than efficiency arguments.

5.1.2 Why European Regional Policy?

Nearly all EU member states pursue some form of regional policy, although there are significant differences in the form and scope of national regional policies across the Union. Why, however, should the EU get involved in regional policy if the member states are already pursuing it? Once again, the literature provides various arguments.

1. The 'solidarity' or 'financial targeting' argument: Because poor member states are unable to target their regional problems themselves, the EU has to provide the necessary resources.

2. The 'vested interest' argument: The solution to regional problems in one member state will also be beneficial for other member states.
3. The 'effects of integration' argument: Because the benefits of integration are not evenly spread across the EU, a redistribution mechanism is required.
4. The 'effects of other EU policies' argument. Since the regional benefits of other policies such as the Common Agricultural Policy (CAP) are not spread evenly, the relative losers should be compensated by means of EU regional policy.

The 'solidarity' or 'financial targeting' argument is relatively undisputed but the 'vested interest' argument is problematic. Rich member states do not necessarily benefit from the fact that other regions are made better off. It can be argued, however, that without compensation for those regions which obtain less than their 'fair' share of the aggregate welfare gains, further integration would be impossible which in turn would cause aggregate welfare losses. This provides a link between the 'vested interest' and the 'effects of integration' arguments. The question of whether there are 'winners' and (relative or absolute) 'losers' of the integration process, is hotly debated and the empirical evidence rather mixed. Lammers (1992), for example, stresses the probability that integration will reduce spatial disparities while Vickerman (1992) is more pessimistic concerning the divergence effects of the Single European Market (SEM). Regardless of the scientific debate, however, 'the division of costs and benefits is central to the political agreements needed to proceed with integration' (Begg and Mayes, 1993).

Finally, the 'effects of other EU policies argument' is frequently and, at least with regard to the CAP, rightly mentioned in order to defend regional transfers. It is mainly the better-off EU regions that benefit from CAP expenditures (European Parliament, 1991). Although the EU has recently tried to reduce this bias (CEC, 1996a) the impact of the last round of CAP reforms on the cohesion countries is likely to be rather limited (Baltas, 1997).

5.1.3 Why 'Bounded' Regional Policy Transfers?

At the moment, EU regional policy operates mainly on the basis of conditional transfers from the EU budget to specific areas within the member states. Which arguments can be used in favour of this system?[3]

1. The 'conditions of the donor' argument: The net contributors to EU regional policy want to make sure that the money is spent in order to improve the growth potential of those regions that are in greatest need for support.
2. The 'insufficiency of regional authorities' argument: Regional authorities in most member states are unable to make sure that the 'right' measures to achieve regional convergence are pursued.
3. The 'co-ordination' argument: Regional policy measures in one member state have spillover effects in other member states which are not sufficiently taken into account if regional policy is conducted on a national level.
4. The 'fear of waste' argument: Purely national regional policy might lead to a wasteful subsidy race between different locations.

The first argument is the main reason for the current set-up of EU regional policy, namely the reluctance of the better-off member states to fund a fiscal transfer system without 'strings' for the recipients. EU regional policy is not officially designed as a system of fiscal federalism, contributing to convergence between the member states or to an equalisation of interpersonal income levels across the EU. Instead, its main purpose is to provide temporary support for those regions of the Union whose present level of competitiveness is insufficient. The net contributors to the EU budget would not have accepted the substantial increase in regional policy funding since the mid-1980s without a substantial degree of control over the use of structural fund resources for what they perceive as the 'right' measures for increasing regional competitiveness (CEPR, 1993; Folkers, 1995).

The second argument is essentially a rationalisation of the first. While the quality of regional authorities in some EU member states leaves much to be desired, it is obviously doubtful whether a centralised European administration is in a better position to design 'suitable' measures to increase regional competitiveness.

An economic rather than political argument for centralised regional policy is provided by the 'co-ordination' argument (Weise, 1995). Some regional policy measures, for example, transport infrastructure investments which also improve international transport links, have cross-border repercussions (external effects). The same applies to human capital formation in conjunction with international migration although, as argued above, international migration within the EU is still very low.

As far as the fear of a subsidy race between different locations is concerned, effective state aid control could prevent this outcome (Lammers, 1992). So far, however, the efficacy of EU state aids control still leaves much to be desired and, as we shall see in Chapter 6, on a per capita basis national regional aids in the supported parts of core member states such as Germany and Belgium are usually far above corresponding values in the cohesion countries (Marques, 1992). The weakness of competition policy, however, is a poor argument in favour of regional policy in general and an even poorer argument for centralised regional policy.

From the point of view of economic theory, it is easier to find arguments against the current regional policy system than arguments in favour of it. Generally speaking, the preferable method of compensation in economics is lump-sum compensation. Since this form of compensation requires that the winners and losers are identifiable and that the sum to be transferred can be calculated, it is impracticable in its perfect form, although the sums to be transferred can be approximated in a bargaining process. After all, the funding actually used for European regional policy is also established in a bargaining process.

Among the most important reasons why direct transfers would be more efficient than the current system is the fact that the current system pursues distributional aims by means of allocational policy. Although EU regional policy is not officially designed as a redistributive policy, it has significant redistributive effects (CEC, 1996a) and its distributional element can hardly be denied. This mix of aims and policies, however, is bound to lead to efficiency losses. From the point of view of economic theory, a system of direct or indirect transfers between the EU member states would therefore be preferable in order to fulfil the redistributive function of EU regional policy (Strain, 1993).

Finally, the current system is not easily compatible with the subsidiarity principle. This principle, included in Article 3b of the Maastricht Treaty (Treaty on European Union; TEU), states that the Community shall take action:

> only if and in so far as the objectives of the proposed action cannot be sufficiently achieved by the member states and can therefore, by reason of the scale or effects of the proposed action, be better achieved by the Community.

While some elements of EU regional policy – notably major infrastructure projects, with inter-regional spillovers such as railway lines or gas pipelines – are compatible with this principle, other forms of structural action undertaken by the EU, for example productive investment support in lagging areas, might as well be performed by the member states. It is thus mainly the 'conditions of the donor' that block the application of the subsidiarity principle in European regional policy.

5.2 EU REGIONAL POLICY – PAST AND PRESENT

5.2.1 The Development of European Regional Policy

The oldest elements of European regional policy today are the European Social Fund (ESF), aimed at 'rendering the employment of workers easier and of increasing their geographical and occupational mobility within the Community' (Article 123, EEC Treaty) and the European Agricultural Guidance and Guarantee Fund, Guidance Section (EAGGF) (Article 40, EEC). Areas encountering economic problems could also obtain loans with below market interest rates from the European Coal and Steel Community (ECSC) and the European Investment Bank (EIB). The geographical focus of early ESF activities was southern Italy – until the 1973 enlargement the unemployment hotspot of the Community. EAGGF funding, however, was mainly distributed to the better-off agricultural areas in the North of the EC. In financial terms all these instruments were very small and there was no clear strategy to promote regional development (Kenner, 1994).

The 1973 oil shock and the first enlargement of the EEC eventually led to a strengthening of the Community's regional policy activities. Regulation 724/75 EEC (Official Journal (OJ) L 73/8, 1975) established the European Regional Development Fund (ERDF) which was later incorporated into primary Community law.

> The European Regional Development Fund is intended to help to redress the main regional imbalances in the Community through participation in the development and structural adjustment of regions whose development is lagging behind and in the conversion of declining industrial regions. (Article 130C, EEC Treaty)

Prior to the 1988 reform, ERDF resources were allocated to member states on the basis of fixed quotas. Member states had to co-finance ERDF-supported projects with national public funding (principle of additionality). Up to 85 per cent of ERDF-funded projects during the 1970s and early 1980s concerned infrastructure improvements with the lion's share being allocated to transport infrastructure.[4]

The design of EU regional policy during the 1975–88 period led to a number of serious problems:

- In order to make sure that the quota allocated to them was used in full, member states frequently compromised the economic efficiency of ERDF-supported project.
- Community funding did not normally lead to additional projects but member states used European funding in order to reduce national expenditures for projects which would have gone ahead anyway (Tsoukalis, 1997).

The European Commission made several attempts to reform this early system of regional assistance. The aim of the Commission was to create a more encompassing regional policy where it would have an increased role vis-à-vis the national authorities. In order to achieve this goal, it was of crucial importance to move away from the member state quotas for ERDF funds. In 1978 and 1985, the Commission launched attempts to scrap the quota system but the European Council left it more or less intact. The member states were not yet willing to change a system that suited them well. They could use EU regional policy funds to reduce national expenditures and they were able to retain the initiative in regional policy-making.

Probably the most important reason for the overhaul of the original system was the EU's southern enlargement which increased regional disparities and led to demands by the existing southern member states to be compensated for their willingness to accept the widening of the Community. The so-called Integrated Mediterranean Programmes (IMP) for Italy, France and Greece were designed to satisfy these demands. The IMPs, launched in 1985, moved beyond the previous project-based approach and towards a more encompassing programme-type policy. They thus became 'pioneer' programmes for the large-scale 1988 EU regional policy reform (Bianchi, 1993).

Another reason for the reform was the 1986 Single European Market (SEM) project. In light of the SEM's uncertain spatial effects, the poorer member states demanded financial assistance by the EU in order to be able to increase their economic competitiveness. The richer member states were willing to satisfy these demands in order to make sure that integration would proceed. However, they wanted to ensure a more efficient use of the ERDF funds. This desire was even stronger than their reluctance to sacrifice the old quota-based system and to increase the influence of the European Commission. As argued above, however, they were not willing to establish a system of unbounded fiscal transfers.

The increased European competence for economic and social measures was also manifested by the insertion of the Title 'Economic and Social Cohesion' (Article 130A–130E, EEC Treaty) into primary European law:

> In order to promote its overall harmonious development, the Community shall develop and pursue its actions leading to the strengthening of its economic and social cohesion.
>
> In particular, the Community shall aim at reducing disparities between the levels of development of the various regions and the backwardness of the least favoured regions, including rural areas. (Article 130A(1), EC Treaty)

Article 130B mentions the most important Community instruments in order to improve social and economic cohesion within the EU. The aims and organisation of the structural policy instruments as well as the co-ordination between these instruments and the European institutions concerned are regulated by Article 130C–E, EC Treaty.

The Commission used its 'window of opportunity' to draw up a policy concept which was a dramatic departure from the previous system.[5] The reform affected not only the role and operations of the ERDF, but also the other Structural Funds (SFs), namely the ESF and the EAGGF. The most important elements of the reform were arranged around four guiding principles, namely 'programming', 'concentration', 'additionality' and 'partnership'. These principles are discussed below.

Economic and social cohesion has gained even more importance after the treaty revisions at Maastricht and the treaties now contain a clear obligation to use suitable policies in order to reduce socio-economic imbalances unless this reduction is likely to come about automatically and within a reasonable time period (Marias, 1994). Given the theoretical and empirical findings outlined above, however, this is very unlikely.

The Maastricht Treaty also led to a number of changes in the instruments of European regional policy. Two further cohesion instruments were created, namely the European Investment Fund (EIF) and the

Cohesion Fund (CF). The EIF is a special credit facility, organically linked with the EIB. The facility is designed to ease the financing of projects in economically backward parts of the EU which involve a higher credit risk than the standard operations of the EIB. The CF is based on Article 130D(2), EC Treaty and provides additional funding for infrastructure and environmental projects in member states with a per capita GDP of less than 90 per cent of the EU average. At present Spain, Portugal, Ireland and Greece are entitled to support from this facility. On top of the income condition, CF support requires the presentation and implementation of a national convergence programme in order to qualify for EMU. Given that the defining criteria are national rather than regional, and in light of the fact that the CF is specifically designed in order to ease cohesion countries' transition to EMU, the Cohesion Fund is strictly speaking not comparable with the Structural Funds (SF) but its purpose is also the promotion of economic development in the weaker parts of the EU.

The sectoral instruments related to the fishing industry have been reorganised in the form of the Financial Instrument for Guidance in the Fisheries Sector (FIFG) adopted as Regulation (EEC) 2080/93 (OJ L 193/1, 1993). Whereas these instruments operated previously outside the scope of the Structural Funds, they have now become an integral part of the SF operations.

A final and potentially far-reaching change was the establishment of the Committee of the Regions (Article 198a–c). So far this committee has merely advisory status, comparable to the Social and Economic Committee and is serviced by the same secretariat. Regardless of its very limited actual power, the mere existence of a committee consisting of representatives of regional and local bodies reflects the growing importance of sub-national levels of government within the EU. Whether the committee will eventually become more influential for the decision-making process regarding EU cohesion policies than originally envisaged remains to be seen (Kenner, 1994).

5.2.2 Principles of European Regional Policy – a Critical Assessment

5.2.2.1 Concentration

One of the guiding principles of the 1988 reform was the concentration of regional policy on those parts of the EU which are in greatest need of structural support. Whereas prior to the reform, areas eligible for national regional support qualified automatically for support from the European structural funds, the Commission used the 1988 reform to develop its own regional policy 'objectives'.

There are two main reasons for this change. First, the definition of eligible regions on a European level makes sure that member states do not unduly expand their national eligibility coverage in an attempt to maximise European structural support payments. Second, a European rather than national perspective as to what constitutes a regional problem is useful for a policy aimed at the reduction of socio-economic disparities at the Union level.

Regulation (EEC) 2052/88 established five priority objectives for regional policy. After the 1989–93 period, the list of objectives was partly revised and, following the accession of Sweden and Finland, a sixth objective, tailor-made for the new Nordic member states, was added. By and large, however, the original list of objectives remained in place.

The Commission proposals for the 2000–6 programming period foresee a reduction of the number of objectives from seven to three. A closer look at these objectives, however, shows that they encompass all existing objectives and even add some new fields of activity, for example urban areas facing structural problems (CEC, 1998a; CEC, 1998b).

Box 5.1 European Regional Policy Objectives

1989–93 Period

1. Development and structural adjustment of lagging regions
2. Conversion of regions or parts of regions seriously affected by industrial decline
3. Combating long-term unemployment
4. Occupational integration of young people

5a. Speeding up the adjustment of agricultural structures
5b. Development of rural areas

1994–9 Period

1. Not altered
2. Not altered
3. Combines former Objectives 3 and 4
4. Facilitating structural change

5a. As before but aid to the fisheries sector included
5b. Development and structural adjustment of rural areas

6. Development and adjustment of areas with very low population density (Nordic regions)

2000–6 Period (Commission proposal)
1. Combines former Objectives 1 and 6
2. Combines former Objectives 2 and 5b plus urban areas in difficulty and depressed areas dependent on fisheries
3. Combines former Objectives 3, 4 and 5a plus support for the participation of women in the labour market

Sources: CEC (1993b); CEC (1998b).

The objectives can be divided into two different categories. As far as the 1994–9 period is concerned, Objective 1, 2, 5b and 6 are 'regional' and refer only to certain eligible areas. Under Objective 3, 4 and 5a, however, it is possible to fund activities in the entire EU. These objectives are therefore called 'horizontal'. From 2000 onwards, Objectives 1 and 2 will be regional and Objective 3 will be horizontal (CEC, 1998b).

In order to make the designation process for region-specific objectives more transparent, a set of designation criteria has been developed. The most precise criteria were set up for the designation of Objective 1 regions. Per capita income in these regions, expressed in PPS, has to be less than 75 per cent of the Community average for the last three years where data are available. Moreover, Objective 1 status can only be granted to NUTS II regions in order to prevent the 'creation' of low-income regions by disregarding regional frontiers. So far, the regulation allows for exceptions from these rules. According to the proposals for the post-1999 period, however, exceptions are foreseen to be limited to the most remote island regions of the Community and areas currently eligible under Objective 6.

Designation criteria for the other objectives are less strict. In order to qualify for Objective 2 status, regions have to have a greater unemployment rate and a higher share of industrial employment than the EU average. Moreover, industrial employment has to be in decline. These criteria have to be satisfied for a couple of years, but they are not clearly quantified in the regulations. In principle the designation should be based on NUTS III regions but parts of NUTS III regions can also qualify.

The criteria for Objective 5b regions are a low level of socio-economic development, a high share of agricultural employment and a low level of agricultural income (Regulation (EEC) 2081/93). Once again, extensions of the eligibility criteria are possible and none of the criteria is quantified which leaves a lot of leeway for 'political' designations.

According to the proposals for the 2000–6 period, the Commission will lay down a population ceiling for the new Objective 2 for each member state. These ceilings will be based on the seriousness of structural problems at the national as well as the regional level (NUTS III regions). Within these ceilings, the member states will propose a list of eligible regions to the Commission which will then draw up the final list of Objective 2 regions. While the criteria differ according to the type of problem to be addressed under Objective 2 – industrial, rural or urban – unemployment will play a very prominent role. The same applies to the allocation of Objective 3 funding to the member states. Funding under Objective 3 can be used in all regions that are not eligible under Objective 1 or 2.

Although it was an explicit aim of the 1988 reform to limit the geographical availability of EU regional assistance, more than 50 per cent of the EU population currently lives in eligible areas. The 1994–9 coverage ratio has even gone up compared to the 1989–93 period and the quantitatively defined criteria for Objective 1 regions have been eroded.

Valenciennois in France, for example, one of the 1994–9 additions to the Objective 1 list, is not a NUTS II region. Hainault in Belgium and the Highlands and Islands region in the UK, two other newly designated lagging regions, were above the 75 per cent relative income threshold. Moreover, the economic problem in regions like Hainault or Merseyside (UK) is not a lack of development but one of industrial decline. Per capita funding for Objective 2 areas, however, is significantly lower than for Objective 1 regions.

Another example for the area designation practice are the Objective 6 areas in Sweden and Finland. These regions obtain EU structural support of a per capita magnitude that is comparable to some of the Objective 1 regions although most of them are well above the 75 per cent threshold. One cannot help forming the impression that the main purpose of Objective 6 is to make EU membership in agricultural areas of northern Sweden and Finland more attractive.

All in all, the level of spatial concentration is frequently regarded as insufficient (Bachtler and Michie, 1993).[6] This is also recognised by the Commission which aims to reduce Objective 1, 2, 5b and 6 coverage

Table 5.1 Population Covered by European Regional Policy Objectives, 1989 and 1994

Objective	1	1/6*	2	2	5b	5b	Total	Total
	1989	1994	1989	1994	1989	1994	1989	1994
Austria	./.	3.7	./.	7.5	./.	28.7	./.	39.9
Belgium	./.	12.8	22.1	14.2	2.7	4.5	24.8	31.5
Denmark	./.	./.	4.9	8.5	2.1	6.8	7	15.3
Finland	./.	16.7	./.	15.7	./.	21.6	./.	54
Germany	20.6**	20.6	12.4	8.8	7.4	9.7	40.4	39.1
Greece	100	100	./.	./.	./.	./.	100	100
Spain	57.7	59.7	22.2	20.4	2.5	4.4	82.6	84.5
Sweden	./.	5.3	./.	11.5	./.	9.2	./.	26
France	2.7	4.4	18.3	25.1	9.7	16.7	30.2	46.2
Ireland	100	100	./.	./.	./.	./.	100	100
Italy	36.4	36.7	6.6	11	5	8.3	47.8	56
Luxemb.	./.	./.	38	34.6	0.8	7.9	38.8	42.4
NL	./.	1.5	9.9	17.4	3	5.4	12.9	24.2
Portugal	100	100	./.	./.	./.	./.	100	100
UK	2.8	5.9	35.5	30.9	2.6	4.9	40.4	41.7
EU12/15	21.7	27	16.8	16.4	5	8.8	43	52.5

* Objective 6 for Sweden and Finland, otherwise Objective 1.
** From 1991 onwards.
Source: CEC (1996a).

from the present 51 per cent of the EU population to 35–40 per cent (new Objectives 1 and 2) (CEC, 1998c). Around half of this reduction can be achieved by applying the 75 per cent threshold for the designation of Objective 1 regions. This would exclude Hainault (B), Berlin (East) (FRG), Valencia (E), Valenciennois and Corse (F), Ireland, Sardegna (I), Flevoland (NL), Lisbon (P) and Highlands and Islands, as well as Northern Ireland (UK) from the list of eligible regions. The only new Objective 1 region would be South Yorkshire (UK) and the current Objective 6 regions (Martin, 1998). The Commission plans a further reduction of the population coverage by limiting Objective 2 eligibility to 18 per cent of the EU population compared to the current 25.2 per cent for Objective 2 and 5b (CEC, 1998b).

It remains to be seen whether the plans of the Commission will pass the European Parliament and the European Council without major changes. Even if they do, however, the financial impact of the reduced population coverage will only be felt after a couple of years. All regions scheduled to be de-designated after 1999 will be eligible for phasing-out payments over a 4–7-year period.

5.2.2.2 Programming

Prior to the 1988 reform, aid from the European Structural Funds was predominantly granted on a project basis. The Framework and Co-ordination Regulations (2052/88 and 2082/88) changed this system into a programming approach. The major advantage of programming is that it allows the integration of different forms of regional support for a particular area into an encompassing development plan. The idea is to improve the coherence between the individual measures and the co-ordination between the different institutions involved at EU, member state and regional level.

During the first phase of the programming, regional or national development plans are drawn up by the national and/or regional authorities concerned. There is a substantial amount of variation as far as these national plans are concerned. The most important differences are between plans for the different objectives. Plans for Objective 2 regions, for example, are obviously rather different from plans for Objective 5b regions. However, there are also major differences between regions covered by the same objective. This is partly because the regional problems of areas covered by the same objective may be very different, but there are also different national preferences for specific regional policy instruments. While some member states or regions put more emphasis on basic infrastructure or education, others prefer to support business-related infrastructures or productive investments.

On the basis of these national or regional plans, the European Commission develops, together with the national or regional authorities, the Community Support Framework (CSF), the second step in the programming process. During the 1994–9 period, the lion's share of CSF expenditures falls under the three categories Productive Investment Support, Human Capital Formation and Infrastructure. Productive Investment Support includes support measures for industry and services, rural development, fisheries, tourism and agricultural structures. Human Capital Formation covers education, training and Research and Development (R&D) and Infrastructure refers to areas such as transport, communication and energy but also water, environment and health. Productive investment support is mainly targeted at

Table 5.2 Functional Distribution of Objective 1 Structural Fund Expenditures in Ireland, Greece, Portugal and Spain, 1994–9*

Type of Expenditure	Ireland	Portugal	Greece	Spain
Productive Environment	36.2	35.7	27.8	30.5
Human Resources	43.9	29.4	24.6	28.4
Infrastructure	19.7	29.7	45.9	40.4

* Figures in per cent.
Source: CEC (1996a).

the firm level whereas investments in human capital and infrastructure try to improve the underlying competitiveness of regions.

Table 5.2 shows the functional distribution of the 1994–9 Structural Fund expenditures in the four cohesion countries.

The third step in the implementation process are the Operational Programmes (OPs), the implementation of which is mainly the task of the national and regional authorities within the member states. Intense consultations between national and European authorities take place during the planning and implementation process, and monitoring committees, made up of national experts as well as Commission officials, are set up for all CSFs and OPs.

Compared to the pre-1989 period this complex arrangement has significantly increased the influence of the Commission in regional policy design. In fact, it is sometimes argued that it is now too strong (Bachtler and Michie, 1993). The changes for the 1994–9 programming period tried to accommodate this critique by introducing various simplifications into the programming process (Regulations 2081 and 2082/93). In particular, member states now have the possibility to submit a single programming document (SPD) replacing the CSF and the OP.

Under the new Commission proposals there will be a clearer distribution of responsibilities between the Commission, the member states and the other actors involved in the SF process. While the strategic responsibility for programming would rest with the Commission, the member states, in consultation with governmental as well as non-governmental organisations, would develop the details of the plans.

Together with some other changes, concerning for example a simplification of the financial management of the SFs, these measures are likely to reduce the administrative burden that is frequently associated with EU regional policy. To locate the strategic decision-making at the level of the Community, however, may reduce the involvement of the member states to an essentially executive role. This, however, would not be easily compatible with the principle of subsidiarity and the fact that the member states are normally in a better position to identify the strategic needs of their economies.

Box 5.2 The Community Initiatives

During the 1994–9 period, the EU is spending 14 billion ECU on so-called Community Initiatives (CIs). The CIs are mainly designed to support regions that suffer from structural changes in specific industries, their location along national borders or the fact that they are located in the extreme periphery of the Union. The CIs are initiated by the Commission and implemented mainly by the regions. Some of them have been well received, especially INTERREG which aims to promote cross-border co-operation, an area where the EU, due to its European rather than national perspective, is clearly in a better position to act than the member states. The large number of CIs, the resulting lack of concentration and the administrative efforts they require, however, have been criticised (Michie and Bachtler, 1994: 11). During the 1994–9 period, the CIs evolved around five core topics:

- Cross-border, transnational and interregional co-operation and networks,
- rural development,
- assistance to the outermost regions,
- employment promotion and development of human resources and
- management of industrial change.

Within these fields, however, no fewer than 13 CIs were launched (CEC, 1996a). For the period after 1999, the Commission envisages a further concentration to only three initiatives, namely:

- Transnational, cross-border and interregional co-operation,
- rural development, and

- transnational co-operation to fight discrimination and inequality preventing access to employment

The Commission proposes to reduce the funding allocated to the CIs from nine per cent during the present programming period to five per cent during the 2000–6 period (CEC, 1998b).

5.2.2.3 Additionality

The additionality principle dates back to the pre-1989 period, and was designed in order to make sure that EU funding actually increases total expenditures for structural purposes. In light of the negative experiences with additionality during the pre-1989 period, the principle was explicitly incorporated into the Co-ordination Regulation.

> the Commission and the member states shall ensure that the increase in the appropriations for the Funds ... has a genuine additional economic impact in the regions concerned and results in at least an equivalent increase in the total volume of official or similar (Community and national) structural aid in the member state concerned, taking into account the macroeconomic circumstances in which the funding takes place. (Art. 9, Regulation (EEC) 4253/88)

Despite its increased legal profile, it is still difficult to put the additionality principle into practice. In fact, it became a cause for frequent disputes between the Commission and the member states during the 1989–93 period. A test case for the additionality debate was the struggle between the Commission and the UK government concerning EU funds for UK regions under the RECHAR CI (McAleavey, 1993; Welfare and Beaumont, 1993). The UK government tried to deduct RECHAR funding from the global local authority spending ceilings for the eligible areas. Since this was at odds with the additionality principle, the Commission withheld money earmarked for the UK under RECHAR, until the government in London partly accommodated the Commission.

The revised Co-ordination Regulation (Regulation (EEC) 2082/93) requires the member states to provide more detailed financial information than before in order to ensure the implementation of the additionality principle. Nevertheless, it remains doubtful whether more subtle attempts to evade the additionality principle than that practised by the UK government in the RECHAR dispute will be detected.

The additionality rules are different for Cohesion Fund – projects where European funding can cover up to 85 per cent of the total project costs. This is in effect a departure from the principle of additionality although an intended one since the CF was designed in order to enable poorer member states to improve their infrastructure endowments and to launch environmental projects without putting further strains on their national budgets in the run-up to EMU.

5.2.2.4 Partnership

The designers of the 1988 reform realised that the successful implementation of EU structural policy depends on close partnership and co-operation between European, national and sub-national authorities. After all the involvement of all these layers of government as well as non-governmental organisations creates a formidable demand for information.

Co-ordination has to take place between the different Structural Funds and between the SFs and related financial instruments of the EU, such as the EIB (Smit and Herzog; 1992, Art. 130D.03). Despite some co-ordination problems between the different services of the Commission, this aspect of partnership does not seem to be a cause of major concern.

The relationship between EU structural policies and non-spatial European and national policies, is much more difficult. The fact that CAP expenditures favour the core member states more than the cohesion countries, for example, is a frequently mentioned example for a non-spatial EU policy compromising the efficiency of the Union's spatial policy (European Parliament, 1991; CEC, 1996a). Further case studies on the link between EU structural policy and non-spatial policies will be elaborated in Chapter 6, 7 and 8.

The third and probably most prominent aspect of partnership concerns the links

> between the Commission and all the competent authorities and bodies including, within the framework of each Member State's national rules and current practices, the economic and social partners, designated by the Member State. (Art. 4, Regulation (EEC) 2081/93)

A definitive judgement on whether the partnership principle has been successfully put into practice is difficult to make. The complex programming system described above certainly creates a large potential for conflicts between the Commission and the member states, which in turn is frequently mentioned as one of the main problems of EU regional policy. During the first few years after the 1988 reform, for example, the absorption of EU commitments by the member states was in some cases rather low, particularly in Italy (CEC, 1997c). This has partly been blamed on the lack of efficiency of the national administrations and partly on the member states unwillingness or inability to provide the necessary co-financing in order to match European commitments. However, it is important to keep in mind that a high level of absorption does not allow any conclusion about the efficient use of resources.

In the case of the Greek CSF (1989–93), for example, there is evidence of shifting expenditures to smaller and thus more easily realisable projects, with lower expected economic returns, in order to reach higher rates of absorption (Tsoukalis, 1997).

Opinions as to how the present division of regional policy power should be altered are mixed. A large number of commentators argue in favour of a reduction of the Commission's influence and in favour of more subsidiarity (Roberts, 1993). As argued above, however, a more consequent application of the subsidiarity principle would face political resistance from the net contributors. Moreover, the Commission should certainly retain enough power to guarantee that EU regional policy is based on a proper 'European' perspective. In some cases it seems even desirable to grant more power to the Commission, for example, in order to prevent the inclusion of 'political' Objective 1 regions like Flevoland.

Another effect of the partnership approach in EU regional policy was the strengthening of the regions vis-à-vis the member states. As a matter of fact, the influence of regional authorities in the Structural Funds implementation is bigger than in most national regional policy schemes. This has been welcomed by most commentators because it brings more local knowledge into the regional policy process (Ryan, 1993; Roberts, 1993).

5.2.3 The Spatial Allocation of Structural Funds Support

The development of the financial allocations for EU regional policy shows the increased importance of structural action within the overall framework of the EU. In the wake of the 1988 reform, the available resources for the structural funds were doubled from ECU 7.2 billion in 1987, the last year before the reform, to ECU 14.5 billion in 1993, at the end of the first programming period. In relation to the EU

Table 5.3 EU Resources Committed to Structural Action, 1994–9: Breakdown According to Member State and Objective*

	Obj. 1	Obj. 2	Obj. 3/4	Obj. 5a	Obj. 5b	Obj. 6	TOTAL
Belgium	730	341	465	195	77	./.	1808
Denmark	./.	119	301	267	54	./.	741
Germany	13640	1566	1941	1145	1227	./.	19519
Greece	13980	./.	./.	./.	./.	./.	13980
Spain	26300	2415	1843	446	664	./.	31668
France	2190	3769	3203	1936	2236	./.	13334
Ireland	5620	./.	./.	./.	./.	./.	5620
Italy	14860	1462	1715	815	901	./.	19752
Luxembourg	./.	15	22	40	6	./.	83
NL	150	650	1079	165	150	./.	2194
Portugal	13980	./.	./.	./.	./.	./.	13980
UK	2360	4480	3377	275	817	./.	11409
Austria	162	99	389	388	403	./.	1432
Finland	./.	179	337	354	190	450	1503
Sweden	./.	157	342	260	174	247	1178
EU15	93991	15352	15184	6155	6860	697	138201
EU15 (%)	68	11.1	11	4.4	5	0.5	100

* Million ECU, 1994 prices.
Source: CEC (1996a).

budget, this represents an increase from 20 per cent in 1987 to 35 per cent by 1993 (Kenner, 1994: 13).

Another significant increase was decided as part of the 1992 Delors II package. It was agreed that 'the resources available for commitment from the Structural Funds and the FIFG shall be ECU 141,471 million at 1992 prices for the period 1994 to 1999' (Regulation (EEC) 2081/91, Article 12/1). In comparison with the 1989–93 period, this represents roughly a doubling of the available resources and an increase of the budget share to 37 per cent.

During the 1994–9 period, slightly over two-thirds of the SF funding goes to lagging regions and a further 11 per cent is earmarked for regions in industrial decline. The remaining 21 per cent is divided between Objectives 3–6. While Spain is the largest total recipient country, Ireland and Portugal have the highest per capita allocations under Objective 1, 262 ECU and 235 ECU, respectively.

Table 5.4 Cohesion Fund Resources, 1994–9

	Transport Infrastructure		Environment		TOTAL
	Mio. ECU	%	Mio. ECU	%	Mio.ECU
Spain	3983	50.1	3967	49.9	7950
Portugal	1380	53.0	1221	47.0	2601
Greece	1235	47.5	1367	52.5	2602
Ireland	665	51.1	636	48.9	1301
EU 4	7263	50.2	7191	49.8	14454

Source: CEC (1996a).

Per capita allocations for Objective 2 and 5b regions are mostly in the range of 30 to 50 ECU, and Objective 6 allocations are around 110 ECU.

Since 1993 additional funding for the four cohesion countries – Ireland, Spain, Portugal and Greece – is available under the CF. In fact, CF funding, by definition earmarked for transport infrastructure and environmental projects, has become a very significant part of the total assistance the cohesion countries receive from the Union. As a proportion of total cohesion funding – SFs, CIs and CF taken together – Cohesion Fund support is around 18 per cent for Spain and Ireland and around 15 per cent for Portugal and Greece.

Over the last decade, the financial allocations for structural policy have steadily increased both in absolute terms and as percentage of the EU budget. According to the new Commission proposals for the post-1999 period this development will come to an end. Expressed in 1997 prices, expenditures on structural operations in the existing member states will go down from 34.3 billion ECU in 1999 to 30.2 billion ECU in 2006. The Objective 1 share is supposed to remain at two-thirds of the total SF expenditures. In conjunction with reduced geographical eligibility this would result in a slight increase of per capita support in Objective 1 regions. For the new Objective 2 regions, however, the per capita figures would be slightly lower than during the 1994–9 period. Additional resources are foreseen for the Central and Eastern European Countries (CEEC) which have applied for membership. This point will be taken up again in Section 5.3.

5.2.4 Explaining the Spatial Allocation of Structural Funds Support

It was argued above that the key purpose of EU regional policy is to improve the competitiveness of the less prosperous parts of the Union. This implies that a strongly negative correlation between relative regional per capita income and per capita regional policy expenditures can be expected which is confirmed by Figure 5.1.

Objective 1 and 2 regions can be easily recognised with Objective 1 regions being located on the left-hand side of the figure and Objective 2 regions on the right-hand side. The figure also shows that per capita figures for the lagging regions differ widely. Differences in per capita allocations for Objective 2 regions, however, are comparatively small. The low figures for the German Objective 1 regions, depicted in the bottom left corner of Figure 5.1, come about because the new Länder were only included into European structural operations in 1991.

In the following regression a number of explanatory variables are used in order to explain the distribution of EU regional policy expenditures; regional per capita income relative to the EU (INC1), relative per capita income of the recipient country (INC2), the size of the recipient region (SIZE), the relative share of industry in the recipient

Figure 5.1 EU Regional Policy Expenditures per capita in Objective 1 and 2 Regions, 1989–93

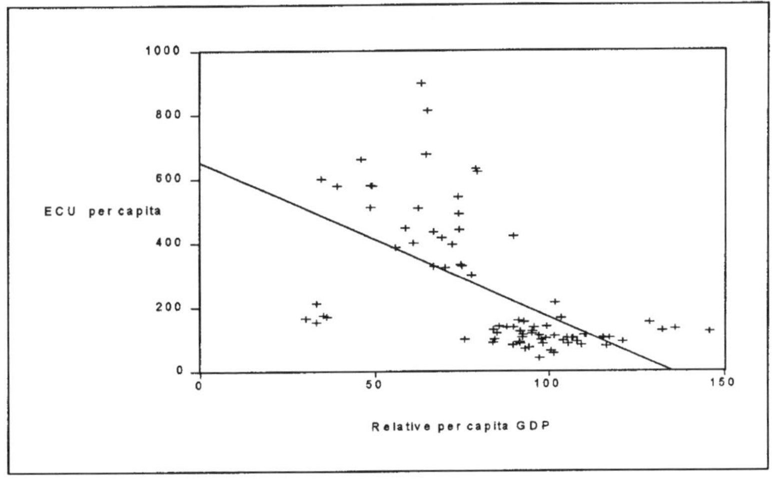

Source: Own calculations.

region (IND) and country dummies. The sample is restricted to Objective 1 and 2 regions only, figures in brackets are *t*-statistics:

$$\begin{array}{lll} EU & = & 19.24 - 0.84\ INC1 - 1.27\ INC2 - 1.00\ IND + 1.00\ DIRL \\ & & (14.28)\ (-5.14) \quad (-5.09) \quad (-5.20) \quad (2.04) \end{array} \qquad (5.1)$$

$R^2 = 0.63$, DW = 1.48, SE Reg. = 0.48, n = 81

All coefficients have the expected sign and the variables are significant. Low relative national and regional income as well as a low share of industrial production in the regional economy are all likely to result in higher structural transfers from the EU. The overall fit of the regression, however, is comparatively poor which suggests that there is a large element of political discretion in the allocation of regional policy funding. This observation applies of course also to the preferential position of Ireland whose country dummy (DIRL) is positive and significant.

The picture looks rather different for the Objective 1 regions only:

$$\begin{array}{lll} EU & = & 10.07 - 0.73\ INC1 - 0.09\ SIZE + 0.72\ DIRL - 1.53\ DG \\ & & (13.76)\ (-5.20) \quad (-3.40) \quad (3.34) \quad (-13.00) \end{array} \qquad (5.2)$$

$R^2 = 0.87$, DW = 2.56, SE Reg. = 0.21, n = 32

Within the sub-sample of lagging regions differences in relative regional income are still a significant explanatory factor. The regression also suggest that small countries and regions receive more funding than the large lagging regions located for example within Spain and in the Mezzogiorno. The negative coefficient for the (East) German Objective 1 regions has been explained above. The favourable treatment of the Republic of Ireland, however, is difficult to explain. It may be that the economic track record of this country in the recent past conveys the impression that SF money is well spent but the skills of the Irish negotiators may also play a part. In light of the recent developments of Irish per capita GDP, however, the country is almost certain to lose its Objective 1 status after 1999.

In the event that the Commission proposals for the next programming period are adopted without major changes, the results of a similar exercise for the 2000–6 period are likely to look rather different. The Commission plans to use unemployment as an indicator for the allocation of funding in Objective 1 as well as Objective 2 regions. This would reduce the per capita allocation in low-unemployment countries like Portugal, the Netherlands and the UK and would increase it in member states with a high rate of unemployment, notably Spain and Italy but also Germany. The usefulness of the unemployment indicator for the allocation of EU structural funding will be briefly discussed in Section 5.4 below.

5.3 REGIONAL POLICY AFTER 1999 AND EASTERN ENLARGEMENT

During the 2000–6 period the Commission is likely to face the challenge to include the first CEECs into the EU regional policy arrangements. In its proposals for the next programming period the Commission aims to do that while keeping the total costs of structural policies as percentage of EU GDP at the 1999 level, namely at 0.46 per cent.

For the old and new member states taken together, the Commission foresees structural expenditures of a magnitude of 275 billion ECU at 1997 prices, 45 billion ECU of which are earmarked for the likely new member states (Poland, Hungary, the Czech Republic, Slovenia and Estonia) and the remaining five applicants from Central and Eastern Europe (the Slovak Republic, Romania, Bulgaria, Latvia and Lithuania) (CEC, 1997b).

Table 5.5 Expenditures on Structural Operations, 2000–6*

	1999	2000	2001	2002	2003	2004	2005	2006
EU15								
Structural Funds	31.4	31.3	32.1	31.3	30.3	29.2	28.2	27.3
Cohesion Fund	2.9	2.9	2.9	2.9	2.9	2.9	2.9	2.9
CEECs								
New Member States		0.0	0.0	3.6	5.6	7.6	9.6	11.6
Pre-Accession Aid**		1.0	1.0	1.0	1.0	1.0	1.0	1.0
Total	34.3	35.2	36.0	38.8	39.8	40.7	41.7	42.8

* ECU billion at 1997 prices.
** In 2000 and 2001 for all CEECs, from 2002 onwards for the remaining candidates only.
Source: CEC (1997b).

The stark difference between the support earmarked for the new member states (38 billion ECU) and the remaining five CEECs (5 billion ECU) has to be regarded with concern. While regional policy transfers to the first group of countries will soon reach three per cent of their GDP, the pre-accession aid foreseen for the remaining CEECs amounts to only about 1 per cent of GDP for the 2002–6 period. Although a full discussion of these different levels of support would require further insights into issues such as the relative utilisation and quality of existing infrastructure in the different CEECs, there is a clear danger that countries that do not become EU member states in the first round will face an uphill struggle to increase their competitiveness not only vis-à-vis the EU15 but also vis-à-vis the first new member states.

For the pre-accession phase the Commission proposes three structural instruments (CEC, 1998c):

- An instrument for Structural Policies pre-Accession (ISPA),
- an agricultural pre-accession instrument, and
- aid under the existing PHARE regulation.

The funding available under the agricultural instrument and the PHARE regulation will make another two billion ECU per year available during the pre-accession period. The assistance will be concentrated on the following areas (CEC, 1998c):

- Reinforcement of the administrative and judicial capacity,
- investments related to the adoption of the 'acquis', mainly in the areas environment and transport infrastructure and
- improvements of agricultural efficiency.

Despite undeniable problems concerning the absorption capacity of the CEECs, the amounts allocated for the pre-accession period seem rather modest. The Commission itself has estimated that in the areas of transport and environment alone investments of a magnitude of 150–90 billion ECU are required (CEC, 1998d). Compared to this needs assessment annual transfers of three billion ECU prior to the accession of the first candidate countries seem rather modest.

As far as the present member states are concerned, the Commission's financial plans ('Agenda 2000') make the effects of the Eastern enlargement on EU regional policy appear far less dramatic than sometimes prophesied (Courchene et al., 1993; Weise, 1997).

While regional policy is certainly not an insurmountable obstacle for enlargement, the Commission's assumption that regional policy expenditures in the CEECs can be fully financed by means of savings and growth-generated resources has to be regarded with some caution. Scenarios based on slightly lower real growth rates than those used in 'Agenda 2000' (2.5 per cent real annual growth for EU15 and 4 per cent for the new member states) and on cautious assumptions concerning the savings potential due to de-designation show that it might be necessary to go beyond the 0.46 per cent EU–GDP threshold for structural action that is currently envisaged by the Commission. However, the shortfall in funding is likely to be temporary and comparatively modest. Martin and Mortensen (1997) argue that by 2006 up to 5.5 billion ECU for structural expenditures in the CEECs may have to be financed by other means than savings and growth. This is still a modest sum indeed compared to the political and economic importance of enlargement.

5.4 CONCLUSIONS

Any assessment of EU regional policy has to take into account that the Union's structural operations are not intended as a regional stabilisation systems such as the German Länderfinanzausgleich (Gordon, 1991). EU regional policy intends to improve the competitiveness and hence the long-term growth prospects of the supported regions. Despite the official denial that EU regional policy is about redistribution, however, its redistributive effects are significant and comparatively easy to identify whereas the identification of long-run changes in the competitiveness of supported regions is a much more difficult task.

According to the Cohesion Report, Community structural assistance equalised per capita income by some three per cent during the 1989–93 period and by 4.5 per cent during the 1994–9 period. These figures seem very high, but since the cohesion countries obtain up to 4 per cent of their GDP from the structural and cohesion funds they are not unrealistic (CEC, 1996a).

The growth effects of EU structural operations have been estimated by means of regional or national macroeconomic models. According to an input–output model used by the Commission's Directorate-General for Regional Policy (DG XVI), GDP growth in Portugal, Greece, Ireland and Spain without the interventions of the Structural Funds would have been on average almost half a percentage point lower than the 2.2 per cent that were actually achieved during the 1989–93 programme period. The input–output model used for these estimations provides a high level of sectoral disaggregation but it suffers from the fact that it is comparative-static. Longer-term supply-side effects are not taken into account (Beutel, 1993).

According to estimates based on the QUEST II macroeconomic model, operated by the Commission's Economic and Financial Service (DG II), the growth effects of the 1989–93 programmes have not been negligible but less pronounced than suggested by the input–output analysis. The QUEST model distinguishes between demand and supply-side effects of the Structural Funds in the short, medium and long run. It is thus more sophisticated than the input–output analysis. It has to be kept in mind, however, that the QUEST II estimates are made on a national rather than regional basis and that the QUEST II model does not differentiate between different sectors of production (Röger, 1996).

Simulations based on the HERMIN macroeconomic model yield estimates closer to or even above the input–output-based estimates (Bradley, 1996). One of the key features of this model is that it assumes positive growth externalities of public investments in human capital and infrastructure, assumptions that are based on endogenous growth theory and research on the economic impact of infrastructure investments.

A recent study by the London School of Economics (LSE, 1997), finally, has identified substantial positive spillover effects from Cohesion Fund investments. This evaluation exercise is based on a number of recent economic modelling techniques, but it is restricted to the economic effects of individual transport infrastructure projects like the Madrid ring road.

Besides macroeconomic modelling, virtually all EU regional policy programmes are now subject to *ex-ante*, ongoing and *ex-post* evaluations. These evaluations provide a more in-depth analysis of the individual programmes than the aggregate simulations reviewed above. Unfortunately, however, the programme evaluations suffer from massive problems (Bachtler and Michie, 1995; Cameron, 1990). Apart from the usual anti-monde problem of policy evaluation, the availability of regionalised data is still very poor. Another formidable evaluation problem is the short time period during which the funds have operated in their present form. Finally, the big variety in approaches towards evaluation has made the creation of a coherent picture even more difficult (MEANS, 1993). However, 'any search for an all embracing methodology applicable to all possible situations is equivalent to the search for the holy grail' (McEldowney, 1991: 264).

Suggestions for improvements of EU regional policy come under two different categories. First, improvements within the present framework. Second, more fundamental changes in the way regional economic imbalances are tackled. The latter will be addressed in the concluding chapter.

As far as the first category is concerned, most analysts demand an increased level of concentration of regional assistance and a simplification of its procedures (Begg, Gudgin; and Morris, 1995). These demands have been taken on board by the Commission. As argued above, 'Agenda 2000' envisages a reduction of the eligible population from 51 per cent to 35–40 per cent. In order to prevent possible opposition by some of the southern member states against the Union's eastern enlargement, however, the Commission has already departed from earlier ideas to abandon the Cohesion Fund and the negotiations concerning regional eligibility for European structural funding are bound to be very controversial. Compared with the thorny issue of de-designations, the proposed changes in the administrative procedures, for example a simplification of the financial arrangements (CEC, 1998b), are certainly easier to realise.

Other measures that could improve the efficiency of the Union's structural operations are the increased use of clearly defined designation criteria, the introduction of quality incentives, inter-regional competition for EU funding and the increased use of financial instruments other than grants.

As argued above, one of the central elements of the 1988 reform of the SFs was the definition of clearly defined eligibility criteria for Objective 1 regions. So far, however, the allocation of funding for other objectives is not based on comparable criteria although suitable indicators could make the debate on regional policy more rational and less focused on distributional issues.

As argued above, the Commission aims to base the allocation of funding during the 2000–6 period on more objective criteria than the allocation during the present period. The excessive reliance on unemployment as a key indicator for all objectives has to be regarded with caution, though. Unemployment is mainly a national and only to a minor extent a regional problem. Moreover, it largely depends on the quality of the national employment policy. 'Rewarding' high unemployment with high per capita allocations of structural resources gives a wrong signal to the member states. Allocation should rather be based on the member state's efforts to fight unemployment, although these are obviously more difficult to quantify than the number of people looking for jobs.

So far, member states have only limited financial incentives to make good use of SF funding. The only existing but implicit mechanism for sanctions is the bargaining process for the allocation of funding between the member states. During the next programming period the Commission thus plans the introduction of a budget reserve of 10 per cent of total SF funding. These resources will be allocated half-way through the next programming period on the basis of the programme performance, for example the absorption of EU resources and their leverage effect (CEC, 1998b). While the idea is to be strongly welcomed, it is important to make sure that the allocation is not primarily based on purely quantitative criteria like budget execution but on indicators like the generation of private funding (foreseen in the proposal) and the long-term economic and social benefits of the programme. This in turn represents a challenge for evaluation.

As far as financial instruments are concerned, EU regional policy still relies almost exclusively on grants. For many of the supported projects, however, alternative methods of finance, for example soft or interest-free loans from the EIB, would be feasible. Recent developments in the financing of transport infrastructure in particular could be applied to many projects that are currently grant-financed. This would also emphasise the 'start-up' character that the funds are supposed to have. It is therefore encouraging that the new Commission proposals argue in favour of alternative financial instruments.

Finally, the co-ordination between EU regional policy, national regional policy and non-spatial European and national policies should be substantially improved. The following chapters illustrate these co-ordination problems, using national state aids, R&D and transport infrastructure as case studies.

6 National and European Regional Policy: an Uneasy Relationship

As argued in Chapters 4 and 5, EU regional policy tries to improve regional competitiveness in three ways: (1) by upgrading the physical infrastructure; (2) by enhancing the regions' human capital endowment; and (3) by supporting the productive sector directly. This last area of regional policy encompasses a large number of measures ranging from direct investment grants to the subsidised provision of industrial estates or financial support for the introduction of advanced technology. In this chapter, however, the emphasis will be on the more direct forms of support, namely investment grants (thereafter usually called regional incentives).

Regional incentives are provided not only on the European level but also by most member states. In fact, they are still the most important regional policy instrument at member state level (Bachtler, 1995). Whether European and national incentive policies are well co-ordinated, however, remains a neglected area of research.

Previous analyses based on data at the member state level (Marques, 1992; Martin and Schulze Steinen, 1995 and 1997) suggest that in relative terms cohesion countries' expenditures for state aids are not significantly below the EU average. Table 6.1 summarises state

Table 6.1 State Aids Expenditures in the Cohesion Countries Relative to the EU Average, 1981–94*

	1981–6	1986–8	1988–90	1990–2	1992–4
Greece	89	141	155	116	100
Ireland	143	123	100	79	88
Spain	n.a.	123	90	68	71
Portugal	n.a.	105	110	74	70

* State aids in per cent of GDP relative to the EU average (= 100).
Source: CEC (various issues A).

aids expenditures reported in the European Commission's periodic Surveys on State Aids.

Although Table 6.1 shows a reduction of relative (and, along with the rest of the EU, absolute) expenditures over time, the cohesion countries still use a sizeable share of their national product for state aids. The unweighted average for the 1992–4 period is 1.4 per cent compared to the Union average of 1.7 per cent. As we will see below, this is in clear contrast with the relative efforts of the cohesion countries in the fields of R&D and transport infrastructure.

The present analysis differs from previous investigations by using a regional data set for the 1989–93 period. This yields more detailed insights into the co-ordination problem than data at the national level.

The first section of this chapter reviews research on the impact of regional incentives on business investments. Section 6.2 presents two hypotheses concerning the spatial distribution of regional incentive funding across European regions. Section 6.3 reviews these hypotheses empirically.

6.1 THE ECONOMIC EFFECTS OF REGIONAL INCENTIVES

When reviewing the literature on the importance of regional incentives for investment decisions, the evidence seems fairly mixed. Shepherd, Silberston and Strange (1985), for example, argue that incentives had only a negligible impact on investment decisions of overseas investors in the UK. In a similar study, focusing on Japanese direct investments in the UK, Dunning (1986) found that incentive schemes had at least some modest impact on the decision to locate in Britain. Faini and Schiantarelli (1987) used Scottish data to estimate the impact of regional policy incentives on investments. They found that during the 1961–78 period the use of incentives increased investments by 14.1 per cent. Looking at outward investment from the UK, Newbould, Buckley and Thurwell (1978) concluded that most investors took the availability of incentives into account when making a location decision.

Another country which, like the UK, has managed to attract significant foreign direct investments is Portugal. Once again there is some indication that incentives were important though not central in attracting foreign capital into the country.

> The Portuguese authorities maintain ... that incentives are needed to attract investment in certain activities and regions, but that

> Portugal's strong workforce, sound economic policies and improving infrastructure remain the more important determinant of FDI inflows. (OECD, 1994a: 34–5)

It should be kept in mind that Portugal also supported investments in its most advanced and attractive regions, such as Greater Lisbon and Porto. This makes it easier to attract foreign direct investments and lowers the ratio of incentive costs to investment attracted. The drawback of this policy, and the subject of an intra-Portuguese policy debate, is the likelihood of a further increase of domestic disparities (Yuill et al., 1994: 114–15).

In the run-up to the Single European Market, the European Commission (CEC, 1990) published the results of a major survey among European companies asking which factors shape the regional competitiveness of problem regions. The study was based on questionnaires sent to companies in lagging, declining and control regions in ten European countries. Lagging and declining regions correspond to Objective 1 and 2 regions whereas the third category represents wealthy, non-problematic regions.

The study looked at the importance of national as well as regional factors. As far as the former were concerned, industrial policy was found to be amongst the most significant positive factors in all three types of regions (CEC, 1990: 26). The term 'industrial policy', however, covers a much wider area of economic policy than only direct public support to the productive sector. In the section looking at regional factors the impact of incentives was addressed separately and, although it was not found to be amongst the most important locational factors, was generally assessed as positive (CEC, 1990: 34). It should be remembered, however, that the survey covered only companies which have been at their location for less than five years when questioned.

A later study (CEC, 1993a) confirmed these findings. About 40 per cent of companies in the manufacturing sector, for example, considered governmental support an 'important' factor in the choice of the country as well as the region. About 30 per cent perceived it as 'critical' for the selection of the region, and 17 per cent as 'critical' for the choice of the country (CEC, 1993a: Table 8.3).[1]

Summarising the debate, three points emerge.

1. Regional incentives cannot compensate for major disadvantages of countries or regions such as the absence of stable macroeconomic policies or a lack of qualified labour.

2. However, regional incentives can 'influence investment decisions within certain large national markets' (Thomsen and Woolcock, 1993: 74) as well as between similar regions in different countries. As it was expressed in the abovementioned study for the European Commission, 'on the basis of cost differentials and financial incentives, various lagging regions have attracted a substantial amount of foreign investment in the recent past, notably in manufacturing'.[2] One may think of a multi-stage decision-making process determining the investment location. At some point towards the end of that process, incentives become an important variable in the final decision.
3. Most factors determining locational decisions can only be changed in the long run. Some of them, like the geographic location and the climate, cannot be changed at all. Regional incentives are, therefore, amongst the few policy instruments that can influence investment decisions in the short run (Wishlade, 1995). They are therefore of considerable importance for assessing the convergence prospects within the EU.

6.2 HYPOTHESES ABOUT THE SPATIAL DISTRIBUTION OF REGIONAL INCENTIVES

In the following, two hypotheses concerning the spatial distribution of regional incentives in Europe are presented. The 'need for support hypothesis' is likely to provide an explanation of the regional distribution of European regional support whereas the 'ability to pay hypothesis' is likely to explain the spatial distribution of national regional support across the EU.

Both hypotheses are based on the argument that the purpose of regional incentives is to compensate potential investors for the economic disadvantages they will face in problem regions. Examples for such disadvantages are poor infrastructure and a shortage of skilled labour. Keeping in mind that most problem regions are also low-income regions, one can expect a negative relationship between relative regional per capita GDP and the availability of regional incentives.

While this negative relationship can be expected for European as well as national regional incentives, the two policies are based on different perspectives. Since EU regional policy aims at assisting regions that face economic problems compared to the European average, EU support is likely to be highest in regions with the lowest per capita income relative to the EU average. This corresponds with the 'need for support hypothesis'. Although it must be emphasised that neither the level of aggregate regional policy spending, including human capital formation and infrastructure, nor the level of productive sector support is a guarantee of economic success, it can be assumed that a spatial distribution following the 'need for support hypothesis' is likely to contribute to economic convergence between European regions.

As far as national incentives are concerned, regional income relative to the national rather than the European average is decisive. While the socio-economic problems of, say, the Dutch region of Limburg are rather small compared to those in many lagging parts of the EU, they are considerable from a Dutch perspective and will be perceived as such by the Dutch government. Moreover, expenditures will depend on the countries' ability to finance national incentive schemes. According to the 'ability to pay hypothesis', a poor region in a poor country is thus likely to receive less than a poor region in a rich country. Unlike the 'need for support hypothesis', this second pattern of regional incentive spending is likely to contribute to divergence rather than convergence among European regions because the poor areas in better-off member states obtain a competitive advantage vis-à-vis regions in poorer member states – an outcome that European competition policy tries to prevent.

Box 6.1 European Competition Policy and the Availability of National Regional Incentives

The availability of national regional incentives is regulated by European competition policy (Martin and Schulze Steinen, 1995: 14–15). Although in principle any kind of state aids which distort, or threaten to distort, fair and free competition between enterprises of the member states is illegal, competition policy foresees two special circumstances under which the Commission can allow the use of state aids as a means to reduce regional disparities. Article 92(3)(a), EC Treaty concerns 'aid to promote the economic development of areas where the living standard is abnormally low or where there is serious underemployment'. Article 92(3)(c), EC Treaty allows the Commission to grant certain sectoral or regional aid intended to improve the economic development in lagging areas of the member states (Bellamy and Child, 1991: 140). The list of regions that qualify for these exceptions is established in highly politicised negotiations between the member states and the European Commission. Although the overlap between areas that are eligible for EU regional policy and those that qualify for national support is high, some discrepancies occur which illustrates the discretionary character of the mapping process (Wishlade, 1993). In the past the European Commission tried to reduce the spatial coverage and the average intensity (the ratio between the money awarded and the total investment costs) of national regional incentives whilst making sure that lagging EU regions benefit more from incentive support than better-off areas of the Union. As far as the spatial coverage is concerned, the Commission was partly successful (CEC, various issues A). Its record concerning average intensity levels and the safeguarding of an advantage for lagging regions, however, is less impressive. Although the permitted maximum incentive levels for investments in poorer regions are higher than in better-off areas, budgetary restrictions normally prevent the poorer member states from using that advantage (Marques, 1994).

In a recent communication (OJ C 74; 10 March 1998) the Commission tried to address these shortcomings by introducing various changes in the state aids regime. First, the future designation practice for Article 92(3)(a) regions follows the practice for Objective 1 regions. Second, the designation practice for Article 92(3)(c) regions follows closely the proposed system for the designation of Objective 2 regions after 1999. Put into practice, these measures are likely to guarantee a high level of coherence between the national and European eligibility maps. As argued above, however, the key problem so far is the wedge between the permitted aid intensity, which is higher in poorer member states, and the realised aid intensity, which is higher in richer member states.

According to the new communication, aid in Article 92(3)(a) areas must not exceed a net grant equivalent of 50 per cent of the total costs of the supported investment. The corresponding figure for Article 92(3)(c) regions is 30 per cent. For both types of regions there are special regulations for outermost areas and support for small and medium-sized enterprises. Whether these new rules are sufficient to have a noticeable impact on the actual distribution of national investment aid across the EU remains to be seen.

Looking at the distribution of aggregate productive sector support, the spatial pattern will depend heavily on the relative importance of national vis-à-vis European support. Where European support dominates, the aggregate distribution is likely to follow the 'need for support hypothesis'. Where national support dominates, poor regions in rich countries are likely to receive the highest amount of support. It is also possible that the combined operation of European and national support leads to a situation where large parts of the EU receive roughly equal amounts of incentives. This situation would not foster the convergence of regions that are lagging from a European perspective and it would lead to substantial welfare losses. If large parts of the Union benefit from similar levels of support, this is unlikely to have an impact on locational decisions but will merely be taken as windfall profits by the investing enterprises.

6.3 AN EMPIRICAL ANALYSIS FOR EUROPEAN REGIONS

The following analysis looks at three different forms of productive investment support, the first being EU incentives spent within the framework of European regional policy in Objective 1 and 2 regions. These funds are partly provided by the EU itself and, according to the principle of additionality, partly by the member states. These cofinancing funds represent the second category of productive investment support. The third category is money spent on national support schemes not normally linked with European regional policy. There is some overlap between EU and national incentives, however, because some member states use European regional policy transfers to finance national incentive programmes. This has been taken into account. Table 6.2 summarises the three different categories of regional incentives to be analysed below.

Table 6.2 Different Forms of Regional Incentives

<table>
<tr><td colspan="2">EU Productive Sector Support</td></tr>
<tr><td>Structural Funds Contribution
(Category 1)</td><td>National (Cofinancing) Contribution
(Category 2)</td></tr>
<tr><td colspan="2">National Regional Incentives
(Category 3)</td></tr>
</table>

Regionalised data on European or national funding allocated to regional incentives are not readily available. It is possible, however, to obtain figures on European productive sector support from the Community Support Frameworks (CSFs) for the various Objective 1 and 2 regions. In the CSFs, European funding and national 'additionality' funding are provided separately, which allows the calculation of 'additionality multipliers'.[3] These data are subject to two limitations:

1. Since they refer to budget allocations foreseen at the beginning of the investigation period, differences between these proposed figures and actual expenditures are inevitable. Due to data limitations, however, actual expenditure figures cannot be used.
2. The exact share of total regional policy expenditures going to the productive sector is difficult to ascertain. The CSFs vary greatly in the headings and descriptions used for different regional policy measures. Overall, however, they allow a reasonable estimation of the division of funding between the different 'pillars' of EU regional policy.

For some member states, data on resources allocated to national incentive schemes are available in Yuill et al. (1994). Most of the data used, however, are unpublished material provided by national authorities.[4] As for European incentives, all data refer to planned budgetary allocations rather than actual expenditures. A list of the national incentive programmes included in the analysis as well as a list of the regions covered by European and/or national support schemes can be found in the Appendix. A large number of NUTS II regions were only partly eligible for European and/or national support. This was taken into account for the calculation of the per capita figures. Population coverage data for national and European incentive schemes were supplied by the European Commission.

Other forms of region-specific support for the productive sector, such as tax relief systems and subsidised investment loans, were not included in the analysis. Nor were horizontal measures such as innovation incentives, environmental support measures or subsidies to firm-specific education taken into account. These programmes were excluded because it is nearly impossible to quantify them, especially on a regional basis. In order to obtain a comparable and reliable picture of the spatial distribution of regional incentives, the analysis was restricted to the two abovementioned categories.

6.3.1 Productive Sector Support within the Structural Funds

It was established in Chapter 5 that the development of prerequisites for economic activity like roads, railways or education takes up a much larger share of total regional expenditures in Objective 1 regions than in Objective 2 regions. The share of total EU resources used for the productive sector is therefore almost by definition higher in Objective 2 regions. This is reflected in Figure 6.1, presenting EU support for the productive sector plus the national additionality payments. The figure looks strikingly different compared to Figure 5.1 which depicted total EU regional policy support.[5]

The link between regional funding and relative regional income has become much weaker and the difference between Objective 1 regions, located left of the 75 per cent mark for relative regional per capita income, and Objective 2 regions has almost totally disappeared. Ireland has the highest expenditure level for EU productive sector support with nearly 500 ECU per capita during the 1989–93 period.

Table 6.3 provides regional averages of per capita EU and additionality support for the productive sector in the different member states. For member states with Objective 1 and Objective 2 regions, average

Figure 6.1 EU Productive Sector Support in European Regions, 1989–93*

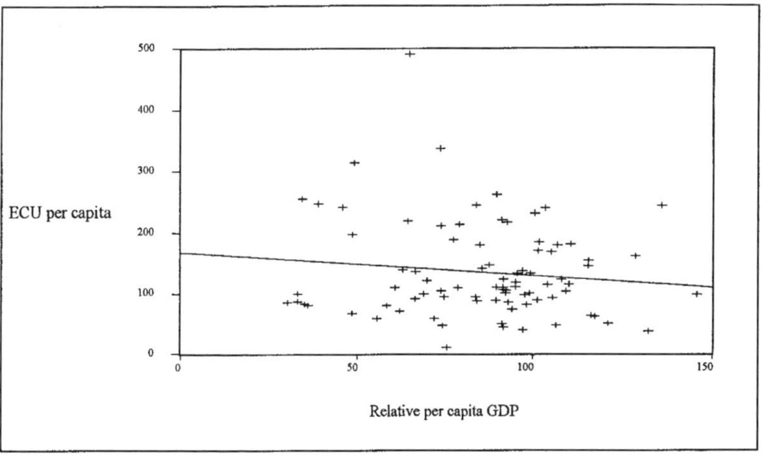

*National additionality payments included.
Source: Own calculations.

Table 6.3 EU Productive Sector Support plus Additionality Funding According to Member State and Regional Policy Objective, 1989–93*

Country	Objective 1 average	Objective 2 average
Belgium	./.	98.65
Denmark	./.	47.30
Greece	196.87	./.
Germany	148.92	83.35
Spain	69.95	69.84
France	109.29	137.57
Ireland	490.85	./.
Italy	141.95	100.75
Luxembourg	./.	161.22
Netherlands	./.	170.02
Portugal	303.68	./.
UK	188.23	100.28

* Average regional value in ECU per capita of covered population during the 1989–93 period.
Source: Own calculations.

figures for both categories are given. In the case of the UK, for example, the Objective 1 figure refers to Northern Ireland only. The Objective 2 figure, however, is the arithmetic average of all UK Objective 2 regions.

As argued above, differences in the percentage share of total EU funds used for productive sector support in Objective 1 and 2 regions explain that EU productive sector support in Objective 2 regions comes on average so close to that in Objective 1 regions. In fact, as summarised in Table 6.4, the share of total EU funding earmarked for the productive sector during the 1989–93 period was almost twice as high in Objective 2 regions as in Objective 1 regions.[6]

Table 6.4 also provides the ratios between EU support for the productive sector and the member state's additionality funding, the so-called 'additionality multipliers'. Although the differences in the multipliers are limited, they are generally higher in better-off member states. Only in the cohesion countries (Greece, Spain, Ireland and Portugal) are the multipliers below 2.

Table 6.4 EU Productive Sector Support as a Share of Total EU Regional Support (in per cent) and Additionality Multiplier According to Member State and Regional Policy Objective, 1989–93

Country	EU Productive Sector Support / Total EU Support		Additionality Multiplier	
	Obj. 1 average	Obj. 2 average	Obj. 1 average	Obj. 2 average
Belgium	./.	45.0	./.	2.33
Denmark	./.	19.7	./.	2.30
Greece	26.7	./.	1.56	./.
Germany	27.3	62.7	2.03	2.62
Spain	9.2	31.5	1.86	2.10
France	8.2	47.9	2.11	2.39
Ireland	33.4	./.	1.66	./.
Italy	18.9	39.2	2.04	2.45
Luxembourg	./.	52.9	./.	2.00
Netherlands	./.	64.4	./.	2.47
Portugal	33.7	./.	1.58	./.
UK	22.7	42.1	2.77	2.50
EU average	22.5	45.04	1.95	2.35

Source: Own calculations.

6.3.2 National Productive Sector Support – Regional Incentives

The regional distribution of allocations for national incentive schemes does not follow a very clear pattern. The level of per capita support varies significantly across the EU and is not strongly correlated with relative regional income.

During the 1989–93 period, the Italian region of Lazio had by far the highest level of national incentive support per inhabitant (1,382 ECU). There is also a small group of regions which received more than 600 ECU per capita. Three of these regions belong to the former German Democratic Republic, namely Thüringen, Sachsen-Anhalt and Brandenburg. Another, somewhat surprising member of this group are the eligible parts of Luxembourg. In the two remaining regions the high level of expenditure comes about due to exceptional circumstances. Abruzzi lost its eligibility for Italian capital investment grants during the period under review. The high level of funding being allocated to this

Figure 6.2 National Support for Productive Investments in European Regions, 1989–93

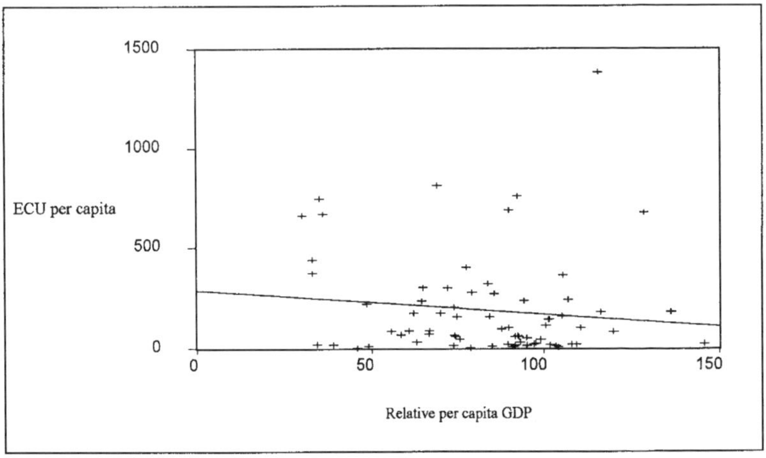

ECU per capita
1500
1000
500
0
0 50 100 150
Relative per capita GDP

Source: Own calculations.

region thus reflects a 'last orders' rush by potential investors. In Murcia, a single major project led to an exceptionally high level of support.

Table 6.5 summarises average per capita national expenditure figures and provides ratios between national and EU support for the productive sector. These ratios illustrate the relative importance of EU support vis-à-vis national sources in different EU regions.

The regional discrepancies are very strong indeed. Those Objective 1 regions that received most national incentives during the 1989–93 period are parts of Germany and the UK, namely the new Länder and Northern Ireland. Lagging countries of the EU, however, in particular Portugal but to a lesser extent also Italy and Spain, used much more limited resources for national regional incentives. The average level of incentive support for the Objective 1 and 2 regions is nearly identical and many eligible regions in the central member states received significantly more national incentive support than regions in the European periphery.

Looking at the ratio between national and EU support for the productive sector, the former exceeds European support in most member states. The difference is especially impressive for Luxembourg, Belgium and (Eastern) Germany. In the new German Länder, the ratio between national and European support for productive investments is more than 10 : 1!

Table 6.5 National Regional Incentives and Average Ratios between National and EU Support According to Member State and Regional Policy Objective, 1989–93*

Country	National Incentives		Ratio National Incentives/EU Productive Sector Support	
	Obj. 1 average	Obj. 2 average	Obj. 1 average	Obj. 2 average
Belgium	./.	337.76	./.	7.98
Denmark	./.	n.a.	./.	n.a.
Greece	n.a.	./.	n.a.	./.
Germany	432.80	136.1	10.32	2.39
Spain	141.05	37.76	3.75	1.13
France	2.92	23.30	0.06	0.48
Ireland	299.49	./.	1.01	./.
Italy	176.51	759.36	2.54	18.5
(Lazio excluded)		158.68		2.76
Luxembourg	./.	675.17	./.	8.38
Netherlands	./.	144.62	./.	2.10
Portugal	13.19	./.	0.07	./.
UK	400.58	143.17	5.89	3.57
EU average	208.22	207.07**	3.38	3.60**

* ECU per person during the 1989–93 period; additionality payments not included.
** Lazio not included.
n.a.: Not available
Source: Own calculations.

6.3.3 Total Public Support for the Productive Sector

Figure 6.3, plotting European and national incentive support taken together vis-à-vis relative regional income, resembles the national support distribution provided in Figure 6.2 above. Given the above ratios of budget allocations, indicating that the magnitude of national incentives is far above that of EU productive sector support, this is not a surprising result.

Lazio remains the biggest recipient, followed by a group of regions comprising the abovementioned new German Länder as well as the Republic of Ireland, Abruzzi, Luxembourg and Murcia. Table 6.6 provides total average per capita incentive figures during the 1989–93 period.

Figure 6.3 Total Support for Productive Investments in European Regions, 1989–93

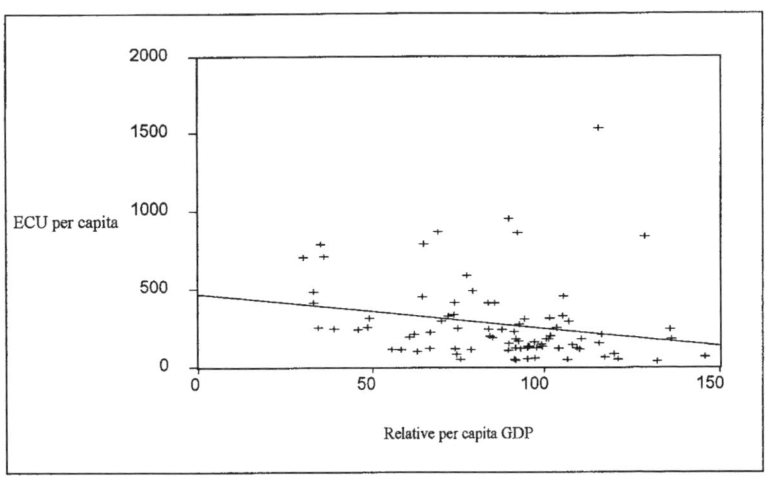

Source: Own calculations.

Total per capita support for productive investments was largest in the supported parts of Luxembourg followed by Ireland. Data for national support in Greece were not available. Generally speaking, Table 6.6 shows that the difference between Objective 1 and Objective 2 is surprisingly small. Moreover, the aggregation of national and European support does not alter the fact that, with the exception of Ireland, only Objective 1 regions that are part of better-off EU member states are among the major recipients of productive sector support. In countries that are entirely or predominantly made up of lagging regions (Spain, Portugal and Greece) relatively low levels of public support for the productive sector prevail.

6.3.4 Regional Incentives and Regional Income: an Econometric Analysis

It was established in Section 6.2 that budget allocations for regional incentives are likely to be negatively related to relative per capita income in the eligible region. In other words, the poorer a region, the more public support for its productive sector it can expect. The key explanatory variables for the spatial distribution of regional incentives are, therefore, regional per capita income relative to the Union average (INC1) and national per capita income relative to

Table 6.6 Average Total Regional Incentives According to Member State and Regional Policy Objective, 1989–93*

Country	Objective 1 average	Objective 2 average
Belgium	./.	436.41
Denmark	./.	47.30**
Greece	196.87**	./.
Germany	464.86	192.92
Spain	178.64	71.09
France	112.20	160.90
Ireland	790.33	./.
Italy***	318.46	259.40
Luxembourg	./.	836.39
Netherlands	./.	314.63
Portugal	303.68	./.
United Kingdom	588.81	243.45
EU average	369.23	284.72

* ECU per capita of covered population during the 1989–93 period.
** National funding does not exist (Denmark) or data on national funding are unavailable (Greece).
*** Lazio excluded.
Source: Own calculations.

the Union average (INC2). INC1 provides an indicator for the regional need for support from a European point of view and INC2 provides information on the national need for support as well as the member-states' ability to pay. Other variables that are likely to have an impact are relative regional unemployment (UNEMP), the relative share of industry in the regional economy (IND) and country dummies.[7]

Regressing EU support for the productive sector plus national additionality payments (EUADD) on INC1, INC2 and country dummies yields the following result:[8]

$$\underset{}{EUADD} = \underset{(-0.60)}{-1.01} + \underset{(0.82)}{0.14\,INC1} + \underset{(3.05)}{1.10\,INC2} + \underset{(3.86)}{2.04\,DIRL} + \underset{(5.28)}{1.75\,DP} + \underset{(2.62)}{1.49\,DGR}$$

$$R^2 = 0.33,\ DW = 1.66,\ SE\ Reg. = 0.50,\ n = 82 \qquad (6.1)$$

The most interesting aspect of Regression 6.1 is that relative regional per capita income is not significant. In fact, the coefficient even has a counter-intuitive (positive) sign, indicating that richer regions received on average more regional incentive support than poorer regions. The explanation for this are the differences in the shares of total EU Structural Funds support devoted to the productive sector. The variables testing for differences in unemployment and the share of industry are not significant but the country-dummies for Ireland (DIRL), Portugal (DP) and Greece (DGR) are strongly significant.

National differences become even more important when member states' regional incentive schemes are analysed.

$$\begin{aligned} \text{NAT} = {} & \underset{(5.36)}{104.67} - \underset{(-2.82)}{0.95\ \text{INC1}} - \underset{(-5.28)}{21.54\ \text{INC2}} + \underset{(2.25)}{0.89\ \text{IND}} + \underset{(6.61)}{2.98\ \text{DG}} \\ & - \underset{(-4.16)}{9.27\ \text{DIRL}} - \underset{(-5.89)}{17.57\ \text{DP}} - \underset{(-4.64)}{7.11\ \text{DE}} + \underset{(6.14)}{6.95\ \text{DLUX}} + \underset{(2.29)}{0.87\ \text{DI}} \end{aligned}$$

$R^2 = 0.70$, DW = 1.93, SE Reg. = 0.85, n = 71 (Lazio excluded) (6.2)

Whereas the coefficients of the INC1 and INC2 variables in Regression 6.2 indicate that high relative regional and national per capita income are negatively correlated with national productive sector support, the country dummies tell a different story. Those for Germany (DG) and Luxembourg (DLUX) are strongly significant and positive, whereas those for Ireland, Portugal and Spain (DE) are strongly significant and negative. Once again it shows that relatively poor regions located in relatively rich member states can expect a disproportionate level of national regional incentives compared to poor regions located in poor countries.

The third regression analyses European and national regional incentives taken together.

$$\begin{aligned} \text{TOT} = {} & \underset{(4.82)}{22.15} - \underset{(-4.07)}{0.94\ \text{INC1}} - \underset{(-2.78)}{2.67\ \text{INC2}} - \underset{(-3.06)}{2.34\ \text{DP}} - \underset{(-3.94)}{1.60\ \text{DE}} \\ & + \underset{(3.28)}{2.12\ \text{DLUX}} \end{aligned}$$

$R^2 = 0.34$, DW = 2.13, SE Reg. = 0.61, n = 71 (6.3)

Both income variables (INC1 and INC2) in Regression 6.3 are significant and their coefficients have the expected sign. The dummy variables for the two cohesion countries Portugal and Spain, however, are now negatively significant, whereas the dummy variable for Luxembourg is positively significant. The other country dummies were not significant which means that in countries such as Ireland high levels of EU support are counterbalanced by relatively limited national support, or vice versa (for example, Germany). (Data on Greek national support are not available.)

All in all, these results provide some comfort from the point of view of European regional policy. After all, a (weak) negative link between relative regional income and total support for the productive sector can still be traced, even after including national incentive schemes. The national ability (and willingness) to pay, however, compromises the link between relative income and regional incentive support significantly. In order to make sure that the two policies do not counteract each other, significant changes in the co-ordination between European regional policy and EU state aids seem therefore advisable.

6.4 CONCLUSIONS

This chapter presented two contrasting views on the spatial distribution of productive sector support across EU regions: the 'need for support' and the 'ability to spend hypotheses'. Whereas the negative link between relative regional income and total EU regional policy funding reported in Chapter 5 is very clear, this is much less so for European support for the productive sector. As far as this part of regional policy is concerned, there is hardly any difference in per capita support between Objective 1 and 2 regions. The empirical analysis also revealed that support under national support schemes depends strongly on the willingness and ability of different countries to finance these schemes. Countries such as Germany, Belgium and Luxembourg are very generous in providing regional support, whereas national funding in the Iberian countries is very modest compared to other parts of the EU. The analysis of national and European support for the productive sector taken together confirmed that in most regions national regional incentives clearly exceed European support for the productive sector.

It should be kept in mind, however, that cohesion countries' state aids expenditures as a per cent of their GDP are far less modest. Table 6.1 shows that some EU4 countries, notably Greece, have even devoted a larger share of their income to the provision of state aids support than the EU average.

Neither the 'ability to spend' nor the 'need for support hypothesis' provides a convincing explanation for the aggregate distribution of regional incentives. The reality is somewhere between the two. In many peripheral as well as central parts of the EU, support levels under national and European incentives taken together are comparable. The privileged position that EU state aids policy tries to grant the periphery does not exist in practice. Moreover, due to data limitations, the analysis above tends to overestimate the actual level of productive sector support in lagging regions and to underestimate the support level in core regions.

- The importance of horizontal support schemes, which, almost by definition, favour the core regions of the EU, rises in most European countries (Frazer, 1995: 12; and Thomsen and Woolcock, 1993). Due to data limitations, these schemes could not be included into the analysis.
- The estimations of the share of total European support going to the productive sector were rather generous because it was often impossible to separate assistance to firms from funding for business-related infrastructure.
- The take-up rate, in other words the share of incentive commitments that is finally used for investments, is likely to be lower in lagging areas due to the less favourable underlying economic conditions. At present, however, empirical research on this topic does not exist.

From the point of view of European regional policy and the prospects for regional convergence, these are sobering results. Although the importance of regional incentives for the convergence process should not be overestimated, regional incentives retain some importance for locational decisions and are one of the few variables that can be influenced in the short run. As far as the aggregate welfare effects are concerned, the results indicate that the regional 'subsidy field' across the EU is too level to have a large impact on intra-EU locational decisions which means that regional aids will frequently be taken as windfall profits.

As far as policy recommendations are concerned, various aspects have to be kept in mind. First, it is a political aim of the EU to grant its periphery privileged use of regional incentives. Second, due to limited budgetary possibilities, additional European incentive transfers to the periphery are unlikely to be committed. Third, in light of the distortionary effects of regional incentives, a further limitation rather than an increase in the aggregate use of regional incentives is desirable. All these arguments point towards a reduction of European and national productive sector support in the core regions and a further concentration of European support on those lagging areas where they are most likely to have positive economic effects. In order to bring this about, a further reinforcement of European state aid rules is of crucial importance. Needless to say, this will be a very difficult political task, not least because it might lead to an initial sharpening of intra-national regional disparities in the richer member states. Whether the recent Commission communication is sufficient to make sure that the use of state aids is restricted to the Union's lagging regions remains to be seen.

At the same time, EU regional policy should concentrate its support on the poorest member states. In the case of the cohesion countries, however, it is not clear whether concentration automatically implies concentration on the weakest regions within these member states. Alternatively, a concentration of productive sector support on those regions within the cohesion countries which have the best prospects for lasting positive effects should be considered. In the case of Portugal, for example, this would imply a concentration on the Lisbon and Porto regions.

In light of the EU's eastern enlargement it is important to keep in mind that most of the present Central and East European countries are in a comparable situation to Portugal. Their economies are focused on a few regions, usually the capitals (e.g. Prague and Budapest). These areas have the best prospects for competing successfully in the Single European Market. Spreading the limited European resources evenly across the entire territory of the CEECs may reduce intra-national disparities in these countries, but it is likely to weaken their economic prospects from a national point of view.

7 Human Capital Investments and Cohesion: the Case of R&D Policy

Human capital formation, the second pillar of EU regional policy, covers very different fields of activity. The largest share of human capital investments is devoted to schooling and continuing education.[1] The focus of the present chapter, however, is on another aspect of human capital formation, namely R&D. In contrast to schooling, the EU plays a very active part in R&D and the potential conflicts between R&D policy and cohesion are considerable.

Three types of R&D policy have to be differentiated:

1. National R&D policies (OECD, 1994b).
2. Non-spatial EU R&D policy ('EU R&D policy proper').
3. EU R&D policy within the framework of regional policy.

Whereas EU R&D policy proper aims primarily to improve aggregate European competitiveness, EU R&D support for lagging regions is focused on cohesion. These different aims are likely to create conflicts because most of the existing R&D capacity in the EU is concentrated in small 'islands of innovation', usually located in central parts of the Union. Hilpert calls this highly unequal spatial distribution 'Archipelago Europe' (Hilpert, 1992). EU R&D policy proper is likely to favour these 'islands' because, due to their R&D capacity, they can absorb additional EU-supported R&D projects more easily. Earlier studies on the link between R&D policy and cohesion were therefore extremely sceptical about the impact of R&D policy on lagging areas of the EU (European Parliament, 1991; Grote, 1993).

The relevant question to be asked, however, is not so much the actual distribution of research funding but rather the longer-term trends in expenditures in the central and lagging parts of the EU and the proportionate involvement of economically lagging areas in European R&D policy. If this involvement exceeds the existing research capacity in the lagging regions, it can be argued that European R&D policy is contributing to a technological catching-up process.

This chapter starts by reviewing some of the empirical literature on the link between R&D, technology and growth, respectively cohesion. This is followed by an analysis of the 'technology gap' between the core of the EU and the lagging regions. In order to illustrate the 'productivity' of R&D, output as well as input indicators will be used. The third section is devoted to the regional distribution of European and national R&D budget appropriations as well as EU co-financed R&D projects.

7.1 R&D AND ECONOMIC GROWTH – A REVIEW

As argued in Chapter 3, the presence or absence of technological differences between locations is of great importance for economic theories on growth and convergence or divergence. While convergence theory assumes that production technologies are identical and exogenously given across countries (and regions), divergence approaches and theories of endogenous growth are frequently based on the assumption of technological differences. Divergence approaches in particular look at the accumulation of physical and human capital.

Bradley et al. (1996: 93–7), for example, use an endogenous growth model with human capital as an additional factor of production in order to demonstrate the link between physical capital, human capital and growth. The model shows that in the long run both physical and human capital are indispensable for growth. If the ratio between physical and human capital is too high, the returns to physical capital will be insufficient to attract outside capital or to induce domestic capital formation. Human capital thus becomes a bottleneck for growth. In principle, the same applies if physical capital is the relatively scarce factor of production. Since human beings, the bearers of human capital, are normally less mobile than physical capital, however, human capital is more likely than physical capital to be in short supply.

Depending on how difficult it is to attract external human capital, it may be meaningful to use public policies to improve the endogenous human capital endowment of locations. As argued above, such improvements may, for example, be realised in the form of a higher educational standard of the workforce or by increasing R&D efforts.[2]

For the reasons outlined above, the focus of this chapter is on R&D only. Although this is just one aspect of human capital, it covers a whole range of measures. Armstrong, for example, distinguishes between original ideas (inventions) and applications of these ideas (innovations) (Armstrong, 1993). For the least developed regions of the EU, the build-up of inventive capacity may not be as useful as improvements of the availability of existing technologies. For lagging regions at a somewhat more advanced level of development, however, for example, the economically advanced regions within the cohesion countries Portugal and Greece, the build-up of capacities to invent and to get involved in the initial application of new technology becomes more useful.

In the following, the question of the most appropriate policy mix will not be looked at in detail. The analysis rests on the, admittedly simplifying, assumption that the marginal utility of R&D investments is comparable across all EU regions and that R&D funding is always used in the most appropriate way.

There are numerous empirical studies on the link between human capital, technology and growth. Most of them can be grouped into three categories:

1. Cross-sectional investigations on the effects of schooling or R&D on growth and convergence in a sample of countries or regions.
2. Studies on R&D spillovers and their repercussions on locational decisions and agglomerations.
3. Empirical work on the link between R&D, productivity and growth in particular countries or regions.

As far as the first category is concerned, useful surveys of empirical cross-sectional studies are Fagerberg (1994) and de la Fuente (1995); Levine and Renelt (1992), testing for the robustness of a large number of explanatory variables for growth, identified human capital as one of the few consistently significant variables. This has also been supported by Fagerberg and Verspagen (1996), as well as the empirical analysis in Chapter 4 of this book.

An encompassing survey of literature on the locational impact of R&D spillovers (Category 2) is Harhoff (1995). A good example for an empirical investigation supporting the importance of spillovers is Jaffe et al. (1993). The positive spillover effects of academic research on commercial innovative activities in the US have been explored by Jaffe (1989) with a subsequent addition by Acs, Audretsch and Feldman (1992). Lichtenberg (1995) investigates the effect of EU R&D policy on research and development spillovers and the evolving pattern of geographical specialisation. The results of these studies show that the importance of R&D spillovers depends to a large extent on factors such as the type of industry, the firm size, the market structure and the type of R&D (basic/applied). All in all, however, the results indicate that a clustering of R&D activity in a particular area is most likely to have a positive impact on the productive sector in this area and to contribute to agglomerative tendencies. This in turn will reinforce existing spatial R&D disparities.

Looking at country- or region-specific empirical studies (III), the impact of technical efficiency on growth and convergence in German labour market regions was recently investigated by Schalk, Untiedt and Lüschow (1995). They argue that technical inefficiencies are responsible for a significant fraction of income differences within Germany. Harris and Trainor (1995) look at innovations and R&D in Northern Ireland and find a positive link between R&D spending and the probability of innovation as well as between R&D and the existence of a sufficiently trained local workforce. In light of the problems to obtain private finance for high risk R&D ventures, they argue cautiously in favour of government provision of R&D aid (Harris and Trainor, 1995: 600).

The empirical studies reviewed above all point towards a significant positive impact of human capital and technology on the economic well-being of a country or region. These findings also underline the importance of R&D policy for the convergence prospects of the lagging regions in the EU.

7.2 R&D ENDOWMENTS IN THE EUROPEAN UNION

A recent study on the link between regional development and R&D in the EU argued that the 'technology gap' between European core and the cohesion countries is even wider than the socio-economic gaps illustrated in Chapter 2 (CEC, 1994c: 151). This section shall illustrate and quantify the relative backwardness of lagging regions, using a combination of input and output indicators which permits some tentative conclusions about regional variations of the 'productivity' of R&D.

7.2.1 Input Differences: R&D Personnel in EU Regions

An important and widely used indicator for regional differences in R&D capacity is the share of the regional workforce employed in the

Table 7.1 Share of R&D Personnel in Total Employees in European NUTS II Regions and Share of Business R&D Personnel

	All Sectors*		Share of Business R&D Personnel**	
	Objective 1 average	National average	Objective 1 average	National average
Belgium	./.	1.11	./.	55.7
Denmark	./.	1.00	./.	59.2
Greece	0.29	0.29	20.6	20.6
Germany	n.a.	1.54	n.a.	69.5
Spain	0.28	0.57	22.8	40.3
France	n.a.	1.38	n.a.	54.8
Ireland	0.74	0.74	48.8	48.8
Italy	n.a.	0.62	n.a.	45.6
Luxembourg	./.	n.a.	./.	n.a.
Netherlands	./.	1.08	./.	44.9
Portugal	0.33	0.33	16.6	16.6
UK	0.44	1.14	31.8	58.6

* Full-time equivalents; for reference periods see the Appendix.
** In per cent of total R&D personnel.
Source: EUROSTAT (1995); own calculations.

R&D sector. Despite differences in the quality of R&D personnel, this indicator is a useful approximation of R&D capacity. After all, it is not obvious, that quality differences are country-specific, which would imply that the researchers in country X are on average inferior to their colleagues in country Y.[3]

Regionalised data on R&D personnel has only recently become available, although not yet for all EU member states and regions.[4] Table 7.1 provides an overview of R&D personnel as a percentage of the total workforce and the share of R&D personnel employed in the business sector.

The lagging economies and the Objective 1 regions within 'rich' member states have a significantly lower share of employees in the R&D sector than the core regions. The only exception is the Republic of Ireland, which has pursued an active R&D policy starting with the Science and Technology Development Programme in 1987 (OECD, 1994b: 67).

The share of R&D personnel working in the business sector is also much lower in lagging parts of the EU, again with the exception of

Ireland and Northern Ireland. The situation in Greece, Spain and Portugal with respect to these two indicators is very similar. Their share of total personnel is less than one third of the average share in the core member states, and the share of R&D personnel working in the business sector less than half of that in the core.[5]

All cohesion countries show a strong dominance of the metropolitan areas. In Greece, 55.4 per cent of all R&D personnel work in the Athens region, while 65 per cent of the Portuguese R&D capacity is located in Lisbon. The situation is somewhat less polarised in Spain, although Madrid and Catalonia taken together account for 53.5 per cent of total personnel. As argued above, however, a concentration of the 'inventive' R&D capacity is likely to be a sensible approach for the cohesion countries as long as the dissemination of R&D results and 'innovative' activity throughout the country is assured.

One of the main reasons for the lesser relative importance of firm R&D in cohesion countries is the smaller average size of enterprises in these countries (Grote, 1993; CEC, 1996b: 72). It also indicates, however, that the productive sector in lagging areas is engaged in less R&D-intensive activities than the productive sector in central parts of the Union, which is likely to have repercussions on the value-added and regional per capita income levels.

The link between relative R&D capacity and regional income is illustrated in Figures 7.1 and 7.2. In Figure 7.1, the share of R&D

Figure 7.1 Relative Regional Income and R&D Personnel as Share of the Regional Workforce in EU Regions*

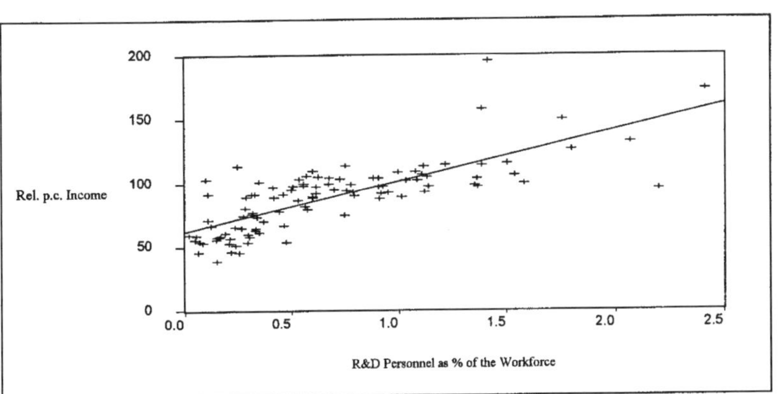

*For year of reference see the Appendix.
Source: EUROSTAT (1995); own calculations.

Figure 7.2 Relative Regional Income and Share of R&D Personnel Working in the Business Sector in EU Regions*

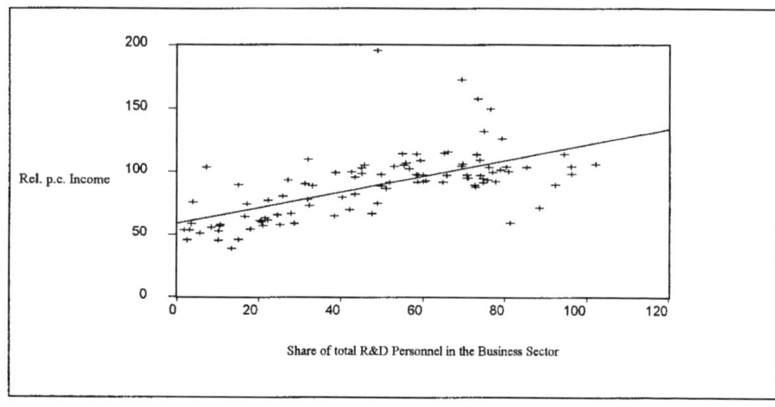

*For year of reference see the Appendix
Source: EUROSTAT (1995); own calculations.

personnel in the regional workforce is plotted against relative per capita income in PPS. Figure 7.2 represents the link between relative regional income and the share of total R&D personnel working in the business sector.

Both links are very clear. Total R&D personnel as well as the share of firm R&D are strongly correlated with relative per capita regional income. Although the existence of a correlation between per capita income and R&D does not allow conclusions about the causality of this correlation, the above review of empirical studies and the convergence analysis in Chapter 4 show that there are good reasons to assume that R&D activity has a positive impact on economic growth and per capita income.

7.2.2 Output Differences: Patents and Publications

The abovementioned reservations concerning qualitative differences within the R&D workforce also apply to the various measures of R&D output. Research and development results like patents or publications are extremely heterogeneous and many R&D efforts may be beneficial in the long run, although they do not lead to a quantifiable result (Griliches, 1990). As argued above, however, these problems are unlikely to operate systematically in favour of particular countries

Table 7.2 Shares of Patents and Publications in EU Member States

	US Patents		European Patent Applications		Scientific Publications	
	Share 1991	Change 1981–91	Share 1991	Change 1981–91	Share 1991	Change 1981–91
Belgium	2.04	–0.12	2.15	–0.12	2.87	–0.14
Denmark	1.02	+0.15	1.19	+0.06	2.51	–0.50
Germany	46.43	–2.06	47.02	–2.23	22.22	–2.59
Greece	0	0	0	0	1.08	+0.32
Spain	1.02	+0.59	0.95	+0.77	5.73	+3.48
France	18.37	+1.48	19.81	–0.65	17.20	+0.66
Ireland	0.51	+0.51	0.24	+0.05	1.08	+0.32
Italy	7.14	+0.22	9.07	+4.71	10.04	+2.14
Netherlands	6.17	+1.36	6.21	+0.52	6.81	+0.79
Portugal	0	0	0	0	0.36	–0.02
UK	16.84	–2.21	13.37	–2.92	29.75	–4.84

Source: CEC (1994c); own calculations.

or types of regions. The combined use of patents and publications allows us to look at two different areas of R&D. While scientific publications are primarily indicators for basic research, patents are more important in order to assess the applicability of R&D.

Table 7.2 lists the 1991 member states' shares of total EU patents granted in the US, the shares of European patent applications and the shares of scientific publications. It also gives the changes in member states' shares since 1981. These data are available at member state level only.

As far as US patents and European patent applications are concerned, Germany, France and the UK are clearly the dominant countries. Their combined share of the total number of patents granted to EU countries is 80 per cent. In contrast, the figures for Greece and Portugal are so low that these countries fail to register. Spain and Ireland combined muster little more than 1 per cent of the patents. Overall, the international distribution during the last decade was quite stable, although there is a small upward trend for most EU countries, mainly at the expense of Germany and the UK.

Scientific publications are more evenly distributed across the EU countries. The German share is less than half that for patents,

Table 7.3 R&D Output Relative to R&D Personnel in EU Member States

	US Patents	European Patent Applications	Scientific Publications
Belgium	0.74	0.77	1.03
Denmark	0.57	0.67	1.41
Germany	1.32	1.34	0.63
Greece	0	0	1.42
Spain	0.20	0.19	1.14
France	0.89	0.96	0.83
Ireland	0.90	0.42	1.91
Italy	0.72	0.91	1.01
Netherlands	1.32	1.34	1.47
Portugal	0	0	0.43
UK	0.94	0.74	1.66

Source: CEC (1994c); own calculations.

suggesting that the comparative advantage of German R&D is more in the field of applied research. The performance of the UK is very impressive, although its performance might be assisted by the fact that English is the leading language in international scientific publications. This obviously also benefits the Irish performance.[6]

Table 7.3 illustrates the link between R&D input and output by calculating the ratio between patents and publications on the one hand, and R&D personnel on the other. A figure below 1 means that the country has a lower share of total EU R&D output than might be expected on the basis of its share of R&D personnel. The opposite applies for a figure greater than 1.

Since Portugal and Greece do not account for a sufficient number of patent applications the patent indicators cannot be constructed. The figures for Spain and, to a lesser extent, Ireland, however, are not encouraging. The Spanish share of full-time R&D personnel, for example, is five times higher than the country's share of patents granted in the US as well as European patent applications. The Irish share in European patent applications is also less than half the country's relative R&D workforce.

The cohesion countries' position concerning the relative share of scientific publications is more positive. With the exception of Portugal, the shares in publications always exceed the shares in R&D personnel. A priori this is to be welcomed, but it suggests a lack of applicability of research and development in these countries which is in line with the low level of business R&D in the cohesion countries.

Summing up, a significant technological gap between core countries and lagging parts of the EU emerges:

- The shares of R&D personnel in the total workforce are much lower in lagging areas of the Union than in the core.
- The relative importance of public vis-à-vis business R&D is stronger in lagging parts of the EU.
- Finally, although this conclusion has to be treated with great caution, the productivity and applicability of research and development in the periphery are lower than in central parts of the Union.

Most of the data used for this analysis refer to the year 1991, two years after the reformed structural funds were launched. In the following, European and national R&D investment data and the spatial distribution of EU-supported research will be used in order to assess whether the existing technological gap is likely to widen or to narrow in the future.

7.3 R&D FUNDING IN THE EUROPEAN UNION

Most public R&D support in the European Union is provided by the member states. EU R&D policy proper account for only 4 per cent of total public civilian research expenditures in the EU (CEC, 1996b: 69). In eligible regions, R&D are also supported within the context of EU regional policy. The following section looks at the spatial distribution of national as well as European R&D funding.

7.3.1 National R&D Budget Appropriations

The availability of regionalised data on national R&D budget appropriations is comparable with the situation concerning R&D personnel. EUROSTAT (1995) provides a regional breakdown for most member states. In some countries, however, national sources had to be used in order to approximate the regional breakdown.[7] Table 7.4 provides an overview of total national R&D funding as well as the shares of business sector expenditures.

R&D funding in the cohesion countries and the Objective 1 regions within core member states are significantly lower than in the core

Table 7.4 National Average Annual R&D Expenditures per Capita in EU Member States*

	Public and Business Expenditures		Public Expenditures		Business Expenditures	
	Obj. 1 average	National average	Obj. 1 average	National average	Obj. 1 average	National average
Belgium	./.	287	./.	110	./.	176
Denmark	./.	341	./.	143	./.	198
Greece	29	29	21	21	8	8
Germany**	n.a.	538	n.a.	163	n.a.	375
Spain	40	94	28	43	12	52
France	16	409	n.a.	154	n.a.	255
Ireland	103	103	40	40	64	64
Italy	78	199	52	86	25	113
Netherlands	./.	291	./.	132	./.	159
Portugal	33	33	24	24	9	9
UK	134	678	43	91	92	587

* ECU per capita (for details of period covered see Appendix).
** The new Länder are not included.
Sources: Expenditure data: EUROSTAT (1995).
Population data: EUROSTAT (1997b).

regions. The discrepancy between core and periphery is less significant for Ireland and Northern Ireland, the only lagging regions, where the total annual amount spent on R&D per capita exceeds 100 ECU.

The ratio between total budget appropriations in the four cohesion countries (EU4) and the seven core member states (EU7),[8] however, is even lower than the corresponding ratio for R&D personnel. The EU4 share of R&D personnel of the total workforce is 37 per cent of the EU7 share, but EU4 per capita R&D funding is only 13 per cent of EU7 funding. This is a worrying finding because it suggests that the technological gap between the core and periphery may widen further in future.

Ireland and Northern Ireland are the only lagging regions with sizeable business R&D expenditures. Expenditures in Greece, Spain, Portugal and the Mezzogiorno are very low. Total and business expenditures in the Italian South, however, are about twice as high as in Portugal, Greece and the Spanish Objective 1 regions.

Another recurrent feature of the spatial distribution of R&D activity within cohesion countries is the dominance of metropolitan areas. Athens accounts for 53.5 per cent of total Greek R&D expenditures and 66.2 per cent of business R&D expenditures. The corresponding figures for Lisbon, the dominant Portuguese R&D location, are 60.6 per cent and 52 per cent respectively. Madrid and Catalonia taken together account for 61.1 per cent of total Spanish funding and 68.6 per cent of business R&D expenditures. These figures are, by and large, comparable to the concentration of personnel and indicate that the spatial distribution within the cohesion countries is likely to remain more or less unchanged.

From the cohesion point of view, the development of national R&D budget appropriations relative to GDP is more encouraging than the per capita expenditure figures above. Average EU4 business R&D expenditures increased from 0.24 per cent of GDP in 1985 to 0.33 per cent in 1991. The comparable EU6/EU7 values are 1.19 per cent in 1985 and 1.21 per cent in 1991.[9] This indicates that the R&D efforts of firms located in lagging parts of the Union are slowly approaching the technological intensity of productive activities in the core.

The increase in public R&D funding in the cohesion countries, however, is not above the increase in the core. The 1985 EU4 value was 0.27 per cent of GDP and increased to 0.38 per cent of 1991 GDP. In the six/seven, core member states, public R&D support increased from 0.66 per cent of GDP in 1985 to 0.75 per cent in 1991. The relative public R&D expenditure gap of the periphery has thus been reduced but the absolute difference remained the same.[10]

All in all, the analysis of national expenditure patterns across different parts of the EU suggests that the technological gap between core and lagging parts of the Union is not likely to be rapidly reduced, neither due to national public R&D policy nor due to increased firm R&D activity in the lagging parts of the EU.

7.3.2 European R&D Policy

7.3.2.1 Key Features of European R&D Policy

European R&D activities were incorporated into primary Community law as part of the 1987 Single European Act (SEA) (Title XV of the EEC Treaty). Article 130f describes the general aim of Community R&D policy:

> The Community shall have the objective of strengthening the scientific and technological bases of the Community industry and encouraging it to become more competitive at international level, while promoting all the research activities deemed necessary by virtue of other Chapters of this Treaty. (Article 130f, 1st para.)

The last sentence of this paragraph asks Community R&D policy to take other chapters of the Treaty, for example the aim of economic and social cohesion (Title XIV), into account. The second paragraph of Article 130f, however, asks for the encouragement of R&D activities 'of high quality', thereby establishing 'excellence' as a key principle of EU R&D policy. Although high-quality R&D can obviously also be found in lagging areas, the excellence principle is likely to bias Community R&D in favour of the Union's core.

According to Article 130i of the Treaty, all R&D-related activities of the Community should be set out in multi-annual Framework Programmes (FPs). The FPs establish the scientific and technological objectives to be achieved, indicate the general lines of activities, the maximum financial contributions and the rules for the Community's financial participation.

While the total amount of money used for FP projects has significantly increased, it still represents only 4 per cent of the total public civilian research effort in the EU. Within the FPs, there is a clear shift away from (nuclear) energy to key industrial technologies. Especially the 3rd and 4th FP were much more diversified than the early FPs.[11] This is not always perceived as a positive development. First, it is argued that EU R&D policy lacks thematic concentration (Ochel and Penzkofer, 1996). Second, the thematic proliferation can be regarded as an indicator of an ever-increasing role for the EU in European R&D which is not easily compatible with the subsidiarity principle (Tomann, 1991 and Schmidt-Aßmann, 1995).

The most important form of EU R&D activity are so called 'shared-cost' actions.

> These actions are mainly put into effect through multinational consortia made up of firms ..., research centres and universities from the European Union. The Commission pays up to 50% of the costs of these precompetitive research projects. (CEC, 1994c, p. 208)

This introduces further principles of R&D policy besides excellence, namely collaboration, cost-sharing and the dominance of precompetitive research.[12] Collaboration is frequently regarded as a positive aspect of EU R&D policy. It improves the dissemination of R&D results and the links established in order to obtain EU R&D support frequently continue to exist after the initial project has been completed (Ochel and Penzkofer, 1996: 77–81).

As far as the lagging regions are concerned, the above principles give rise to two serious problems.

1. SMEs find it more difficult to participate in EU R&D programmes than do large firms. In the lagging regions of the Union, however, SMEs are of greater importance than in the EU as a whole.
2. The emphasis on pre-competitive research does not suit the needs of lagging regions. In these areas, the dissemination of marketable technologies and the conduct of applied research are more pressing needs than basic research.

These problems are also acknowledged by the Commission, and efforts are being made to rectify them, for example, in the form of the Innovation Programme, established as part of the 4th FP (CEC, 1996b). The results of these efforts remain to be seen.

The above discussion of EU R&D policy focused on R&D policy proper. The provision of R&D infrastructure in disadvantaged parts of the EU, however, is essentially the task of the Structural Funds (SF). This 'division of labour' has to be kept in mind when the spatial distribution of R&D expenditure data is analysed. It is not the task of R&D funding within the FPs to upgrade the scale and quality of research in lagging parts of the EU. Henceforth, two questions concerning the link between European R&D policy and cohesion have to be asked:

1. To what extent does SF R&D funding contribute to a narrowing of the technological North–South divide diagnosed in Section 7.2?
2. Is this divide widened by European R&D policy operated within the FPs?

7.3.2.2 R&D Support within the Structural Funds

As argued in the introduction to this chapter, support for research and development is one of the measures summarised under the regional policy heading 'human capital formation'. The shares of total regional policy funding earmarked for R&D are usually fairly small. During the 1989–93 period, the average R&D share exceeded the 20 per cent mark only in Italian Objective 2 regions. The share in Objective 1 regions was never above 5.5 per cent.[13]

Table 7.5 Average Annual EU Regional Policy Support for R&D during the 1989–93 Period According to Member State and Regional Policy Objective*

	Support for R&D as % of total SF Funding		Total CSF Funding**		EU Funding within the CSFs**	
	Obj. 1 average	Obj. 2 average	Obj. 1 average	Obj. 2 average	Obj. 1 average	Obj. 2 average
Belgium	./.	13.3	./.	7.9	./.	2.4
Denmark	./.	12.8	./.	10.0	./.	2.6
Germany	n.a.	14.1	n.a.	6.5	n.a.	2.6
Greece	1.9	./.	3.39	./.	1.8	./.
Spain	2.0	9.7	3.27	5.3	1.7	1.6
France	1.1	10.7	3.49	7.8	1.4	2.2
Ireland	4.0	./.	16.8	./.	7.1	./.
Italy	4.9	20.9	7.6	25.64	3.6	4.4
Netherlands	./.	7.9	./.	4.6	./.	1.4
Portugal	5.5	./.	16.5	./.	6.3	./.
UK	2.1	5.3	3.8	2.8	1.6	1.0

* ECU per capita (allocations under the STRIDE Community Initiative included).
** National additionality funding included.
n.a.: Not available.
Source: R&D shares in CSFs: CEC (1994c, Table 6.1).
Amounts: own calculation (see Appendix).

Table 7.5 shows a marked difference between the CSF shares allocated to R&D in lagging (Objective 1) and declining (Objective 2) regions. The average unweighted share in lagging regions (3.1 per cent) is just about one-quarter of the share for declining regions (11.8 per cent). This is mainly due to differences in the development needs and priorities. Whereas a large share of the funding in lagging regions is devoted to basic infrastructure like transport and telecommunications, these are less pressing requirements in Objective 2 regions. Henceforth, the declining regions have more financial flexibility for investments in research and development.

The shares for the Republic of Ireland (4 per cent) and Portugal (5.5 per cent) are significantly above the Objective 1 average. In Ireland, this builds on a longer-term programme to improve the R&D potential of the country. In Portugal, the creation of R&D infrastructure, for example, by establishing a significant number of higher education institutions, was an important element of the country's development programme during the 1989–93 period.

The ratios between national R&D allocations and European SF R&D support show that EU regional policy has a significant impact on total R&D spending levels in the cohesion countries. SF allocations in Portugal, for example, are 25.9 per cent of the available national R&D funding. This is a cautious estimate, based on EU funding only and excluding national funding used to co-finance EU-supported projects.[14] Next in line are the Republic of Ireland (17.9 per cent), Greece (8.5 per cent), the Mezzogiorno (6.9 per cent) and the lagging regions of Spain (5.9 per cent).[15]

As far as the 'additionality multipliers' for SF R&D support are concerned, the situation is similar to Chapter 6. The multipliers are much larger in Objective 2 regions and the lagging regions in 'rich' member states than in the cohesion countries. Figure 7.3, plotting SF R&D support per capita in Objective 1 and 2 vis-à-vis relative income suggests a weak negative link between income and SF R&D funding.[16] This turns into a positive correlation if national additionality money is added (Figure 7.4).

Figure 7.3 Average Annual EU R&D Support within the CSFs during the 1989–93 Period in ECU per capita

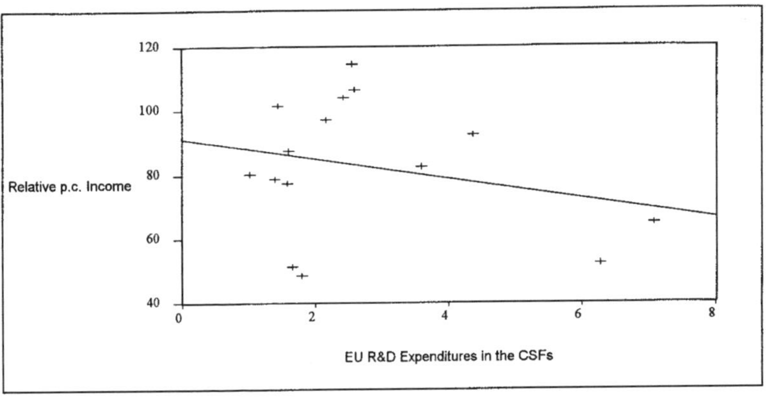

Sources: R&D shares: CEC (1994c, Table 6.1).
Amounts: own calculations (see Appendix).
GDP: EUROSTAT (1997b).

Figure 7.4 Total Average Annual R&D Support within the CSFs during the 1989–93 Period in ECU per capita

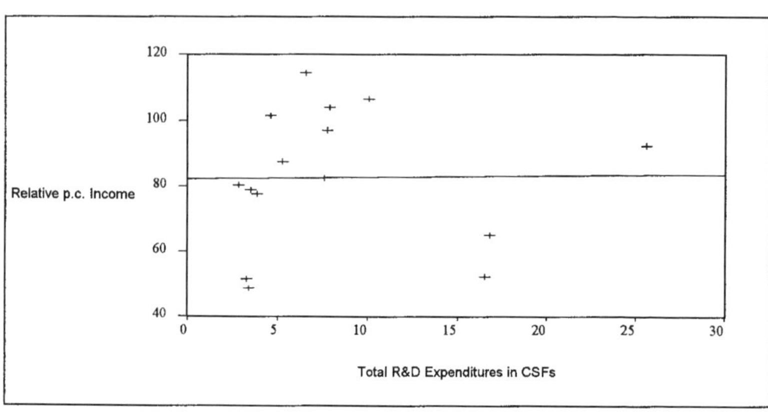

Sources: R&D shares: CEC (1994c, Table 6.1).
Amounts: own calculations (see Appendix).
GDP: EUROSTAT (1997b).

Summing up, EU regional policy support for R&D in lagging regions is on average below that in declining regions, mainly due to regional differences in development needs. In some cohesion countries, however, EU R&D allocations provide a significant part of total public R&D funding.

7.3.2.3 The Spatial Distribution of R&D Projects Supported by the EU

EU contributions towards the costs of R&D projects are in principle awarded on a basis of excellence rather than according to political goals. Given the wording of Article 130i, however, EU R&D policy proper should also contribute to the build-up of research and development capacity in the lagging parts of the Union. If it is assumed that a quality gap between R&D in the lagging and the more advanced parts of the Union exists, an assumption that builds not only on the indicators provided in Section 7.2 but also on most of the relevant literature in the field, the relation between research excellence and cohesion is conflictual and requires compromises.

The following analysis uses a simple indicator to assess this question. In light of an assumed quality gap between R&D in the South and North of the EU, one would expect that the proportion of EU 'shared-cost' projects in the periphery is below the proportion of the periphery's R&D capacity, approximated by the number of R&D personnel. The excellence principle dominates if the ratio between R&D personnel and shared-cost projects in lagging areas is below one. Alternatively, if the shared-cost actions are biased in favour of the cohesion countries, the ratio should be above one. Table 7.6 provides personnel / project ratios for the 2nd and 3rd Framework Programmes.[17]

The results indicate that the FPs are increasingly biased in favour of the lagging regions.[18] All Objective 1 regions and member states except the Spanish lagging regions had a larger share of shared-cost projects than one might expect on the basis of their share of R&D personnel. This is particularly remarkable for Greece, Ireland and Portugal, and even more so for Greek and Portuguese business sector projects.

Germany and the UK, however, are involved in fewer shared-cost projects than one might expect on the basis of their R&D capacity. The ratio for France is about 1. Belgium, Denmark and the Netherlands do very well in attracting shared-cost projects. The ratio for these three countries is around 2, with fewer significant differences between the total number of projects and business projects only.

All in all, and despite the obvious limitations of an analysis based on a simple project count, this is a surprising result. Although one might have expected that the FPs would not worsen the existing technological core–periphery divide within the EU, they actually seem to contribute to intra-EU cohesion. Even if it is assumed that the projects in the periphery are on average more limited than the size of projects in core member states, the links established by shared-cost actions are likely to have a beneficial effects on the transfer of technology between core and periphery.

From the point of view of cohesion this is to be welcomed, but there is also a negative aspect to this finding, namely the likelihood of a quality compromise in the selection of shared-cost projects. As argued above, EU R&D policy has different elements. In order to build up and improve R&D capacity in the periphery, EU R&D policy proper is the wrong instrument. It aims at strengthening the EU's competitiveness vis-à-vis third countries and not at reducing intra-European regional imbalances. In order to achieve this second goal, it is more sensible to strengthen R&D infrastructure in lagging regions through SF support.

Table 7.6 Ratio between EU-supported R&D Projects and Regional Shares of R&D Personnel in EU Member States

	2nd Framework Programme				3rd Framework Programme			
	All Projects		Business Sector		All Projects		Business Sector	
	Obj. 1 average	Nation. average	Obj. 1 average	Nation. average	Obj. 1 average	Nation. average	Obj. 1 average	Nation. average
Belgium	./.	1.98	./.	1.57	./.	1.82	./.	1.45
Denmark	./.	1.98	./.	1.97	./.	2.20	./.	2.12
Greece	5.41	5.41	14.55	14.55	6.66	6.66	16.91	16.91
Germany	n.a.	0.52	n.a.	0.51	n.a.	0.56	n.a.	0.53
Spain	0.89	1.40	1.94	2.09	0.99	1.26	2.74	1.72
France	n.a.	0.94	n.a.	1.04	n.a.	0.85	n.a.	1.04
Ireland	4.21	4.21	3.44	3.44	4.69	4.69	4.66	4.66
Italy	n.a.	1.04	2.33	1.54	n.a.	1.08	2.17	1.64
Netherlands	./.	1.49	./.	1.49	./.	1.70	./.	1.70
Portugal	3.79	3.79	7.94	7.94	3.42	3.42	9.95	9.95
UK	1.15	0.92	0.98	0.83	1.36	0.89	1.97	0.73

n.a. Not available.
Sources: Personnel: EUROSTAT (1995).
Projects: Unpublished material supplied by the European Commission, DG XII.

7.4 CONCLUSIONS: PUBLIC R&D POLICIES AND COHESION

The findings of this chapter confirmed the existence of a large R&D gap within the EU, in particular with regard to applied R&D in the cohesion countries.

Data on national budget appropriations do not point towards a significant catch-up of the periphery. In EU4, the share of GDP used for R&D is still well below the share in the rest of the EU. This, however, is not due to shortcomings of European policies or a lack of policy co-ordination. It is rather the cohesion countries themselves that are to blame. As the example of the Republic of Ireland shows, there are no good reasons why the cohesion countries should not be able to use a proportion of their national income for R&D that is comparable to the budget appropriations in the core member states.

EU regional policy contributes significantly to total budgetary allocations for R&D in the periphery. However, even national and European funding in EU4 taken together fall short of the funding allocated to R&D in the core member states. This highlights the shortcomings of national R&D policies but also, as discussed in Chapter 5, the problem of insufficient EU regional policy concentration. By focusing more clearly on lagging parts of the Union, the Structural Funds could have a more significant impact on the periphery's technological catching-up process.

The analysis of the link between EU R&D policy proper and cohesion suggests a 'periphery bias' of EU R&D policy. While such a bias is likely to foster convergence, it is problematic from the point of view of aggregate European welfare. Instead of compromising the excellence principle of European R&D support, a principle that was introduced in order to safeguard the competitiveness of European R&D vis-à-vis third countries, the intra-EU R&D gap should rather be closed by investments in the quantity and quality of R&D infrastructure in lagging regions.

On the basis of these findings, the following policy recommendations can be given:

- In order to make sure that the technological gap within the Union is not going to widen, lagging member states should be strongly encouraged to improve their domestic R&D efforts.
- EU regional policy efforts to improve the quantity and quality of research and development in the periphery should be continued. The principle of concentration, however, should be taken more seriously.

- The excellence principle of EU shared-cost R&D activities should not be compromised by introducing a 'periphery bias' in the project selection process.

Although a detailed investigation as to which R&D measures are most useful for the economic prospects of the periphery was neither intended nor provided in this chapter, it is intuitive that R&D efforts in the lagging parts of the EU should focus primarily on technology transfer and applied rather than purely academic research. Literature on the importance of economies of scale for R&D suggests that within the cohesion countries a concentration of R&D activities in a limited number of 'islands of innovation' is not only unavoidably but desirable.

In brief, the periphery's backwardness in R&D is very substantial and, taken together with investment data, casts doubts on the prospects for regional convergence within the EU. These problems, however, are not primarily attributable to insufficient co-ordination between EU regional policy and EU R&D policy. It is mainly the cohesion countries themselves that are responsible for improvements of the present situation.

8 Transport Infrastructure Policies

This chapter investigates the link between transport infrastructure policy within EU regional policy, non-spatial EU transport policy ('EU transport policy proper') and national transport infrastructure policy. Section 8.1 reviews theoretical considerations on the link between transport infrastructure and economic performance, followed by quantitative assessments of infrastructure endowment differences in EU regions. Section 8.3 investigates the national and regional distribution of member states' transport infrastructure investments and Section 8.4 focuses on the different elements of EU Transport Policy.

8.1 INFRASTRUCTURE, PRODUCTIVITY AND CONVERGENCE – A REVIEW

Before investigating the various aspects of the link between (transport) infrastructure, productivity and convergence it is necessary to define what is meant by the term infrastructure and to review some of its economic particularities.

The definition that makes the most sense from an economics standpoint consists of large, capital-intensive, natural monopolies such as highways, other transportation facilities, water and sewerage, and communications systems (Gramlich, 1994: 1177).

According to the terminology of Munnell (1993: 24), these facilities are called 'core infrastructure'. A wider definition of 'infrastructure' would include additional facilities such as schools, hospitals, nursing homes and theatres. Core infrastructure, however, constitutes not only the largest part of total infrastructure,[1] it is also the economic impact of core infrastructure that has attracted the most academic interest. Henceforth, this chapter focuses on core infrastructure and in particular on transport infrastructure.

What are the economic particularities of transport infrastructure?

- Transport infrastructure cannot be separated from transport services, although the degree of complementarity is weaker for transport modes such as cars which are predominantly used on an individual basis. It is particularly strong, however, for railways and air services but also for road haulage and freight transport on inland waterways.

- There are some public goods characteristics to transport infrastructure (Vickerman, 1994). The use of uncongested roads for example is non-rival. The public goods aspect is weaker for other modes. Air transport services to major airports, for example, face limitations in the form of take-off and landing slots.
- Transport infrastructure frequently causes significant positive and negative external effects. A transit route like the Swiss Gotthard Pass, for example, has significant positive external effects for Switzerland's neighbouring countries. Within Switzerland, however, substantial negative external effects due to environmental problems and congestion on the approach routes will occur. As a result, infrastructure links are a frequent cause for intra- and international negotiations.

With regard to the EU, it is important to note that positive spillover effects of infrastructure can provide an economic rationale for European involvement in certain areas of transport policy. EU support for the construction of cross-border transport infrastructure, for example, can be justified if positive international external effects of such infrastructures are not taken into account in national transport infrastructure investment plans. These considerations are related to a fourth economic characteristic of most forms of transport infrastructure, namely their network character. A number of recent infrastructure projects in the EU illustrate this aspect.

The commercial viability as well as the development impact of the Spanish high-speed rail link between Madrid and Seville have been regarded rather critically (Ross, 1994: 203). This is largely due to the absence of links between the Madrid-Seville line and the rest of the Spanish and European rail system.[2] The second example is the UK Channel Tunnel link. Due to poor connections with the rest of the UK rail network, the positive effects of through rail services to continental Europe for rail traffic in the UK and regional development in the south-east of England are significantly reduced (Simmons, 1991).

Having established the key economic particularities of transport infrastructure, its various economic effects will now be disentangled.

8.1.1 Direct Effects of Infrastructure

Direct effects of transport infrastructure are primarily the economic consequences of the construction, servicing and maintenance of infrastructure. In most EU countries, the economic importance of the transport sector is considerable and these effects can become even more important on a regional level.[3] Recent examples of major infrastructure projects such as the construction of the Channel Tunnel or the upgrading of the transport infrastructure in the new German Länder illustrate this point. However, the direct economic effects of transport infrastructure construction are usually temporary and will not be analysed in detail.

8.1.2 Indirect Non-Spatial Effects of Infrastructure

In the last few years a significant number of empirical studies on the productivity effect of public investments have been made, pioneered by the work of Aschauer (1989) and further contributions by Munnell (1990) and others. Aschauer argues that there is a causal link between the decline of US public infrastructure investment from the early 1970s onwards and the parallel productivity slowdown. Aschauer estimated that the marginal product of government capital was very high. In fact his estimates were so high, up to 100 per cent or more per annum, that they had to appear implausible. While a number of other authors arrived at very similar results, at least for the US, Ford and Poret (1991), using a similar methodology but longer data-sets than Aschauer for a number of OECD countries, find little support for the public capital hypothesis.[4]

Other analysts criticise Aschauer's approach on methodological grounds. They argue, for example, that first differences rather than aggregate values should be used for the specification of the equations (Tatom, 1991; and Hulten and Schwab, 1993). Tatom (1993), using co-integration estimations, also fails to find a significant positive link between infrastructure and growth. The second line of critique looks at the causality problem. Do economies grow because they spend a lot on infrastructure or do they spend a lot on infrastructure, because they are rich? Whereas Blomström, Lipsey and Zejan (1993) find more evidence in favour of the link from growth to infrastructure expenditures than vice versa, Munnell (1993) finds that the robustness of the original estimates is not seriously compromised by the simultaneity problem.

Most of the empirical analyses so far consider at the US states or national cross-section data sets. Recent contributions looking at EU regions are Seitz and Licht (1995) for the (old) German Länder (NUTS I regions) and Mas et al. (1996) for Spanish NUTS II regions. Seitz and Licht, covering the 1971–88 period, find that public capital indeed has cost-reducing effects for the private sector. Mas et al. (1996), looking at the 1964–91 period, also find evidence in favour of public infrastructure-led increases in private productivity. They obtain much more significant results for productive infrastructure (roads, water and sewer facilities, urban structures and ports) than for social infrastructure (education and health). However, the authors themselves admit that the results concerning education should be re-examined in greater detail (Mas et al., 1996: 647). Their findings also support the hypothesis of positive inter-regional spillovers of public infrastructure (network effects) and they argue that the positive productivity elasticity associated with the provision of public infrastructure declines over time. In other words, as the infrastructure endowment of more and more regions reaches a satisfactory level, its relative importance vis-à-vis other factors declines (Mas et al., 1996: 648).

Summing up, despite the large differences in the empirical findings, none of the authors denies the importance of at least a satisfactory transport infrastructure endowment for the economic well-being of a country.

8.1.3 Indirect Spatial Effects of Infrastructure

This third effect of transport infrastructure is of crucial importance for locational decisions. Krugman and Venables (1990) use a numerical example with two regions, 'core' and 'periphery' to illustrate the link between transport costs, economies of scale and the location of production sites. Their example is based on the following assumptions:

- If the core and the periphery are supplied by one single production site, transport costs have to be taken into account. Since the market in the core is bigger than in the periphery, only a small part of the total production has to be transported if production takes place in the core, and vice versa.
- Factor costs in the periphery are lower than in the core.
- Production takes place under firm-specific increasing returns to scale as described in Chapter 3.

According to Krugman and Venables, production will take place in both locations if transport costs are high. At an intermediate level of transport costs, it becomes profitable to exploit economies of scale by concentrating the production in one region. Due to its bigger size, this will be the core. With low transport costs, however, the lower factor prices in the periphery outweigh the disadvantage of a small domestic market. Production will now be located exclusively in the periphery.

Looking at the real-life importance of transport infrastructure, the conclusions of this numerical example have to be regarded with more caution. First, the relative importance of transport costs vis-à-vis production costs declines steadily and is now usually only 2–3 per cent of total costs (Button, 1993; and Plassard, 1991: 49). Second, due to mayor improvements in transport, at least in industrialised countries like the EU, practically all regions have become accessible in absolute terms. Third, however, relative accessibility and transport costs are becoming more important. While transport links may be good in most places they are always relatively better in some areas out of which, *ceteris paribus*, a location will be selected.

From the point of view of EU regional cohesion, these considerations would suggest that infrastructure investments should be focused on the periphery. From the point of view of aggregate welfare, however, it is more efficient to invest in transport infrastructure where it is most intensively used. These are usually the densely populated central part of the EU.

In this context, the work by Biehl is quite important (CEC, 1986; and Biehl et al., 1991). On the basis of quasi-production functions he investigates the relative over- or underutilisation of transport and other infrastructure in EU regions. According to his findings, overutilised infrastructure is more often a constraint for growth in core regions than in lagging regions. In fact, he finds apparent overcapacity in many lagging regions.

Although it is easy to criticise Biehl's approach on grounds of data selection and methodology, his findings support the argument that infrastructure on its own does not have a major impact on convergence and divergence among EU regions. Without accompanying improvements of the attractivity of a region, improved accessibility may even have negative effects for the region's productive sector. According to ECMT (1994: 122) for example, motorway construction in the Mezzogiorno made it easier for the more competitive industry in the north of Italy to supply the southern regions. This in turn damaged the productive sector in the south.

8.2 TRANSPORT INFRASTRUCTURE ENDOWMENTS IN EUROPEAN REGIONS

Attempts to quantify EU infrastructure endowments across a larger sample of regions are rare. The most encompassing regional infrastructure indicator, covering not only transport infrastructure but also

Figure 8.1 Relative Infrastructure Endowments in EU NUTS II Regions and Relative Regional per capita Income*

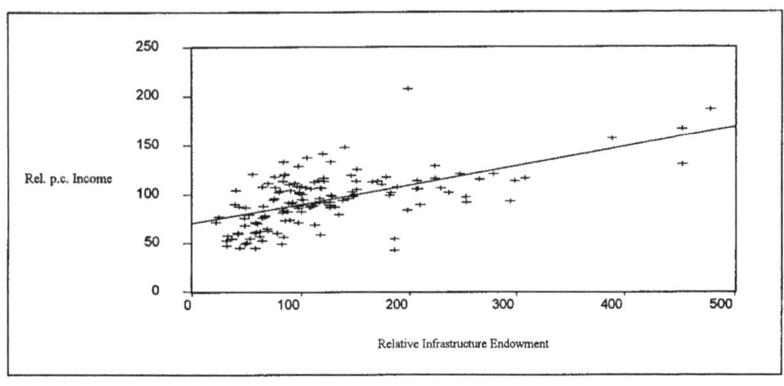

*Income is measured in PPS relative to the EU12 average. The infrastructure indicator encompasses transport, energy and telecommunications.
Sources: Infrastructure: Biehl et al. (1991).
Income: EUROSTAT (1997b).
Own calculations.

social, cultural and environmental facilities, was constructed in the mid-1980s (CEC, 1986; Biehl et al., 1991). A 'physical infrastructure indicator' encompassing transport infrastructure, energy and communication, but excluding social infrastructure, was constructed on the basis of this material and used for the convergence estimations in Chapter 4. Figure 8.1 uses this indicator to illustrate the link between relative regional income and regional infrastructure endowments.

As expected on the basis of the analysis in Chapter 4, the figure shows a very clear link between relative regional per capita income and regional endowments with physical infrastructure. The regions with indicator values between 400 and 500 are the port cities of Hamburg, Bremen and Antwerp and the capital region, Brussels. Average values for the different member states are provided in Table 4.7.

Since the above indicator is based on data collected around 1980, it could be argued that regional infrastructure endowment differences may have become less significant over time. While it is not possible to assess the development since 1980 for all types of infrastructure, the REGIO database (EUROSTAT, 1997b) provides annual information on the length of road and rail networks in European NUTS II regions as well as some information concerning network quality. As far as

Figure 8.2 Changes in Transport Infrastructure Endowments in Cohesion Countries during the 1980s*

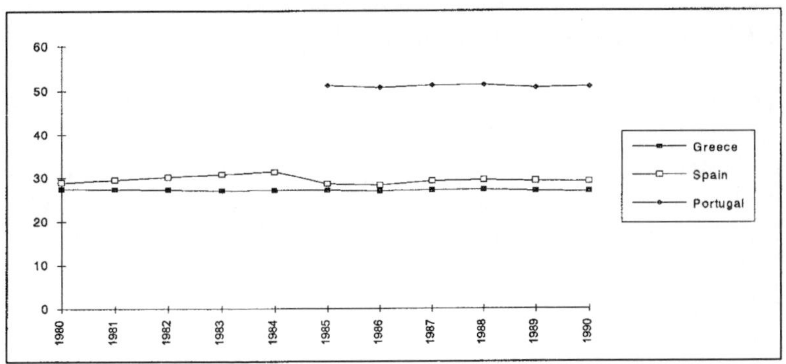

*The transport indicator encompasses regional endowments with roads and railways relative to the EU12 average.
Sources: Networks: EUROSTAT (1997b).
Modal Split: OECD/ECMT (1992).
Own calculations.

roads are concerned, the lengths of the normal road and motorway networks are given separately. For railway lines, it is reported whether they are single or double track and whether electric traction is in operation. Based on this information, it is possible to construct a 'rail and road transport indicator'.[5] Figure 8.2 shows this indicator for the cohesion countries Spain, Portugal and Greece, relative to the EU average.[6]

All three countries remain far below the EU12 average. The position of Portugal appears somewhat more favourable than that of Spain and Greece whose 'rail and road transport indicator' value remains below one third of the European average. Despite a number of shortcomings, including the neglect of air and sea transport facilities and the insufficient treatment of the quality aspect of infrastructure, the indicator illustrates that cohesion countries' disadvantages concerning transport infrastructure are very persistent, at least in quantitative turns. This does not contradict the abovementioned finding by Biehl that there is an actual oversupply in some lagging regions. Unfortunately, however, the available data do not allow a more detailed analysis of developments in the recent past.

8.3 NATIONAL TRANSPORT INFRASTRUCTURE INVESTMENTS IN THE EU

8.3.1 Investments on a National Level

The most important sources of information on transport infrastructure investment in the EU member states are OECD/ECMT (1992) and Bukold et al. (1996). These publications cover all EU countries as well as a number of other OECD member states. OECD/ECMT (1992) provides statistical material for the 1980–9 period, whereas Bukold et al. (1996) provide data up to 1994. For some countries, however, the series in Bukold et al. start only in the mid-1980s.

Figure 8.3 shows a marked difference between national infrastructure investment values in the cohesion countries Ireland, Greece, Spain and – to a lesser extent – Portugal (EU4) and investments in the rest of the pre-1995 EU (EU8). This suggests that not only is the spatial distribution of infrastructure endowments strongly related to relative income, but also the relative level of infrastructure investments. Figure 8.3 shows also that European funding has become an important source for transport infrastructure investments in the

Figure 8.3 National and European Transport Infrastructure Investments in EU Member States, 1989–93*

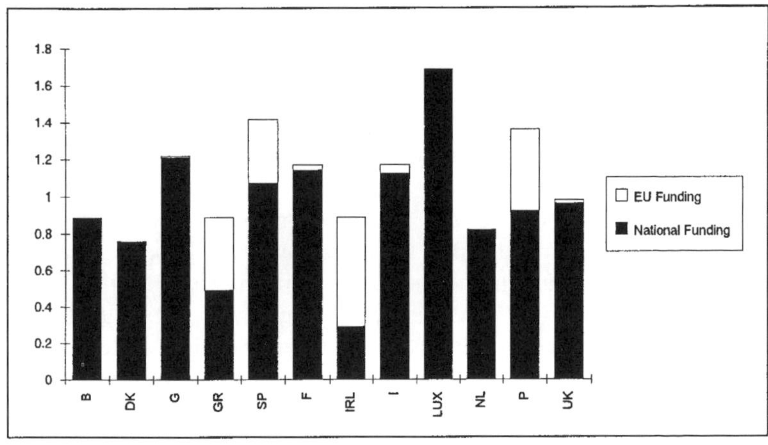

*In per cent of GDP.
Source: Bukold et al. (1996).

Table 8.1 Average Annual Transport Infrastructure Investments as Share of EU Countries' GDP, 1980–93

	EU12	EU4**	EU8	EU8–EU4
1980–4	1.03	0.88	1.10	0.22
1985–9	1.02	0.93	1.07	0.14
Change 1985/89–1980/84	–0.01	+0.05	–0.03	–0.08
1989–93	1.05	0.75	1.09	0.34
Change 1989/93–1985/89	+0.03	–0.18	+0.02	+0.20

* Spain, Portugal, Greece and Ireland
Source: OECD/ECMT (1992) for 1980–9 data; Bukold et al. (1996) for 1989–93 data; own calculations.

cohesion countries. In the case of Ireland, for example, national funding for transport infrastructure is about 50 per cent of EU funding.

Table 8.1 reports the GDP shares used for infrastructure investments by EU4 and EU8. For the 1989–93 period, this table contains only national investments but no EU funding.

It turns out that EU12 aggregate investments declined slightly from the first to the second period and increased again from the second to the third period. All in all, however, Table 8.1 shows that aggregate EU12 investments as a percentage of GDP were quite stable over time. From the point of view of cohesion within the EU, the difference between EU4 and EU8 infrastructure expenditures is the most interesting aspect of Table 8.1. During the 1980–4 period, EU4 transport infrastructure investments as share of GDP were on average 0.22 per cent below the comparable EU8 value. During the 1985–9 period, the cohesion countries reduced this lag by around two-fifths to 0.14 per cent of GDP.[7] During the 1989–93 period, however, the gap widened again. In fact, transport infrastructure investments in the EU4 countries are now merely two-thirds of comparable investments in the periphery. In light of Figure 8.3, it seems likely that the cohesion countries, with the exception of Portugal, have significantly reduced their national efforts to upgrade their transport infrastructure and replaced national funding with EU support. While none of the countries has formally failed to comply with the additionality requirements for EU structural funding, the figures suggest that a reduction of national efforts in this field has taken place.

The following section investigates the intra-national distribution of national transport infrastructure expenditures in Spain and Italy, two large EU member states that encompass lagging as well as non-lagging regions.

8.3.2 Investments on a Regional Level

For most EU member states regionalised transport infrastructure investment data are not available. As far as Spain and Italy are concerned, however, two studies on the regional distribution of public national expenditures have recently been produced. These studies provide statistical information for the years 1989–91 (Spain) and 1991 (Italy) and can be used in order to investigate whether the spatial distribution of national public expenditures in these countries is biased in favour of or against Objective 1 regions.

The study on Spain (de Lucio and Jimeno, 1994) provides a functional disaggregation for regional and communal budgets. Although it does not include the central government level, it covers about 60 per cent of all public investments in Spain during the 1989–91 period. The figures reported for Spain in Table 8.2 refer to the functional category 'Economic Public Goods', which encompasses among other types of expenditures basic infrastructure, transport and communications.

The study on Italy (IGFSPA, 1993) tries to regionalize public expenditures at all levels of government. The category reported in Table 8.2 is 'Investments in Transport and Communication'.[8]

Table 8.2 provides unweighted averages of relative regional per capita income levels and relative per capita investments for lagging and non-lagging Italian and Spanish NUTS II regions. All values are calculated relative to the Spanish and Italian national averages and not the EU average.

The results seem to indicate a weak bias against lagging regions in Spain and Italy. This is confirmed by correlating relative income and expenditures. The correlation value for Italy is 0.334 and for Spain 0.174, indicating a (weak) positive link between income and infrastructure investment.[9] In Spain, however, the positive link between income and infrastructure investments is mainly attributable to the exceptionally high investment level in Navarre. Excluding Navarre from the Spanish non-Objective 1 group reduces the relative investment figure to 89.75 and the correlation value becomes negative (–0.316).

Table 8.2 Relative per capita Transport Infrastructure Investments in Spanish and Italian NUTS II Regions*

	Type of Region	Relative per capita Income 1991 (PPS)	Relative per capita Transport Investments
Spain	Objective 1 Regions	86.1	105.7
	Non-Objective 1 Regions	118.5	135.7
	Non-Objective 1 Regions (Navarre excluded)	117.6	89.75
Italy	Objective 1 Regions	72.0	48.4
	Non-Objective 1 Regions	114.0	125.6

* All reported values are expressed relative to the national average.
Sources: Investments: de Lucio and Jimeno (1994), IGFSPA (1993).
Income: EUROSTAT (1997b).
Own calculations.

While the scope and quality of the data provided in these studies are insufficient to allow more general conclusions, it indicates that lagging regions within these two large member states do not face significant disadvantages with regard to public investments. Insufficient infrastructure investments in lagging EU regions seem to be caused by low investments on the national level rather than intra-national discrimination against Objective 1 regions.

8.4 EUROPEAN TRANSPORT POLICY

8.4.1 Transport Liberalisation – Effects on Core and Periphery

The EU's Common Transport Policy (CTP) remained embryonic until the mid-1980s.[10] Its main emphasis was on transport market liberalisation, but any major progress in this field was blocked by the inactivity of the Council.[11] It is mainly for two reasons that things changed from the mid-1980s onwards:

1. The European Parliament challenged the Council for its inactivity before the European Court of Justice (Case 13/83) and the Court

reminded the Council on its obligation to liberalise the European transport market.
2. The Single Market programme made transport liberalisation a more pressing need for the European economy (Ross, 1994: 193).

In the following, a brief overview of the liberalisation record in the road, rail and air transport sectors is provided. This is followed by considerations on the effects of transport liberalisation on cohesion.

Whereas the liberalisation of the European road haulage sector is approaching its completion,[12] deregulation in international road passenger transport is far less advanced, mainly due to political resistance by the member states. However, the permission of passenger (and goods) transport within a member state by a haulier based in another member state ('cabotage') is the final aim in this area as well (Regulation 2454/92, OJ L 251/1 1992).

The liberalisation of European railways has made limited progress, although Regulation 95/19 (OJ L 143/75 1995) provides a legal basis for the distribution of track access rights for national and foreign rail operators. Based on these regulations, rail operators should in future have track access in all member states.

Regulation 2408/92 (OJ L 240/8 1992) led to the liberalisation of scheduled air services within the EU on 1 April 1997. The full effect of this liberalisation, however, has not been realised yet, partly because the Commission failed to make sure that the allocation of take-off and landing slots as well as airport ground-handling facilities are liberalised as well (*European Voice*, 1997a).

It can be expected that the liberalisation of the European transport market will lead to positive aggregate welfare effects for the EU because increased competition will lead to lower prices and a higher consumer surplus. These effects also emerge in empirical assessments of the effects of transport deregulation in other countries. Morrison and Winston (1989), for example, looking at the deregulation of air transport in the US, emphasise strongly its benefits for consumers.

The impact of air transport liberalisation is of particular importance for peripheral EU regions, where air transport is often the only meaningful transport mode for business purposes. However, since serious liberalisation measures in the EU were only recently implemented, there is still a lack of empirical research in the field. First preliminary investigations indicate that the absolute regional effects of liberalisation were positive.

> The single aviation market has helped to facilitate the creation of new air links to and from peripheral parts of Europe and between them, with positive economic effects, such as the development of tourism. (CEC, 1996a, p. 77)

The lion's share of air transport liberalisation benefits, however, accrue to a limited number of locations in the core of the EU, an effect that is also acknowledged in the Cohesion Report (CEC, 1996a). While the air transport position of peripheral locations within the Single Market is likely to be improved in absolute terms, it will be worsened in comparison with the core regions of the Union.

Additional research on regional effects has taken place in the UK, where (national) transport liberalisation started earlier than in most other member states. Tyson (1990) looks at the regional effects of long-distance bus and coach service deregulation in the UK. He finds an improvement of services and a fall in prices on the routes to and from London. These improvements led to price reductions and service improvements on British Rail's London services. Between provincial regions, however, the level and quality of services tended to be reduced after deregulation (Tyson, 1990: 43–4). The negative effects that transport deregulation can have for services within and between peripheral regions, have also been recognised by the European Parliament which asked the Commission to review whether additional Community rules concerning public transport services in such areas are needed (Transport Europe, 1997).

The regional deregulation effects of road haulage services were more positively assessed. By reducing the costs of road freight, deregulation

> made a further contribution to promoting regional transport, especially when the importance of road haulage and of traffic originating in the outer regions is taken into account. (Tyson, 1990: 45)

This is of particular importance for the cohesion countries, where roads are by far the most important transport mode, for passenger as well as freight transport (CEC, 1996a). So far, EU road transport liberalisation had only limited effects on the distribution of market shares between operators from cohesion countries and core member states. Most routes in the EU periphery are not sufficiently profitable to attract haulage companies from the core member states into the periphery and cohesion country operators, despite lower operating costs, do not have the productivity to penetrate the core markets of the EU (CEC, 1996b). While freight cabotage is likely to be positive for the core as well as the periphery of the Union, more detailed conclusions on regional effects of road transport liberalisation would require the availability of more empirical research.

8.4.2 Transport Infrastructure Support within the Structural Funds

Infrastructure expenditures feature very prominently within EU regional policy, especially in Objective 1 regions. During the 1989–93 period, the average share of total regional policy support earmarked for infrastructure in Objective 1 regions was between 25 per cent (Germany) and 42 per cent (Spain and Greece). The shares in Objective 2 regions are usually much lower except for the UK and Spain.[13]

The main reason for the difference between lagging and declining regions are infrastructure endowment differences between Objective 1

Table 8.3 Average EU Regional Policy Support for Infrastructure According to Member State and Regional Policy Objective, 1989–93*

	Infrastructure as Share of total Support (%)		Total CSF Support*		EU Support within the CSFs*	
	Obj. 1 average	Obj. 2 average	Obj. 1 average	Obj. 2 average	Obj. 1 average	Obj. 2 average
Belgium	./.	10.6	./.	31.3	./.	9.7
Denmark	./.	4.7	./.	18.4	./.	4.7
Germany	25.2	4.2	186.6	9.7	37.9	3.8
Greece	40.9	./.	364.6	./.	193.4	./.
Spain	41.2	34.2	336.5	92.7	170.3	28.1
France	24.8	6.5	393.4	23.6	156.4	6.6
Ireland	26.9	./.	565.6	./.	237.9	./.
Italy	31.6	10.3	244.4	63.2	116.1	10.8
Luxembourg	./.	4.6	./.	33.4	./.	7.0
Netherlands	./.	10.4	./.	30.2	./.	9.4
Portugal	26.9	./.	404.5	./.	153.4	./.
UK	32.3	23.3	295.3	61.8	121.3	22.2

* Average annual amount in ECU per capita.
Source: Own calculations (see Appendix).

and Objective 2 regions. As seen above, there is a very strong correlation between relative per capita income and relative regional infrastructure endowments. In most Objective 2 regions, investments in basic infrastructure are therefore a less pressing need than in lagging EU regions.

The ratios between EU funding in the CSFs and national additionality funding are similar to those for productive investments and R&D. Member states contribute a much larger share to regional development programmes in Objective 2 regions than in lagging regions. However, the national co-financing bias in favour of declining regions is not so strong that it changes the basic link between the amount committed and per capita income. Even if national additionality support is included, poorer regions receive significantly larger EU infrastructure commitments per head of population than the better-off regions of the Union.

Using data on 'EU expenditures within the CSFs' provided in Table 8.3, Figure 8.4 depicts EU regional policy infrastructure commitments in Objective 1 and 2 regions against relative regional income per capita. Objective 1 and Objective 2 regions can be clearly identified, with Objective 1 regions being located on the right-hand side of Figure 8.4.

Figure 8.4 EU Infrastructure Support within the CSFs during the 1989–93 Period in ECU per capita

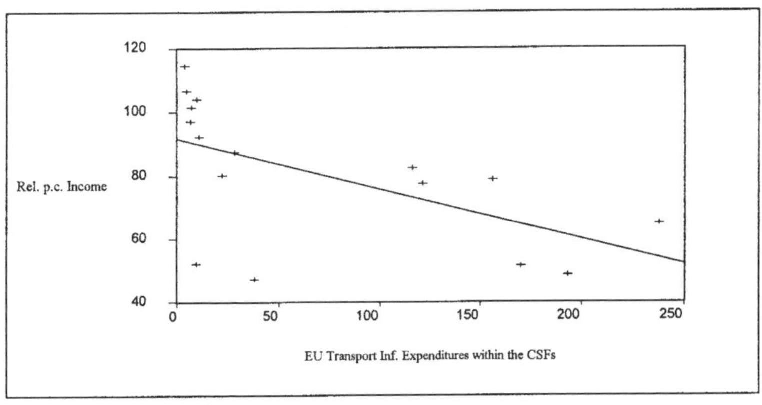

Source: Amounts: Own calculations (see Appendix).
GDP: EUROSTAT (1997b).

The Cohesion Fund (CF), established in the Maastricht Treaty, channels further European resources into cohesion country infrastructure projects as well as the TETN projects described below. Since this fund only became operational in 1993, its impact on the 1989–93 period investigated above was still limited. Table 8.4 below provides an overview of the available CF funding for infrastructure projects in cohesion countries.

For the cohesion countries, these commitments are or special importance because the additionality requirement for CF-supported projects is much weaker than for most SF-supported projects. The provision that up to 90 per cent of the total project costs can be covered by the CF has been included in anticipation of the budgetary pressures that the cohesion countries would face in the years prior to EMU. While this gives more flexibility to the recipient countries, it obviously has the negative side-effect that moral hazard problems are more serious for CF-funded projects than for EU regional policy projects funded by the Structural Funds.

Summing up, EU regional policy is of considerable importance for infrastructure investments in supported regions and in particular for the lagging regions of the Union. An importance that was increased by the creation of the CF. From the point of view of lagging regions long-term catch-up prospects, these findings may at first appear very

Table 8.4 Transport Infrastructure Commitments within the Cohesion Fund, 1993 and 1994–9

	1993		1994–99	
	Mio. ECU*	per cent of total CF funding	Mio ECU**	per cent of total CF funding
Spain	606	71.0	3983	50.1
Portugal	161	57.0	1380	53.0
Greece	105	38.0	1235	47.5
Ireland	86	61.0	665	51.1
Total	958	61.0	7662	50.2

* Current prices.
** Estimate at 1994 prices.
Source: CEC (1996a, Table 27).

positive. It should be kept in mind, however, that it is difficult to justify why the EU should become the main provider of infrastructure in cohesion countries. The provision of such facilities should primarily remain with the member states. Henceforth, it is mainly the task of the cohesion countries to make sure that the qualitative and quantitative insufficiency of their infrastructure endowments are no longer perceived as an obstacle to socio-economic development (CEC, 1990 and 1993a). While the solidarity principle in the EU provides a rationale for assisting parts of the Union that are not in a position to undertake the necessary investments themselves, it is much more difficult to understand why the cohesion countries should be unable to dedicate at least the same GDP share for investments in infrastructure as the core member states.

The final section of Chapter 8.4 looks at the TETNs, the third pillar of EU transport policy, and in particular at the likely effects that they will have on the relative accessibility of peripheral parts of the EU compared to the more central locations of the Union.

8.4.3 Trans-European Transport Networks and the Periphery – Absolute Improvements and Relative Decline in Accessibility?

Over the past years the TETNs have become an important element of EU transport policy. Their origins date back to the mid-1980s when it was diagnosed that European transport infrastructure in general and cross-border infrastructure in particular was insufficient to meet the growing demand (Roundtable of European Industrialists, 1984).[14] These arguments were taken on board by the Commission, and the EU was eventually given competence for the creation of TETNs in the Maastricht Treaty (Article 129b TEU). Plans for the TETNs became more concrete in 1994 when the Commission produced network maps for all transport modes (COM (94) 106 final). From the large number of projects included in these maps, a list of priority infrastructure projects was presented at the Essen Summit in 1995. Table 8.5 provides an overview of these priority transport projects (CEC, 1995a).

Most of these projects are high-speed or conventional railway lines and the blueprints often foresee combined transport facilities. In peripheral areas, however, road projects dominate. This reflects the fact that the relative importance of road transport vis-à-vis rail is much higher in the peripheral parts of the Union although the quality of the road network is largely insufficient (Button, 1992: 30).

Table 8.5 Trans-European Transport Networks – Priority Transport Projects Included in the Report to the Essen European Council

No.	Project	Countries concerned	Costs (Mio ECU)	Mode
1.	Berlin–Munich–Verona	D, A, I	21 925	High-Speed Rail, combined transport
2.	Paris–Brussels–Cologne–Amsterdam–London (PBKAL)	F, B, D, NL, UK	15 754	High-Speed Rail
3.	Madrid–Montpellier/Dax	E, F	12 870	High-Speed Rail
4.	Paris–southern Germany	F, D, (LUX)	5 100	High-Speed Rail
5.	Rotterdam–Emmerich	NL, D	4 117	Conventional Rail, combined transport
6.	Lyons–Turin–Trieste	F, I	13 230	High-Speed Rail, combined transport
7.	Greek motorways	EL	6 360	Road (Motorway)
8.	Lisbon–Valladolid	P, E	970	Road (Motorway)
9.	Larne–Belfast–Dublin–Cork	IRL, UK	238	Conventional Rail
10.	Milan (Malpensa)	I	1 047	Airport
11.	Copenhagen–Malmö (Oresund)	DK, SV	3 647	Road/Rail sea crossing
12.	Nordic Triangle	DK, SV, N, SF	8 780	Road and Rail
13.	Ireland–UK–(Benelux)	IRL, UK	3 340	Road
14.	London–Birmingham–Glasgow	UK	2 160	Conventional Rail

Source: CEC (1995a), European Voice (1997b).

The main idea behind the TETNs is to improve accessibility across the whole EU and to overcome the network barriers that still exist at national frontiers within the EU. What, however, will be the impact of the TETNs on relative accessibility in core and periphery of the EU? As argued above it is not absolute accessibility that has an impact on the locational competition between regions but relative accessibility (Plassard, 1994).

A recent study for the European Commission estimated TETN-induced market access improvements in different types of cities. The definition of market access used in this study is the increase of population that can be reached within a six-hour round trip, using the fastest available mode of transport.

Table 8.6 Trans-European Transport Networks – Improvements in Market Access for Different Types of City (in per cent)

Major Cities % – Core		Major Cities % – Periphery		Medium Cities % – Core		Medium Cities % – Periphery	
Paris	5	Madrid	20	Liège	61	Cuenca	10
Frankfurt	11	Barcelona	20	Utrecht	35	Umea	11
Brussels	28	Lisbon	26	Lille	29	Alexandropoul.	11
Amsterdam	19	Athens	16	Odense	61	Mede	5

Source: CEC (1996a, Table 17).

Table 8.6 summarises some of the results of this study, which are broadly in line with other research looking at the impact of the emerging European HST network in particular.[15]

Generally speaking, the strongest benefits will accrue to intermediate cities in the core of the EU, a limited number of major cities in the periphery and some major cities in the core. In absolute terms, most peripheral areas will also benefit from high-speed transport but to a lesser extent than other parts of the EU. As Plassard put it:

> The new infrastructure will have an amplifying effect: the most dynamic and economically-developed towns, regions and firms will derive the most benefit from the new transport infrastructure that will be progressively built, thereby accentuating the existing polarisation. There is thus obviously a risk of a dual spatial pattern emerging. (Plassard, 1991: 66)

Their are two main reasons for these effects:

1. Many peripheral areas will not be directly served by high-speed transport because high-speed transport has to link major conurbation in order to be profitable. This condition, however, can not be satisfied in many peripheral regions.
2. The 'corridor effect' has to be kept in mind. Many regions are crossed by high speed trains but the services do not stop in these areas. In consequence, HSTs do not generate any economic activity in these regions (Vickerman, 1994).

Since the relative decline in the periphery's accessibility can have negative effects on its development prospects, it is important to make sure that the TETNs are supplemented by national network extensions. HST lines, for example, should be sufficiently linked with regional lines (feeder services) in order to make sure that the benefits are not restricted to the HST terminals and their immediate surroundings. Given the large costs of HST, there is a risk that regional components of the transport networks will be neglected. Ross (1994: 203) mentions the examples of France and Spain, where the costs of high-speed trains are blamed for the backwardness of regional rail services.

The risk that TETN-induced development effects remain restricted to the network hubs emerges in assessment studies looking at the effects of the Channel Tunnel on Kent. These studies predict that most positive effects will occur in those parts of the county that are close to London. The eastern parts of Kent, however, are likely to suffer from the abovementioned 'corridor effect' (Simmons, 1991: 81). In the case of Kent, this effect was not cushioned by linking the Channel Tunnel with regional services.

Positive examples of regional development effects due to HST are the areas around Lille (TGV Nord) and Lyons as well as Rhône-Alpes in general (TGV Méditerranée) (Plassard, 1991). In both cases an encompassing regional development plan was pursued and, especially in the case of Lille, the geographical situation is very favourable with Lille becoming a hub of the emerging PBKL network.

All in all, the construction of European high-speed transport networks will not be a major obstacle to cohesion, but nor will it speed up cohesion either. Within the periphery, it is primarily some central locations that will benefit which is likely to increase intra-national differences of spatial activity within the cohesion countries.

8.5 CONCLUSIONS: PUBLIC TRANSPORT POLICY AND COHESION

Summarising the effects of national and European transport policy on cohesion, one has to keep in mind that the provision of transport infrastructure is an important but not a sufficient requirement for regional economic development (ECMT, 1991). This is the main result that emerged from the theoretical discussion in Section 8.1. It can therefore be assumed that the significant disadvantages of the periphery in terms of its relative infrastructure endowment vis-à-vis the core of the EU represent a problem for the convergence process of the lagging parts of the Union.

Section 8.3 established that the main reason for the relatively inferior position of the cohesion countries is their own policy. EU4 countries are spending a smaller share of their GDP on infrastructure than the core member states. Moreover, there is evidence that EU infrastructure funding is used in order to reduce national investments. As far as intra-national investment patterns are concerned, case studies for Spain and Italy indicate that there is no serious investment bias against the lagging parts of these countries.

As far as non-regional EU transport policy is concerned, its relation with the Cohesion aim is uneasy and the problems that occur are to a large extent unavoidable. Looking at transport liberalisation, core and periphery of the EU are both set to gain but the larger gains are likely to accrue to central parts of the Union where the most profitable markets are located. A policy issue that has to be addressed in this context is the provision of public transport services in areas where they would not be sustainable on the basis of market considerations only. These concerns have also become part of a recent Commission publication on the citizens network (CEC, 1995b).

The spatial effect of EU high-speed transport networks will be similar to those of transport market liberalisation. Core and periphery are set to gain in absolute terms but most of the periphery is set to lose in relation to the core of the EU. Analysts of the accessibility changes uniformly argue that the effects of these changes on the distribution of economic activity in the EU will not be dramatic, but they will make the aim of cohesion more difficult in the years to come. In light of these findings, supplementary infrastructure measures such as the provision of feeder roads, provincial rail services and regional airports are required in order to make sure that the relative disadvantages that the cohesion countries are likely to face are limited. In this respect the idea of a European infrastructure fund (Vickerman, 1994: 15) or an infrastructure agency (*European Voice*, 1997b) has been considered. In principle, such an agency could balance out the conflicting infrastructure aims of core member states and cohesion countries and develop a more integrated approach towards European infrastructure investments, encompassing SFs, CF and EU TETN funding. As argued above, however, the main responsibility for the provision of transport infrastructure should remain with the member states. The involvement of the EU in this area should be restricted to two main fields of activity. First, cross-border infrastructure that is not sufficiently accounted for in national infrastructure plans; and second, support for infrastructure improvements in lagging regions provided that the cohesion countries use an appropriate amount of national funding for infrastructure and if the investment can be expected to provide a significant contribution to the competitiveness of the location. The latter condition obviously require detailed cost-benefit analyses that go far beyond the general considerations on the link between transport and cohesion provided in this chapter.

9 Conclusions and Policy Recommendations

With respect to key economic indicators like per capita income and employment the European Union is characterised by very significant socio-economic regional disparities. Can a natural reduction of these disparities be expected? Economic theory does not provide a clear answer to this question. According to convergence theory economic integration leads to an equalisation of factor returns within an economically integrated area like the EU as long as sufficiently strong adjustment mechanisms, namely goods or factor movements, exist. Divergence theory, however, predicts that technological differences, external effects and transport costs will lead to the development of a heterogeneous economic landscape made up of agglomerations with high factor returns and high factor utilisation on the one hand, and peripheral areas where returns and utilisation rates are much lower on the other hand.

In Chapter 4 the problem of regional convergence and divergence is approached from a national as well as a regional perspective. The analysis of national determinants of economic competitiveness shows that there are clear differences between the four cohesion countries Greece, Spain, Portugal and Ireland (EU4). Whereas the macroeconomic performance of Ireland is good, at least from the late 1980s onwards, the performance of Spain and Portugal is mixed and that of Greece disappointing. The difference in national economic performance are also reflected in the growth performance of Objective 1 regions during the 1980–94 period. However, there are not only national but also region-specific determinants of growth.

1. The initial regional income lag ('natural' convergence), has the strongest impact on regional convergence, but
2. 'Natural' convergence is very slow and likely to exclude some regions. This creates strong political pressure in favour of regional policy interventions.
3. Relatively good endowments with human capital and infrastructure are most likely to have a positive influence on regional economic development. This implies that regional policy can in principle be used to foster the growth performance of lagging regions.

There is no clear evidence for a threshold of economic development below which European economic integration is harmful for countries or regions. Chapter 4 suggests, however, that structurally backwards regions find it more difficult to benefit from the economic gains of integration, especially in periods of sluggish aggregate growth in the EU. This should be kept in mind with regard to the proposed eastern enlargement of the EU. While enlargement should take place in the foreseeable future, the competitiveness of the candidate countries has to be carefully assessed prior to accession.

As argued in Chapter 5, economic support for disadvantaged parts of the Union is by now firmly embedded in primary Community legislation and has to be regarded as a political imperative. Judgements on the welfare effects of European structural operations, however, differ widely and economic evaluations of the Union's structural operations are plagued by the limited availability of regionalised data and the short time period during which the funds have operated in their present form. Moreover, the evaluation practice so far has been eclectic which reduces the comparability of the different studies. Nevertheless, some points of critique emerge clearly.

1. The present level of spatial and thematic concentration is insufficient. Too many parts of the EU and too many different projects are supported simultaneously which reduces the potential positive impacts that regional policy might have.
2. With the exception of Objective 1 regions there is a lack of clear designation criteria. This makes a rational designation practice nearly impossible and compromises the concentration principle.
3. The involvement of regional authorities into the decision-making process is often insufficient and there is a heavy administrative burden for what are frequently small-scale projects.
4. Selecting the 'right' projects and implementing them efficiently is obviously rewarded by good results but – so far – not by additional funding. By the same token poor performance, is not punished.

In its proposals for the new programming period, the European Commission addresses most of these points although, as argued in Chapter 5, some of the Commission's ideas, for example the emphasis on the unemployment rate as allocation criterion, are not convincing.

Chapters 6, 7 and 8 provide case studies for the co-ordination between EU regional policy on the one hand, and non-spatial national and European public policies on the other hand.

Chapter 6, investigating the co-ordination between EU and national regional incentives for productive investments finds that the magnitude of European vis-à-vis national support is in most regions rather limited and that in many peripheral as well as central parts of the EU expenditure levels for national and European incentives taken together are comparable. In short, the privileged position that EU state aids policy tries to grant the periphery does not exist in practice.

Although most economists argue that the importance of regional incentives for the convergence process should not be overestimated, regional incentives are of some importance for locational decisions and they are one of the few variables that can be influenced in the short run.

Chapter 7 confirmed the existence of a large quantitative and qualitative R&D gap between core and periphery of the EU. Moreover, national investment data do not point towards a rapid catch-up of the periphery. Unlike in the case of state aids, the GDP share used for R&D in EU4 is well below the European average. The core–periphery gap in R&D is therefore mainly attributable to the cohesion countries themselves, a result that is very different from the result of Chapter 6. EU regional policy contributes significantly to total R&D expenditures in the periphery but it is insufficient to close the gap between EU4 and EU8.

The analysis of the link between non-spatial EU R&D policy and cohesion indicates a slight 'periphery bias' of EU R&D policy. While such a bias is likely to be useful for cohesion, it may compromise the 'excellence principle' of European R&D support, introduced in order to safeguard the competitiveness of European R&D vis-à-vis third countries. The intra-EU R&D gap should rather be closed by national investments in the quantity and quality of peripheral R&D infrastructure supported – but not replaced – by the Union's structural operations.

The results of Chapter 8, looking at transport infrastructure, are very similar to those of Chapter 7. Rich countries invest a significantly larger share of GDP in infrastructure than the cohesion countries. This investment gap is narrowed by EU regional policy, but it seems that the cohesion countries used the recent increase in EU transfers to lower their national investments in transport infrastructure.

The impact of non-spatial European transport policy on regional cohesion is difficult to establish and remains so far an under-researched area. However, the liberalisation of transport services as well as the recent TETN initiative seem to favour core parts of the Union relatively more than the periphery. With regard to transport policy, the 'effects of other EU policies' argument can hence justify European regional policy interventions.

Three types of policy recommendations can be given on the basis of the present analysis: (1) recommendations based on the key features of the present system; (2) recommendations concerning the links between EU structural operations and non-spatial European policies; and (3) recommendations that would result in major changes of the current system.

1. Recommendations Based on the Present System

- Regional assistance should be more concentrated. During the present planning period more than 50 per cent of the EU population live in eligible areas. Some Objective 1 regions have passed the current eligibility threshold which will lead to some 'natural' concentration. Beyond that, however, the 35–40 per cent mark given in Agenda 2000 should be a yardstick for the post-1999 period.
- The 'delivery system' has to be improved. The present multi-stage, multi-fund, multi-level procedures are cumbersome, lack transparency and require a major bureaucratic effort. Compared to the 1989–93 period the present programming period has already brought some progress, for example with the introduction of Single Programming Documents, but more remains to be done.
- The reliance on grants should be reduced. Many of the SF projects that are now grant-financed, especially infrastructure investments but also support measures for the productive sector like the construction of business parks, could be financed on the basis of soft or interest-free loans. This would not only reduce the financial burden for the EU but it would also exert stronger pressure on the national and regional authorities to identify projects that are bankable, at least for investment banks rather than commercial banks.
- Competition should become an element of the structural operations. As argued above, it should become possible to reward excellence in regional development and penalise poor results. An acceptable incentive system, however, has to ensure that member states or regions are not being punished for poor results for which they cannot be blamed. This in turn requires the development of clear and comparable performance indicators on which programme evaluations and the resulting decisions on the allocation of performance incentives can be based.

2. Recommendations Concerning Policy Co-ordination

- CAP guarantee expenditures are still biased in favour of the core regions of the Union. Further changes of the CAP, required mainly due to the next round of WTO/GATT negotiations as well as the accession of some Central and East European countries to the EU, should therefore take co-ordination with the Union's structural operations more explicitly into account.
- Current EU state aids regulations grant the periphery privileged use of regional incentives vis-à-vis more central regions. However, this privilege is not translated into practice. Since state aids are costly contra-market interventions, causing significant distortions on goods and factor markets, their aggregate use should be limited as much as possible. A tightening of the current rules concerning the eligibility of non-peripheral areas and the maximum level of support permitted would therefore have two effects. It would provide the peripheral areas with a policy variable that would be exclusively at their disposal and it would result in significant reductions of European and national expenditures. Henceforth, the policy change does not only mean a 'stick' for the core member states, but also a 'carrot'.
- With regard to the Common Transport Policy, the analysis in Chapter 8 suggests that the liberalisation of transport services and the TETNs tend to favour the core regions of the EU more than the remote areas. More detailed research into these issues is required – after all, both policy areas have only recently been launched and gained momentum – but it can be assumed that the design of European transport policy has significant repercussions on economic cohesion within the Union.

3. More Fundamental Changes

Before turning to suggestions for more fundamental changes of the system it has to be kept in mind that an EU-wide inter-personal redistribution system will remain politically impossible for the foreseeable future. An unbounded inter-country redistribution system is also likely to be unacceptable, not least because it would mean that poor citizens of rich countries would pay for rich citizens of poor countries. (Thomas, 1997). Nevertheless, a number of more far-reaching proposals for change should be seriously considered.

- The elimination of two-way transfers. The EU budget is artificially inflated by two-way transfers, for example transfers from Germany to the EU budget which are then returned to Germany in the form of Structural Fund expenditures. In order to improve the transparency of the system, member states should have the option to forgo their eligibility for support from the Structural Funds and other expenditure-related policies, mainly the CAP. In return they should be offered a budget rebate. This would increase the transparency of the Union's budget and force the Commission to come up with regional policy solutions that are sufficiently attractive for the member states to be demanded. It would be important, however, to involve the regional level into the decision-making process concerning a possible opting-out. Otherwise, member state governments may be tempted to improve their balance sheets without taking regional interests into account.
- Regional versus national competitiveness. It is obvious that European regional support should be concentrated on the poorest areas of the Union. These in turn are concentrated within the cohesion countries. An overemphasis of EU regional policy on 'balanced' spatial development within the cohesion countries, however, may compromise their national growth prospects. In national economic terms, it may be more meaningful to support those regions within EU4 that hold the best prospects for becoming competitive within the EU rather than the most backward regions. For the time being these considerations apply primarily to Portugal and Greece. The economies in these countries may slow down if European funding can no longer be used in economic centres like Lisbon, Porto or Athens. While the increased income in these regions should obviously be taken into account in the allocation of structural funding to these countries, it is less obvious whether 'poor' member states should be forced to spend structural transfers only outside their most dynamic areas. In order to avoid that, a larger share of structural funding could be allocated on the basis of national criteria with the possibility to use it throughout the territory. This approach has already been chosen for the Cohesion Fund. The discussion on the intra-national distribution of regional support is likely to become an important issue after the Eastern European candidate countries will have joined the Union. The economies in many CEECs, for example the Czech Republic and Hungary, are largely driven by their capital regions which, by the time of accession, may no longer be eligible for structural support.

- The introduction of more elements of conditionality into European Structural Operations. Assistance under the Structural Funds so far is conditional only with regard to the additionality principle and EU rules on issues like market access and public procurement. In future, however, the allocation of funding should include also other aspects of member states' economic policy.

1. Wage-setting systems and labour mobility. Many EU countries have centralised wage-setting systems which do not sufficiently account for regional productivity differences. This, however, increases regional unemployment problems. Moreover, labour migration within the EU, even within most of the member states, remains very low. While migration propensities are difficult to influence member states and the Union should at least make sure that the costs of migration are not artificially increased, for example by means of bureaucratic procedures.
2. Macroeconomic framework policies. It is of crucial importance for lagging regions to operate within a stable national macroeconomic framework. For most member states this is now more or less guaranteed, but one cannot be sure that macroeconomic stability will not become an issue again once some of the present candidate countries have joined the Union.
3. Expenditure-based macro-policies. In light of empirical and theoretical findings on the link between growth, human capital and infrastructure, the periphery has to catch up with regard to these locational factors in order to improve its competitiveness vis-à-vis the core regions and its prospects for convergence. However, there is a shortfall of national growth-inducing investments like education and R&D in the cohesion countries. While it can be argued that some member states do not have the financial means for above EU average investment levels relative to GDP, below-average expenditure levels for human capital and infrastructure are difficult to justify and undermine the solidarity argument, one of the key rationales for European structural operations. The cohesion countries should thus be strongly encouraged to improve their efforts in these fields.

These arguments do not contradict previous suggestions that the member states should have a stronger influence in the design and implementation of regional policy. It is obvious, that member states are in a better position to assess their national needs and to identify their priorities than the European Commission. So far, however, some national governments have failed to provide fundamental prerequisites for growth like a stable macro-economic environment, sufficient infrastructure or education facilities. These failures are only partly attributable to a lack of resources. A possibly even more important part of the explanation are misguided economic policies due to short-term political interests. A concentration of national efforts on state aids rather than human capital formation, for example, may lead to positive short-term results like the rescue of threatened enterprises. In the long-run, however, it will only preserve an outdated economic structure. Obvious economic policy failures of this kind should not be 'rewarded' with structural transfers from Brussels.

Despite the fact that the accession of the first CEECs during the next decade is unlikely to lead to unbearable financial pressure on the EU budget, even if the current system of structural policy is left in place, enlargement will intensify regional disparities within the EU significantly. In light of this challenge it is more important than ever to look not only at improvements within the confines of the present structural operations of the Union but also to think about more substantial – and politically unpopular – policy changes in order to make the European structural operations a more effective and efficient instrument for the reduction of regional socio-economic disparities within the EU.

Appendix

A.1 THE FUNCTIONAL DISAGGREGATION OF EU REGIONAL POLICY EXPENDITURES

The Community Support Frameworks for Objective 1 and 2 regions, together with the annual publication 'Regional Development Programmes' (CEC various issues B), provide a functional breakdown for nearly all operational programmes (OPs) in the Objective 1 and 2 regions as well as for most programmes under the Community Initiatives (CIs). This allows the identification of EU regional policy support for the productive sector (used in Chapter 6), for infrastructure improvements (used in Chapter 8) and for human capital formation. The results are summarised in Table A1. The figures reported in Chapter 7 refer to commitments for R&D only, which is a sub-category of human capital formation as reported in Table A1.

Some OPs are multi-regional and cover larger areas than NUTS II regions, for example the entire Mezzogiorno. For these programmes, a regional breakdown based on 1989 regional population shares was calculated. CI programmes not included in CEC (various issues B) were not taken into account. For two reasons the figures reported in Table A1 are not identical with the results of a comparable functional breakdown in Table 28 and 30 of CEC (1996b).

- Expenditures summarised under 'others' in Table A1 have been assigned to one of the three categories used in CEC (1996b).
- Many regional policy measures are not easily attributable to one of the main categories, business-related infrastructure versus 'normal' infrastructure being a good example.

All in all, however, the breakdown given in Table A1 is quite consistent with the results in CEC (1996b).

A.2 NATIONAL REGIONAL INCENTIVES AND THE ELIGIBILITY OF REGIONS FOR PRODUCTIVE SECTOR SUPPORT

The data used in Section 6.3.2 includes commitments under the national regional incentive schemes listed in Table A2. Other forms of national regional support for the productive sector were not taken into account, largely because it proved to be impossible to quantify their financial impact on a regional basis.

Table A3 summarises which EU regions were fully or partly eligible for national and/or European regional support for the productive sector during

Table A1 Functional Breakdown of EU Regional Policy Support According to Member State and Regional Policy Objective, 1989–93*

Country	Productive Investment Support		Human Capital Formation		Infrastructure		Others**		Total	
Objective	1	2	1	2	1	2	1	2	1	2
Belgium	./.	45.0	./.	15.4	./.	10.6	./.	29.0	./.	100
Denmark	./.	19.7	./.	53.5	./.	4.7	./.	22.1	./.	100
Greece	26.7	./.	17.6	./.	40.9	./.	14.8	./.	100	./.
Germany	27.3	62.7	20.6	25.1	25.2	4.2	26.9	8.0	100	100
Spain	9.2	31.5	10.8	12.5	41.2	34.2	38.8	23.8	100	100
France	8.2	47.9	19.0	18.9	24.8	6.5	48.0	26.7	100	100
Ireland	33.4	./.	35.7	./.	26.9	./.	4.0	./.	100	./.
Italy	18.9	39.2	10.0	23.8	31.6	10.3	39.5	26.7	100	100
Luxembourg	./.	52.9	./.	11.5	./.	4.6	./.	31.0	./.	100
Netherlands	./.	64.4	./.	8.8	./.	10.4	./.	16.4	./.	100
Portugal	33.7	./.	34.8	./.	26.9	./.	4.6	./.	100	./.
UK	22.7	42.1	6.6	11.3	32.3	23.3	38.4	23.3	100	100

* Percentage of total expenditures during the 1989–93 period.
** For example expenditures for agriculture, environment and tourism.
Source: Own calculations.

the 1989–93 period. The regional disaggregation depended largely on data availability in the different countries. In many cases only parts of the country or region were covered. This has been taken into account in the calculation of the per capita figures. In the case of Luxembourg, for example, 38.64 per cent of the population lived in areas that where eligible for support under Objective 2 and 79.65 per cent lived in areas eligible under national regional support. The French Objective 1 regions except Corse as well as Madeira and Açores were excluded due to data limitations.

A.3 DATA ON R&D PERSONNEL AND EXPENDITURES

The data source for R&D personnel is EUROSTAT (1995). The year of reference is 1991, except for Germany (1989), France (1992), Portugal (1990) and the UK (1993). The regional breakdown is NUTS II except for Belgium, Denmark, Ireland, Italy and the Netherlands (NUTS 0) and for

Table A2 National Incentive Schemes Included in the Analysis*

Country	Incentive	Period	Source
Belgium	Interest Subsidy/Capital Grant (Flanders)	1989–93	Yuill et al. (1995)
	Investment Grant (Wallonia)		
Germany	Investment Grant	1989–93**	BMWi
Greece	n.a.	n.a.	n.a.
Spain	Regional Investment Grant	1989–93	MEH
France	Regional Policy Grant (PAT)	1989–93	DATAR
Ireland	New Industry Programme	1988–92	Yuill et al. (1995)
	Small Industry Programme		
	International Traded Services Programme		
Italy	Capital Grant (Assistance for Development Areas)	1988–92	MBPE
Luxembourg	Capital Grant	1988–92	Yuill et al. (1995)
Netherlands	Investment Premium	1989–93	Yuill et al. (1995)
Portugal	Regional Incentive System (SIR)	1989–93	DGDR
UK	Regional Selective Assistance (RSA)	1989–93	Industrial Development
	Regional Enterprise Grant (REG)		Act 1992,
	Selective Financial Assistance (Northern Ireland)		Annual Reports

* Denmark has abolished most forms of national regional support in 1990.
** New Länder, 1991–3.
Abbreviations: BMWi = Bundeswirtschaftsministerium
MEH = Ministerio de Economia y Hacienda
DATAR = Delegation a l'amenagement du territoire et a l'action regionale
MBPE = Ministero del Bilancio e della Programmazione Economica
DGDR = Dirreção Geral do Desenvolvimento Regional
n.a. = data not available

Table A3 Disaggregation and Regional Incentive Coverage

Country	NUTS	Joint Coverage (Objective 1)	Joint Coverage (Objective 2)	National Coverage only	EU Coverage only (Objective 2)	No Coverage
Belgium	I		Flanders, Wallonia			Brussels
Denmark	0				Entire country	
Germany	I	Berlin, Brandenburg, Meckkenburg-V., Sachsen, Sachsen-Anhalt, Thüringen	Bremen, Niedersachsen Nordrhein-Wetfalen, Rheinland-Pfalz, Saarland	Bayern, Hessen, Schleswig-Holstein		Baden-Württemberg, Hamburg
Greece	0	Entire country				
Spain	II	Galizia, Asturias, Castilla-La Mancha, C.-Leon, Extremadura, Com. Valencia., Andalucia, Murcia, C. y M., Canarias	Cantabria, Pais Vasco, Aragon		Navarre, Rioja, Madrid, Catalonia	Baleares
France	II	Corse	Haute-Normandie, Basse-Normandie, Bourgogne, Nord-Pas de Calais, Lorraine, Franche-Comte, Pays de la Loire, Bretagne, Poitou-Charente, Aquitaine, Midi-Pyr., Rhone-Alpes, Auvergne, Languedoc-R., Provence-A. Cote-d'Azure		Picardy	Ile de France, Champagne, Centre, Alsace
Ireland	0	Entire country				
Italy	II	Campania, Abruzzi, Molise, Puglia, Basilicata, Calabria, Sicilia, Sardegna	Marche, Lazio		Piedmont, Valle d'Aosta, Liguria, Lombardy, Veneto, Tuscany, Umbria	Emilia-Romagna

Table A3 *(contiuned)*

Country	NUTS	Joint Coverage (Objective 1)	Joint Coverage (Objective 2)	National Coverage only	EU Coverage only (Objective 2)	No Coverage
Luxembourg	0		Entire country			
Netherlands	0		Entire country			
Portugal	II	Entire country				
UK	I	Northern Ireland	North, Yorkshire + Humberside, East Midlands, West Midlands, North West, Wales, Scotland	South West		East Anglia, South East

Germany and the UK (NUTS I). Data for Eastern Germany and Corse is not available.

For details on R&D support within EU regional policy see Appendix A.1. In order to make EU and national expenditure data comparable, annual expenditure figures instead of figures for the total 1989–93 period are being used.

The main data source for national R&D budget appropriations is also EUROSTAT (1995). For some countries, information on the regional breakdown had to be obtained from additional sources. These references and the years of reference for the different countries are provided in Table A4.

The section on EU-supported R&D projects is based on unpublished material providing a regional breakdown of shared-cost actions under the second and third framework programme (FP). The statistical material was kindly supplied by the European Commission (DG XII).

Table A4 Regional Breakdown of National R&D Appropriations and Time Periods Covered

Country	Period*	Note
Belgium	1991	Regional breakdown for public sector from OECD (1994b).
Denmark	1989, 1991, 1993	
Germany	1990 to 1992	Public sector Länder shares from BMFT (1993), business shares for 1990 and 1992 are average of 1989 and 1991.
Greece	1989, 1991, 1993	
Spain	1990 to 1992	
France	1991 and 1992	Business sector 1990 to 1992.
Ireland	1990 to 1992	
Italy	1990 to 1992	1990 regional shares average of 1991 and 1992, higher education regional shares by IGFSPA (1993).
Netherlands	1991	
Portugal	1990 and 1992	
UK	1990 to 1992	1990 and 1991 regional shares are average of 1992 and 1993 shares (public sector) respectively 1993 shares (business).

* Expenditure data is annual but might be the average of up to three years.

Notes

CHAPTER 1

1. The origins of the EU can be traced to three different communities: the European Coal and Steel Community (ECSC), the European Economic Community (EEC) and the European Atomic Energy Community (EURATOM). Later these three communities taken together were usually called the European Community (EC). After adoption of the Maastricht Treaty, the EC became one of the pillars of the European Union (EU). In order to simplify the terminology, the term EU is used throughout this book unless specific reference to one of the founding treaties is required.

CHAPTER 2

1. On the economic effects of labour migration from southern European countries, see Straubhaar (1988).
2. These issues will be looked at in more detail in Chapter 5.
3. In 1980 Athens' per capita income, expressed in purchasing power standards, was 59 per cent of the EU average, Lisbon's was 69 per cent. Madrid, the richest region in Spain except for the industrialised north-east, had a per capita income of 81 per cent of the EU average (EUROSTAT, 1997b).
4. A definition of the term 'competitiveness' is provided in Chapter 3.
5. It is also argued that Community policies such as the Common Agricultural Policy (CAP) and the R&D programmes favour high-income regions. While this bias is clearly discernible for the CAP, Chapter 7 shows that it is debatable with respect to R&D policy.
6. As far as per capita income is concerned, Boltho reports a standard deviation of 0.151 for 48 US States during the 1985–7 period. The 1983 EU12 figure (member state level), however, was 0.378 (Boltho, 1994: 109–10).

CHAPTER 3

1. This is an implicit assumption since HOS theory does not have an explicit spatial dimension.
2. For a more detailed analysis of this mechanism, see Fischer and Straubhaar (1996).
3. For an overview of microeconomic migration theory, see Fischer, Martin and Straubhaar (1997).

4. The importance of potential member states' capital market structure and interest rate sensitivity is analysed in Nölling (1997).
5. It is possible to construct situations where, due to different relative scarcities of production factors, one factor may be better paid in the technologically inferior location. However, such a situation will not be a stable equilibrium.
6. A similar argument can be made for goods rather than factor movements.
7. For a further discussion of models of sustainable growth and implications of the brain drain, see Findlay (1993), Dolado et al. (1994) and Wolburg (1996).
8. See also Grossman and Helpman (1991, Chapter 13).
9. Recent papers investigating the location of cities are Fujita (1993), Krugman (1993) and Fujita and Krugman (1993). These papers draw heavily on Lösch's and Christaller's pioneering contributions.
10. For details on state aids, see Chapter 6.

CHAPTER 4

1. Recent analyses of the Irish economic performance can be found in CEC (1996b) and OECD (1997). Developments in Spain are analysed in CEC (1994b), OECD (1996a) and Peñalosa (1994), whereas OECD (1996b) and Alogoskoufis (1995) look at the Greek and OECD (1998) at the Portuguese economy. Useful comparative studies for Spain, Portugal and Greece are Larre and Torres (1991) and Bliss and de Macedo (1990). Hallet (1995) compares the impact of economic integration in Greece and Portugal. A good collection of country studies and comparative analyses on postwar growth in Europe is Crafts and Toniolo (1996).
2. FDI shifted the focus of Irish manufacturing from the slow-growing British export market towards more dynamic economies in the rest of Europe and beyond. The 1960 UK share in Irish exports was above 70 per cent, the corresponding figure for 1995 is less than 30 per cent (Barry and Bradley, 1997).
3. This typology is also used by Galor (1996: 1056). On the link between β- and σ-convergence, see Sala-i-Martin (1996). On the underlying theoretical reasoning see also the section on neoclassical growth theory in Chapter 3.1.
4. A dissenting view is Fagerberg and Verspagen (1996: 437). They argue that for the 1980–90 period, 'there is no contribution whatsoever from the catch-up [convergence R.M.] factor when dummies are included'.
5. The per capita income of Groningen is artificially inflated because Dutch North Sea gas is brought ashore and accounted for in this province. Henceforth changes in the gas price are the main determinant for changes in Groningen's per capita GDP.
6. Some of the regressions were also run using relative productivity, defined as output per employee, in 1980 as explanatory variable. For

the full sample and the contrast regions, the results are broadly comparable with those reported in Table 4.4. Regions with a low level of productivity in 1980 grew more rapidly than regions with a high level of productivity. For all three samples, the 1980 productivity level is a significant explanatory variable for the change of productivity.

7. A major shortcoming of the study by Fagerberg and Verspagen (1996), for example, is that it does not cover the cohesion countries.
8. As far as the Objective 1 sample results for R&D are concerned, it should also be kept in mind that in many of these regions no sizeable R&D activities take place.
9. As far as the country dummies are concerned, those for Ireland and Luxembourg remain positively significant. When the relative size of the workforce with low or intermediate educational attainment is taken into account, the dummy variable for Portugal becomes also positively significant.

CHAPTER 5

1. This in turn leads to the question whether it might not be more sensible to change the set-up of regional policy into an inter-personal redistribution system (Hansen, 1995).
2. A notable exception is the recent Commission Communication 'Agenda 2000' (CEC, 1997b) which explicitly laments the lack of labour mobility within the EU and asks for political action to increase it.
3. See for example Armstrong (1993) and Weise (1995).
4. Information on the pre-1989 regional distribution of all funds and the project types supported is available in EUROSTAT (various issues).
5. The legal Acts establishing the new system were the 'Framework' Regulation 2052/88 (OJ L 185/9, 1988), the 'Co-ordination' Regulation 4253/88 (OJ L 374/1, 1988) and regulations for the three funds, namely 4254/88 for the ERDF, 4255/88 for the ESF and 4256/88 for the EAGGF (all in OJ L 374, 1988).
6. For a dissenting view on the concentration issue, see Cuny (1997). He argues that a further reduction of the non-Objective 1 share of the Structural Funds would impede the political acceptance of EU regional policy in the better-off member states.

CHAPTER 6

1. Percentage values refer to the categories 'financial assistance' and 'promotion/attitude of government, etc.', combined and not to investment grants only.
2. CEC (1993a: 12). See also CEC (1990) and PA Economic Consultants (1989). All these studies are based on business surveys.

3. The additionality multiplier is calculated by dividing total public CSF funding for the productive sector with the structural funds contribution towards these commitments. A multiplier of 2 means that 50 per cent of the funding originates from European sources and the remaining 50 per cent from the member state.
4. National authorities also communicated whether EU regional policy transfers are used in order to part-finance national incentive schemes. This information was required to avoid the double counting of European commitments.
5. Due to the similarity of the results, EU regional incentives without additionality payments are not analysed separately.
6. Bachtler and Taylor (1996: 727–8), using a more detailed expenditure typology for Objective 2 regions, calculate that 38 per cent of Objective 2 allocations were used for 'economic infrastructure' and 'aid to firms'.
7. All variables in the following equations are logged.
8. Very similar results are obtained by looking at EU support without national additionality funding.

CHAPTER 7

1. On economic aspects of primary and secondary schooling, see the contributions to the 'Primary and Secondary Education Symposium' in *Journal of Economic Perspectives*, Vol. 10(4), Fall 1996.
2. While these arguments are acknowledged by Brockhoff (1992), he argues that a large share of public R&D funding for industry merely constitutes windfall profits for the participating companies.
3. This point will be taken up again in Section 7.2.2.
4. For details see the Appendix.
5. Regional data for the Mezzogiorno, Eastern Germany and Corsica are not available.
6. The allocation of publications to different countries follows the author country principle. For details see the methodological index in CEC (1994c).
7. Data for Luxembourg are not available. For details see the Appendix.
8. EU4 = Greece, Spain (Objective 1 regions), Ireland and Portugal; EU7 = Belgium, Denmark, Germany, France, Italy, the Netherlands and the UK.
9. 1985 R&D expenditure data for France are not available.
10. All calculations are based on EUROSTAT (1995).
11. For a more detailed review of the different FPs see CEC (1994c: 211–20).
12. There are also other forms of European R&D activity. First, the Joint Research Centre (JRC) of the European Communities, dating back to the EURATOM Treaty. The JRC currently operates at various sites in the EU and is mostly, but not exclusively, financed out of the FPs (CEC, 1994c: 209). Secondly, the EUREKA initiative, launched in 1985, which aims at facilitating European R&D co-operation in areas closer to the

market than those supported within the FPs. Its membership includes also non-EU countries. Financial support for EUREKA projects does not originate from the EU but from national sources (OECD, 1994b).

13. These are not actual expenditures but projected figures given in the CSFs.
14. If co-finance funding is included, CSF support constitutes 68.4 per cent of the national funding. However, it is very unlikely that all or, in fact, much of the co-finance funding is truly additional and would not be spend on R&D in the absence of SF funding.
15. It is not possible to obtain data on national R&D support in Objective 2 regions. Henceforth, per capita R&D allocations in the NUTS II region which contains he Objective 2 region were used as an approximation. In some cases this will lead to an under- or overestimation of national R&D efforts.
16. he observations in the figure refer to the two right-hand columns in Table 7.5. The R&D share of total CSF funding is not separately available for all regions but only according to member state and type of Objective.
17. Needless to say, using the number of projects rather than expenditures has the disadvantage that the size of the projects is not taken into account which might result in a misleading picture. Regionalised FP expenditure data, however, are confidential.
18. At the time when the data was made available only about 85 per cent of the total available funding for shared-cost actions of the 3rd FP had been spent.

CHAPTER 8

1. According to Munnell (1993: 24), core infrastructure constituted 60.7 per cent of total US infrastructure capital in 1990.
2. The AVE uses the European standard gauge which is different from the gauge used in the rest of the Spanish network.
3. In 1992, the transport service sector (NACE 7) accounted for 6,036,000 jobs in EU12. The gross value-added produced by the transport sector in the same year was 211,743 Mio ECU (CEC, 1995c).
4. A useful survey of these studies is Munnell (1993: 33).
5. The available quality differentiations have been taken into account. The relative weight of roads and railways in the indicator was allocated on the basis of the combined average passenger and freight modal split between roads and railways. The indicator was adjusted for population density.
6. The results for Ireland are not reported because the large number of small roads in Ireland leads to implausible results.
7. Especially during the second half of the 1980s, European regional policy had some impact on cohesion countries' investment levels. Given the limited resources available prior to 1989, however this impact is insufficient to explain the reduction of the gap in EU4 infrastructure expenditures relative to EU8 infrastructure expenditures.

8. IGFSPA failed to regionalise about two-thirds of Italian public transport and communication investments, which reduces the explanatory value of the report.
9. This is not attributable to higher tax revenues in richer regions. Regional authorities in Spain and Italy have only limited powers of taxation and rely largely on grants from the central government.
10. Overviews of the development of EU transport policy can be found in Nicolaysen (1996, §42) and Button (1992).
11. Besides its efforts to liberalise the transport market, the European Commission has also pursued the harmonisation of social and technical standards. These aspects of the CTP, however, are of lesser importance for the purposes of the present study and will not be elaborated. For an overview see Nicolaysen (1996, §42).
12. Road haulage liberalisation is mainly based on Regulation 684/92 in OJ L 74/1 1992 and Regulation 3118/93 in OJ L 279/1 1993.
13. These figures refer to total infrastructure rather than transport infrastructure only. Some of the infrastructure investment shares reported in CEC (1996a, Table 30) are above those reported in Table 8.5. For Objective 2 regions, infrastructure expenditures are not reported separately in CEC (1996a). For further details, see the Appendix.
14. Ross (1994: 192–6) provides a good overview of the development of EU transport infrastructure policy, focusing on the HST network.
15. The results of these studies are summarised in Bruinsma and Rietveld (1997).

References

Acs, Z. J., D. B. Audretsch and M. P. Feldman (1992), 'Real Effects of Academic Research: Comment', *American Economic Review*, 82(1), 363–7

Alesina, A. and D. Rodrik (1994), 'Distributive Politics and Economic Growth', *Quarterly Journal of Economics*, CIX, 465–90

Alogoskoufis, G. (1995), 'The Two Faces of Janus: Institutions, Policy Regimes and Macroeconomic Performance in Greece', *Economic Policy*, April, 147–92

Armstrong, H. W. (1993), 'EC Regional Policy', in A. M. El-Agraa (ed.), *The Economics of the European Community*, 4th edn, Allen Unwin, 349–75

Armstrong, H. W. (1995a), 'Convergence among Regions of the European Union 1950–1990', *Papers in Regional Science*, 74(2), 143–52

Armstrong, H. W. (1995b), 'An Appraisal of the Evidence from Cross-sectional Analysis of the Regional Growth Process within the European Union 1950–1990', in H. W. Armstrong and R. W. Vickerman (eds), *Convergence and Divergence among European Regions*, London: Pion, 40–65

Armstrong, H. and J. Taylor (1993), *Regional Economics and Policy*, 2nd edn, London: Harvester

Aschauer, D. A. (1989), 'Is Public Expenditure Productive?', *Journal of Monetary Economics*, 23, 177–200

Bachtler, J. (1995), 'Regional Policy and Cohesion in the European Union', in H. W. Armstrong and R. W. Vickerman (eds), *Convergence and Divergence among European Regions*, London: Pion, 219–30

Bachtler, J. and R. Michie (1993), 'The Restructuring of Regional Policy in the European Community', *Regional Studies*, 27, 719–25

Bachtler, J. and R. Michie (1995), 'A New Era in EU Regional Policy Evaluation? The Appraisal of the Structural Funds', *Regional Studies*, 29/8, 745–51

Bachtler, J. and S. Taylor (1996), 'Regional Development Strategies in Objective 2 Regions: a Comparative Assessment', *Regional Studies*, 30, 723–32

Balassa, B. (1961), *The Theory of Economic Integration*, London: Allen & Unwin

Baldwin, R. (1989), 'The Growth Effects of 1992', *Economic Policy*, October, 248–81

Baltas, N. C. (1997), 'The Restructured CAP and the Periphery of the EU', *Food Policy*, 22/4, 329–43

Barro, R. and X. Sala-i-Martin (1991), 'Convergence across States and Regions', *Brookings Papers on Economic Activity*, 1/91, 107–79

Barro, R. and X. Sala-I-Martin (1995), *Economic Growth*, New York: McGraw Hill

Barry, F. and J. Bradley (1997), 'FDI and Trade: The Irish Host-Country Experience', *The Economic Journal*, 107, 1798–811

Bayoumi, T. and B. Eichengreen (1992), *Shocking Aspects of European Monetary Unification*, Discussion Paper (DP) 643, London: Centre for European Policy Research (CEPR)

Begg, I. and D. Mayes (1993), 'Cohesion in the European Community – a Key Imperative for the 1990s?', *Regional Science and Urban Economics*, 23, 427–48

Begg, I., G. Gudgin and D. Morris (1995), 'The Assessment: Regional Policy of the European Union', *Oxford Review of Economic Policy*, 11/2, Summer 1995, 1–18

Bellamy, C. and G. Child (1987), *Common Market Law of Competition*, 3rd edn, London: Sweet & Maxwell

Beutel, J. (1993), *The Economic Impacts of the Community Support Frameworks for the Objective 1 Regions 1989–93*, Report prepared for the European Commission, DG XVI

Bianchi, G. (1993), 'The IMPs: a Missed Opportunity?', in R. Leonardi (ed.), *The Regions and the European Community*, London: Frank Cass, 47–70

Biehl, D. et al. (1991), 'Kapazitätsausstattung und Kapazitätsengpässe an großräumig bedeutsamer Infrastruktur', *Materialien zur Raumentwicklung*, 40, 237–84

Blanchard, O. and L. Katz (1992), 'Regional Evolutions', *Brookings Papers of Economic Activity*, 1/92, 1–75

Bliss, C. and J. de Macedo (1990), *Unity with Diversity in the European Economy: the Community's Southern Frontier*, Cambridge: Cambridge University Press

Blomström, M., R. E. Lipsey and M. Zejan (1993), 'Is Fixed Investment the Key to Economic Growth?', Working Paper 4436, Cambridge, Mass.: NBER

BMFT (1993), *Bundesbericht Forschung*, Bonn: BMFT

Boltho, A. (1994), 'A Comparison of Regional Differentials in the European Community and the United States', in J. Mortensen (ed.), *Improving Economic and Social Cohesion in the European Community*, Basingstoke: Macmillan, 41–53

Boyer, G. R. et al. (1993), *The Impact of Emigration on Real Wages in Ireland 1850–1914*, DP 854, London: CEPR

Bradley, J. et al. (1996), *Regional Aid and Convergence*, Aldershot: Avebury

Brockhoff, K. (1992), *Forschung und Entwicklung – Planung und Kontrolle*, München: Oldenbourg

Bruinsma, F. and P. Rietveld (1997), 'The Accessibility of European Cities – Theoretical Framework and Comparison of Approaches', *Environment and Planning*

Bukold, S. et al. (1996), *The State of European Infrastructure 1996*, Rotterdam: Centre for European Infrastructure Studies

Button, K. J. (1992), 'Das integrierte europäische Verkehrskonzept', in K. J. Button et al. (eds), *Europäische Verkehrspolitik – Wege in die Zukunft*, Gütersloh: Bertelsmann, 27–81

Button, K. J. (1993), *Transport Economics*, Aldershot: Edward Elgar

Caballero, R. and R. Lyons (1990a), 'Internal versus External Economies in European Manufacturing', *European Economic Review*, 34, 805–30

Caballero, R. and R. Lyons (1990b), 'External Effects and Europe's Integration', in L. A. Winters and A. Venables (eds), *European Integration: Trade and Industry*, Cambridge: Cambridge University Press and CEPR, 34–51

Cameron, G. (1990), 'First Steps in Urban Policy Evaluation in the UK', *Urban Studies*, 27, 475–95

Caporale, G. M. (1993), 'Is Europe an Optimum Currency Area? Symmetric versus Asymmetric Shocks in the EC', *National Institute Economic Review*, May 1993, 95–103

CEC (various issues A), *Survey on State Aid in the European Community in the Manufacturing and Certain Other Sectors*, Brussels: CEC

CEC (various issues B), *Regional Development Programmes*, Luxembourg: Office for Official Publications of the European Communities (OOPEC)

CEC (1986), *The Contribution of Infrastructure to Regional Development*, Luxembourg: OOPEC

CEC (1988), *The Economics of 1992*, European Economy No. 35, Luxembourg: OOPEC

CEC (1990), *An Empirical Assessment of Factors shaping Competitiveness in Problem Regions*, Luxembourg: OOPEC

CEC (1993a), *New Location Factors for Mobile Investments in Europe*, Regional Development Studies 6, Luxembourg: OOPEC

CEC (1993b), *Community Structural Funds 1994–99 – Regulations and Commentary*, Luxembourg: OOPEC

CEC (1994a), *Competitiveness and Cohesion: Trends in the Regions*, 5th Periodic Report on the Social and Economic Situation and Development of the Regions in the Community, Luxembourg: OOPEC

CEC (1994b), *The Economic and Finanacial Situation in Spain*, European Economy: Reports and Studies 7/1994, Luxembourg: OOPEC

CEC (1994c), *The European Report on Science and Technology Indicators 1994*, Luxembourg: OOPEC

CEC (1995a), *Trans-European networks – the Group of Personal Representatives of the Heads of State or Government – Report*, Luxembourg: OOPEC

CEC (1995b), *Das Bürgernetz*, Bulletin der Europäischen Union, Beilage 4/1995

CEC (1995c), *Panorama of EU Industry 1995/96*, Luxembourg: OOPEC

CEC (1996a), *First Report on Economic and Social Cohesion 1996*, Luxembourg: OOPEC

CEC (1996b), *The Economic and Financial Situation in Ireland: Ireland in the Transition to EMU*, European Economy: Reports and Studies 1/96, Luxembourg: OOPEC

CEC (1997a), *AMEKO-Database*, Directorate-General for Economic and Financial Affairs, Brussels

CEC (1997b), *Agenda 2000 – For a Stronger and Wider Union*, Doc/97/6, Strasbourg, 15 July

CEC (1997c), *Implementation of the Structural Funds 1994–1996*, Paper prepared by the European Commission, DG XIX, Brussels, 16 June

CEC (1998a), *Agenda 2000: The Legislative Proposals, Overall View*, Brussels, 18 March, COM (1998) 182 final

CEC (1998b), *Proposal for a Council Regulation Laying Down General Provisions for the Structural Funds*, Brussels, 18 March

CEC (1998c), *Agenda 2000: the Legislative Proposals*, IP/98/258, Brussels, 18 March

CEC (1998d), *ISPA Explanatory Memorandum*, Brussels, 18 March

CEPR (1993), *Monitoring European Integration 4 – Making Sense of Subsidiarity: How Much Centralization for Europe*, London: Centre for Economic Policy Research

Christaller, W. (1933), *Die zentralen Orte in Süddeutschland*, Jena: Fischer

Courchene, T. et al. (1993), 'Stable Money – Sound Finances', *European Economy*, No. 53

Crafts, N. and G. Toniolo (eds) (1996), *Economic Growth in Europe since 1945*, Cambridge: Cambridge University Press and CEPR

Cuny, R. H. (1997), 'Reform der Europäischen Strukturfonds', *Wirtschaftsdienst*, 1997/IV, 227–33

de Grauwe, P. and W. Vanhaverbeke (1993), 'Is Europe an Optimum Currency Area? Evidence from Regional Data', in P. R. Masson and M. P. Taylor (eds), *Policy Issues in the Operation of Currency Unions*, Cambridge: Cambridge University Press, 111–29

de la Fuente, A. (1995), *The Empirics of Growth and Convergence: a Selective Review*, Discussion Paper 1275, London: CEPR

de la Fuente, A. and X. Vives (1995), 'Infrastructure and Education as Instruments of Regional Policy: Evidence from Spain', *Economic Policy*, April, 12–51

de Lucio, J. J. and J. F. Jimeno (1994), *Functional Analysis of Spanish Public Expenditure (1989–94)*, Study for the European Commission, DG II, January

Decand, G. (1996), *The Nomenclature of Territorial Units for Statistics (NUTS)*, Paper presented at the ÖSZ/DGXVI/EUROSTAT Seminar on Regional Statistics, Baden/Vienna, 5–8 March

di Palma, M. and C. Maziotta (1998), *Some Suggestions for More Detailed Statistical Information in the Service of Community Regional Policy*, Paper presented at the 4th CEIES Seminar on 'Regional Information Serving Regional Policy in Europe, Rennes, 30 and 31 January

Dolado, J. et al. (1994), 'The Growth Effects of Migration in the Host Country', *Journal of Population Economics*, 7, 133–56

Dunning, J. H. (1986), *Japanese Participation in British Industry*, London: Croom Helm

ECMT (1991), *Transport and Spatial Distribution of Activities*, Round Table 85, Paris: ECMT/OECD

ECMT (1994), *Regional Policy, Transport Networks and Communications*, Round Table 94, Paris: ECMT/OECD

European Parliament (1991), *The Regional Impact of Community Policies*, DG for Research, Regional Policy and Transport Series 17, Luxembourg: OOPEC

European Voice (1997a), 'Tense Countdown to Open Skies', 30 January–5 February

European Voice (1997b), 'New Route Chartered to Fund TENs Initiatives', 30 January–5 February

EUROSTAT (various issues), *Regions – The Community's Financial Participation in Investments*, Luxembourg: OOPEC

EUROSTAT (1994), *Earnings 1993*, Luxembourg: OOPEC

EUROSTAT (1995), *Research and Development – Annual Statistics 1995*, Luxembourg: OOPEC

EUROSTAT (1997a), *Regions – Statistical Yearbook*, Luxembourg: OOPEC

EUROSTAT (1997b), *REGIO-Database*, Luxembourg: EUROSTAT

Fagerberg, J. (1994), 'Technology and International Differences in Growth Rates', *Journal of Economic Literature*, XXXII, 1147–75

Fagerberg, J. and B. Verspagen (1996), 'Heading for Divergence? Regional Growth in Europe Reconsidered', *Journal of Common Market Studies*, 34 (3), September, 431–48

Faini, R. (1983), 'Cumulative Process of Deindustrialisation in an Open Region: the Case of Southern Italy 1951–73', *Journal of Development Economics*

Faini, R. and F. Schiantarelli (1987), 'Incentives and Investment Decisions: the Effectiveness of Regional Policy', *Oxford Economic Papers*, 39, 516–33

Faini, R., G. P. Galli and C. Gianninni (1992), 'Finance and Development: the Case of Southern Italy', in A. Giovanninni (ed.), *Finance and Development: Issues and Experience*, Cambridge: Cambridge University Press

Findlay, A. (1993), 'New Technology, High-Level Labour Movements and the Concept of the Brain Drain', in OECD, *The Changing Course of International Migration*, Paris: OECD, 149–59

Fischer, P. and T. Straubhaar (1996), *Migration and Economic Integration in the Nordic Common Labour Market*, Copenhagen: The Nordic Council of Ministers

Fischer, P., R. Martin and T. Straubhaar (1997), 'Should I Stay or Should I Go?', in T. Hammar et al. (eds), *International Migration, Immobility and Development*, Oxford: Berg, 49–90

Folkers, C. (1995), 'Welches Finanzausgleichssystem braucht Europa?', in H. Karl and W. Henrichsmeyer (eds), *Regionalentwicklung im Prozess der Europäischen Integration*, Bonner Schriften zur Integration Europas Band 4, Bonn: Europa Union Verlag, 87–108

Ford, R. and P. Poret (1991), 'Infrastructure and Privat-Sector Productivity', *Economic Studies*, 17, 63–89

Frazer, T. (1995), 'The New Structural Funds, State Aids and Interventions on the Single Market', *European Law Review*, 21(1), 3–19

Fujita, M. (1993), 'Monoplistic Competition and Urban Systems', *European Economic Review*, 37, 308–15

Fujita, M. and P. Krugman (1993), 'Urban Systems and Regional Development', in CEPR, *The Location of Economic Activity: New Theories and Evidence*, Report of a Conference in Vigo, 17–19 March, London: CEPR, 583–608

Galor, O. (1996), 'Convergence? Inferences from Theoretical Models', *The Economic Journal*, 106, 1056–79

Galor, O. and J. Zeira (1993), 'Income Distribution and Macroeconomics', *Review of Economic Studies*, LX, January 1993, 35–52

Giersch, H. (1989), 'Anmerkungen zum weltwirtschaftlichen Denkansatz', *Weltwirtschaftliches Archiv*, 125(1), 1–16

Giersch, H. (1990), 'Thünen Vorlesung', *Zeitschrift für Wirtschafts- und Sozialwissenschaften*, 110, 1–19

Gordon, J. (1991), *Structural Funds and the 1992 Program in the European Community*, Fiscal Affairs Department, Working Paper WP 91/65, Washington, D.C.: International Monetary Fund

Gramlich, E. M. (1994), 'Infrastructure Investment: a Review Essay', *Journal of Economic Literature*, XXXII, 1176–96

Griliches, Z. (1990), 'Patent Statistics as Economic Indicators: A Survey', *Journal of Economic Literature*, XXVIII, 1661–707

Gros, D. and N. Thygesen (1992), *European Monetary Integration*, London: Longman

Grossman, G. and E. Helpman (1991), *Innovation and Growth in the Global Economy*, Cambridge, Mass.: MIT Press

Grossman, G. and E. Helpman (1994), 'Endogenous Innovation in the Theory of Growth', *Journal of Economic Perspectives*, 8 (1), 23–44

Grote, J. R. (1993), 'Diseconomies in Space: Traditional Sectoral Policies of the EC, the European Technology Community and their Effects on Regional Disparities', in R. Leonardi (ed.), *The Regions and the European Community*, London: Cass, 14–46

Grubel, H. and P. Lloyd (1975), *Intra-Industry Trade*, London: Macmillan

Hallet, M. (1995), 'Wirkungen wirtschaftlicher Integration auf periphere Regionen: Die EG Integration Griechenlands und Portugals', *Konjunkturpolitik*, 41(2), 115–47

Hansen, N. (1995), 'Addressing Regional Disparity and Equity Objectives through Regional Policies: a Sceptical Perspective', *Papers in Regional Science*, 74(2), 89–104

Harhoff, D. (1995), *R&D, Spillovers and Productivity in German Manufacturing Firms*, Paper presented at the CEPR Workshop on R&D Spillovers, Lausanne 27–28 January

Harris, R. and M. Trainor (1995), 'Innovations and R&D in Northern Ireland Manufacturing: a Schumpeterian Approach', *Regional Studies*, 29 (7), 593–604

Hilpert, U. (1992), *Archipelago Europe – Islands of Innovation. Synthesis Report*, FAST document FOP 242, Brussels

Hulten, C. R. and R. M. Schwab (1993), *Endogenous Growth, Public Capital and the Convergence of Regional Manufacturing Industries*, Working Paper 4538, Cambridge, Mass.: NBER

IGFSPA (Ispettorato Generale per la Finanza del Settore Pubblico Allargato) (1993), *La Spesa Statale Regionalizzata, Anno 1991, 1*, Study for the European Commission, DG II, December

Jaffe, A. B. (1989), 'Real Effects of Academic Research', *American Economic Review*, 79(5), 957–91

Jaffe, A. B., M. Trajitenberg and R. Henderson (1993), 'Geographic Localization of Knowledge Spillovers as Evidenced by Patent Citations', *Quarterly Journal of Economics*, 63(3), 577–98

Katseli, L. T. (1990), 'Economic Integration in the Enlarged European Community: Strategic Adjustment of the Greek Economy', in Bliss, C. and J. de Macedo (eds), *Unity with Diversity in the European Community: the Community's Southern Frontier*, Cambridge: Cambridge University Press, 235–309

Kenen, P. (1969), 'The Theory of Optimum Currency Areas: An Eclectic View', in A. Swoboda (ed.), *Monetary Problems of the International Economy*, Chicago

Kenner, J. (1994), 'Economic and Social Cohesion – the Rocky Road Ahead', *Legal Issues of European Integration*, 1/1994, 1–36

Krugman, P. (1991), *Geography and Trade*, Leuven and Cambridge, Mass.: Leuven Univerity Press and MIT Press

Krugman, P. (1992), *A Dynamic Spatial Model*, Working Paper 4219, Cambridge, Mass.: NBER

Krugman, P. (1993), 'On the Number and Location of Cities', *European Economic Review*, 37, 293–8

Krugman, P. and A. Venables (1990), *Integration and the Competitiveness of Peripheral Industry*, Discussion Paper 363, London: CEPR

Lammers, K. (1992), 'Mehr regionalpolitische Kompetenz für die EG im Europäischen Binnenmarkt?', in Akademie für Raumforschung und Landesplanung (ed.), *Regionale Wirtschaftspolitik auf dem Weg zur europäischen Integration*, Forschungs- und Sitzungsberichte 187, Hannover 1992, 70–82

Langhammer, R. (1987), *Hat der europäische Integrationsprozeß die Integration der nationalen Märkte gefördert?*, Kiel Discussion Papers 130, Kiel: Institut für Weltwirtschaft

Larre, B. and R. Torres (1991), 'Is Convergence a Spontaneous Process? The Experience of Spain, Portugal and Greece', *OECD Economic Studies*, 16, 169–98

Leonardi, R. (1995), 'Regional Development in Italy: Social Capital and the Mezzogiorno', *Oxford Review of Economic Policy*, 11(2), 165–79

Levine, R. and D. Renelt (1992), 'A Sensitivity Analysis of Cross-Country Growth Regressions', *The American Economic Review*, 82(4), 942–63

Lichtenberg, F. R. (1995), *R&D Collaboration and Specialisation in the European Community*, Wissenschaftszentrum Berlin für Sozialforschung (WZB), Discussion Paper 95–18

LSE (1997), *Study of the Socio-Economic Impact of Projects Financed by the Cohesion Fund – Modelling Report for the European Commission DG XVI*, London: LSE

Lucas, R. (1988), 'On the Mechanics of Development Planning', *Journal of Monetary Economics*, 22(1), 3–42

Mankiw, N., D. Romer and D. Wei (1992), 'A Contribution to the Empirics of Economic Growth', *The Quarterly Journal of Economics*, 107, 407–37

Marias, E. A. (1994), 'Solidarity as an Objective of the European Union and the European Community', *Legal Issues of European Integration*, 1994/2, 85–114

Markusen, J. (1983), 'Factor Movements and Commodity Trade as Complements', *Journal of International Economics*, 14, 341–56

Marques, A. (1992), 'Community Competition Policy and Economic and Social Cohesion', *Regional Studies*, 26, 404–47

Marques, A. (1994), 'Regionalbeihilfen und Kohäsion. Tragweite und Grenzen gemeinwirtschaftlicher Maßnahmen', in *Raumforschung und Raumordnung*, 2/52, 127–37

Marshall, A. (1890), *Principles of Economics* (reprint of 1986), Basingstoke: Macmillan

Martin, R. (1998), 'Financing EU Cohesion Policy in Central and Eastern Europe – a Budgetary Timebomb?, *Intereconomics*, May/June, 103–11

Martin, R. and J. Mortensen (1997), 'Economic and Social Cohesion and EU Enlargement', *CEPS-Review*, 5, 10–22

Martin, R. and M. Schulze Steinen (1995), *Regional Policy and Competition Policy in the European Union – Are they Consistent?*, Europa-Kolleg Hamburg, Discussion Paper 2/95

Martin, R. and M. Schulze Steinen (1997), 'State Aids, Regional Policy and Locational Competition in the European Union', *European Urban and Regional Studies*, 4(1), 19–31

Mas, M. et al. (1996), 'Infrastructure and Productivity in the Spanish Regions', *Regional Studies*, 7 (30), 641–9

McAleavey, P. (1993), 'The Politics of European Regional Development Policy: Additionality in the Scottish Minefields', *Regional Politics and Policy*, 3/2, 88–107

McEldowney, J. J. (1991), 'Evaluation and European Regional Policy', *Regional Studies*, 25 (3), 261–4

McKinnon, R. (1963), 'Optimum Currency Areas', *American Economic Review*, 53, 717–25

MEANS (1993), *Methods to Give Meaning to the Evaluation Obligation: the Conclusions of the MEANS programme*, MEANS/93/13/EN, CEOPS, Lyons

Michie, R. and J. Bachtler (1994), 'Recent Developments in EU Regional Policy', *Regions*, No. 194, December 1994, 8–11

Morrison, S. A. and C. Winston (1989), 'Enhancing the Performance of the Deregulated Air Transport System', *Brookings Papers on Economic Activity, Microeconomics 1989*, 61–112

Mundell, R. A. (1961), 'A Theory of Optimum Currency Areas', *American Economic Review*, 51, 657–64

Munnell, A. H. (1990), 'Why has Productivity Growth declined? Productivity and Public Investment', *New England Economic Review*, Jan/Feb, 3–22

Munnell, A. H. (1993), 'An Assessment of Trands in and Economic Impacts of Infrastructure Investment', in OECD (ed.), *Infrastructure Policies for the 1990s*, Paris: OECD

Neven, D. J. and C. Gouyette (1994), *Regional Convergence in the European Community*, Discussion Paper 914, London, CEPR

Newbould, G. D., P. J. Buckley and J. C. Thurwell (1978), *Going International: the Experience of Smaller Companies Overseas*, London: Associated Business Press

Nicolaysen, G. (1996), *Europarecht II – Das Wirtschaftsrecht im Binnenmarkt*, Baden-Baden: Nomos

Nölling, P. (1997), *Großbritanniens Geldordnung im Konflikt mit der Europäischen Währungsunion*, Schriftenreihe des Europa-Kollegs Hamburg Band 12, Baden-Baden: Nomos

North, D. (1994), 'Institutionnal Competition', in H. Siebert (ed.), *Locational Competition in the World Economy*, Tübingen: Mohr, 27–37

Ochel, W. and H. Penzkofer (1996), *Internationale Wettbewerbsfähigkeit und ihre Implikationen für die europäische FuE-Politik*, ifo studien zur europäischen wirtschaft, München: ifo Institut für Wirtschaftsforschung

OECD (1994a), *OECD Reviews on Foreign Direct Investment: Portugal*, Paris: OECD

OECD (1994b), *Science and Technology Policy, Review and Outlook*, Paris: OECD

OECD (1996a), *OECD Economic Surveys: Spain*, Paris: OECD

OECD (1996b), *OECD Economic Surveys: Greece*, Paris: OECD

OECD (1997), *OECD Economic Surveys: Ireland*, Paris: OECD

OECD (1998), *OECD Economic Surveys: Portugal*, Paris: OECD

OECD/ECMT (1992), *Investment in Transport Infrastructure in the 1980s*, Paris: OECD

Ó Gráda, C. and C. O'Rourke (1996), 'Irish Economic Growth, 1945–88', in N. Crafts and G. Toniolo (eds), *Economic Growth in Europe since 1945*, Cambridge: Cambridge University Press, 388–426

Owen, N. (1983), *Economies of Scale, Competitiveness and Trade Patterns within the European Community*, Oxford: Oxford University Press

PA Cambridge Economic Consultants (1989), *The Efficiency of Regional Policy in Member Countries of the European Community*, Study prepared for the CEC – Directorate General for Regional Policy (DG XVI)

Peñalosa, J. M. (1994), *The Spanish Catching-up Process: General Determinants and Contribution of the Manufacturing Industry*, Banco de España, Documento de Trabajo 9428, Madrid

Plassard, F. (1991), 'France', in ECMT (ed.), *Transport and Spatial Distribution of Activities*, Round Table 85, Paris: ECMT/OECD, 40–74

Plassard, F. (1994), 'High Speed Transport and Regional Development', in ECMT (ed.), *Regional Policy, Transport Networks and Communications*, Round Table 94, Paris: ECMT/OECD, 31–83

Predöhl, A. (1925), 'Das Standortproblem in der Wirtschaftstheorie', *Weltwirtschaftliches Archiv*, 21/1, 294–321

Quah, D. (1993), 'Empirical Cross-section Dynamics in Economic Growth', *European Economic Review*, 426–34

Quah, D. (1996), 'Twin Peaks: Growth and Convergence in Models of Distribution Dynamics', *The Economic Journal*, 106, 1045–55

Quah, D. (1997), 'Regional Cohesion from Local Isolated Actions: Part I and II', in London School of Economics, *Modelling Report to DG XVI*, April 1997, London: London School of Economics

Rebelo, S. (1991), 'Long-Run Policy Analysis and Long-Run Growth', *Journal of Political Economy*, 99(3), 500–21

Roberts, P. (1993), 'Managing the Strategic Planning and Development of Regions: Lessons from a European Perspective', *Regional Studies*, 27/8, 759–68

Roeger, W. (1996), *Macro-Economic Evaluation of the Effects of Community Structural Funds (CSF)*, Paper presented at the European Conference on Evaluation Methods

Romer, P. (1986), 'Increasing Returns and Long-run Growth', *Journal of Political Economy*, 94, 1002–37

Ross, J. F. L. (1994), 'High-Speed Rail: Catalyst for European Integration', *Journal of Common Market Studies*, (2) 32, 191–214

Roundtable of European Industrialists (1984), *Missing Links*, Paris: Roundtable of European Industrialists

Ryan, J. (1993), 'The Regional Policies of the European Commission, the United Kingdom and Germany', *Journal of Regional Policy*, 13 (3/4), 457–67

Sala-i-Martin, X. (1994), 'Cross-Sectional Regressions and the Empirics of Economic Growth', *European Economic Review*, 38, 739–47

Sala-i-Martin, X. (1996), 'The Classical Approach to Convergence Analysis', *The Economic Journal*, 106, 1019–36

Schalk, H. J., G. Untiedt and J. Lüschow (1995), 'Technische Effizienz, Wachstum und Konvergenz in den Arbeitsmarktregionen der Bundesrepublik Deutschland (West)', *Jahrbuch für Nationalökonomie und Statistik*, Bd. 214, 25–49

Schmidt-Aßmann, E. (1995), 'Organisationsfragen der europäischen Forschungspolitik, in O. Due, M. Lutter and J. Schwarze (eds), *Festschrift für Ulrich Everling Bd. II*, Baden-Baden: Nomos, 1281–95

Seidenfuss, H. (1989), 'Regionalpolitik zwischen Strukturlenkung und marktwirtschaftlicher Ordnungspolitik', in C. Andrae et al. (eds), *Wettbewerb als Herausforderung und Chance – Festschrift für Werner Benisch*, Köln: Heymanns, 135–52

Seitz, H. and G. Licht (1995), 'The Impact of Public Infrastructure Capital on Regional Manufacturing Production Cost', *Regional Studies*, (3) 29, 231–40

Shepherd, D., A. Silberston and R. Strange (1985), *British Manufacturing Investment Overseas*, London: Methuen

Simmons, M. (1991), 'United Kingdom', in ECMT, *Regional Policy, Transport Networks and Communications*, Round Table 94, Paris: ECMT/OECD, 75–107

Sinn, S. (1989), *Internationale Wettbewerbsfähigkeit von immobilen Faktoren im Standortwettbewerb*, Arbeitspapier No. 361, Kiel: Institut für Weltwirtschaft

Smit, H. and P. E. Herzog (1992), *The Law of the European Community – a Commentary on the EC Treaty*, New York

Solow, R. (1957), 'Technical Change and the Aggregate Production Function', *Review of Economics and Statistics*, 39, 312–20

Solow, R. (1994), 'Perspectives on Growth Theory', *Journal of Economic Perspectives*, 1/8, 45–54

Soltwedel, R. et al. (1988), *Subventionssysteme und Wettbewerbsbedingungen in der EG. Theoretische Analysen und Fallbeispiele*, Kiel, Institut für Weltwirtschaft

Strain, J. F. (1993), *Integration, Federalism and Cohesion in the European Community: Lessons from Canada*, Policy Research Series Paper No. 16, Dublin: The Economic and Social Research Institute

Straubhaar, T. (1988), *On the Economics of International Labour Migration*, Bern and Stuttgart: Haupt

Ströhl, G. (1994), 'Zwischenörtlicher Vergleich des Verbraucherpresiniveaus in 50 Städten', *Wirtschaft und Statistik*, 6/1994, 415–35

Tatom, J. A. (1991), 'Public Capital and Private Sector Performance', *The Federal Reserve Bank of St. Louis Review*, May/June 1991, 3–15

Tatom, J. A. (1993), 'Paved with Good Intentions: the Mythical National Infrastructure Crisis', *Policy Analysis*, Cato Institute, 12 August

Temple, M. (1994), *Regional Economics*, New York: St. Martin's Press

Thomas, I. P. (1997), *Ein Finanzausgleich für die Europäische Union*, Kieler Studien 285, Tübingen: Mohr

Thomsen, S. and S. Woolcock (1993), *Direct Investment and European Integration – Competition among Firms and Governments*, London: Frances Pinter and Royal Institute of International Affairs

Tomann, H. (1991), *Technologiegefälle in Europa und Europäische Technologiepolitik: Was kann Europa zum Abbau der Strukturunterschiede leisten?*, Eurokolleg 13, Bonn: Friedrich Ebert Stiftung

Transport Europe (1997), *Promoting the Notion of Public Service in Transport Policy*, 2/97

Traud, G. R. (1996), *Optimale Währungsräume und die europäische Integration*, Wiesbaden: Deutscher Universitäts Verlag

Tsoukalis, L. (1997), *The New European Community – the Politics and Economics of Integration Revisited*, Oxford: Oxford University Press

Tyson, W. (1990), *Recent Experiences in the United Kingdom, in ECMT, Promoting Regional Transport*,Round Table 82, Paris: ECMT/OECD, 33–50

Vickerman, R. W. (1992), *The Single European Market – Prospects for Economic Integration*, New York: St. Martin's Press

Vickerman, R. W. (1994), 'Transport Infrastructure and Region Building in the European Community', *Journal of Common Market Studies*, (1) 32, 1–24

Weise, C. (1995), 'EU-Politik zur Steigerung regionaler Wettbewerbsfähigkeit', *Vierteljahreshefte zur Wirtschaftsforschung*, 64 (2), 266–77

Weise, C. (1997), 'Der EU-Beitritt ostmitteleuropäischer Staaten: Ökonomische Chancen und Reformbedarf für die EU, *Integration*, 20, 3/97, 175–9

Welfare, D. and K. Beaumont (1993), 'All You Ever Wanted to Know about Additionality but were Afraid to Ask', *European Information Service*, 142/1993, 3–6

Williamson, J. and A. Taylor (1994), *Convergence in the Age of Mass Migration*, Working Paper 474, Cambridge, Mass.; NBER

Wishlade, F. (1993), 'Achieving Coherence in European Community Approaches to Area Designation', *Regional Studies*, 28/1, 79–87

Wishlade, F. (1995), *Regional Incentives and Inward Investment in the European Union: Some Recent Trends and Future Issues*, Paper presented to the General Assembly of the European Association of Development Agencies, Brussels, 6–7 April

Wolburg, M. (1996), *On Brain Drain, Brain Exchange, Division of Labour and Economic Growth within a Common Market*, Institut für Wirtschaftspolitik – Discussion Papers in Economic Policy Nr. 66, Hamburg: Universität der Bundeswehr

World Bank (1991), *World Development Report 1991: the Challenge of Development*, New York: Oxford University Press

Yuill, D. et al. (1994), *European Regional Incentives, 1994–95*, 14th edition, London: Bowker-Saur

Yuill, D. et al. (1995), *European Regional Incentives, 1995–96*, 15th edition, London: Bowker-Saur

Index